SACHEVERELL SITWELL'S ENGLAND

SACHEVERELL SITWELL'S ENGLAND

EDITED BY MICHAEL RAEBURN
Photographs by Edwin Smith

ORBIS·LONDON

© 1986 by Sacheverell Sitwell and Michael Raeburn
Edwin Smith's photographs reproduced by courtesy of
Olive Cook
First published in Great Britain by
Orbis Book Publishing Limited, London 1986

Printed in England by The Bath Press
ISBN 0 85613 508 9

CONTENTS

AUTHOR'S PREFACE

Like many Englishmen, and I suspect it is a trait in our national character, my youthful enthusiasm was for abroad and for Italy in particular, and I found more to admire in buildings seen under the Italian sun than, let us say, Amiens Cathedral on a rainy day of which there are enough and to spare in Picardy. This love for the warm south and its buildings, whether on the Mediterranean or further afield, has remained with me, but the great works of art of the Western world are not all Italian or even French. For there are many marvellous experiences to be had much nearer home, for an Englishman, that is to say, and for many visitors from abroad.

I find that I can lie awake, and perhaps get to sleep, in thinking of English cathedrals; beginning from Canterbury, and going round through Winchester and Wells (the most beautiful of all) to Salisbury; or moving up the east coast paragons, Ely, Lincoln, York, to culminate at Durham. I have written of these and other treasures of our ecclesiastical architecture in *Gothic Europe* and *Monks, Nuns and Monasteries* and in my introduction to Mrs Esdaile's *English Church Monuments, 1510-1840*, while in *British Architects and Craftsmen* I wrote of our domestic architecture in its prime from 1660 to 1830. The present work draws on these four books and on others written over a period of nearly fifty years, mapping out a journey in the imagination that starts in the town on the North Sea coast where I was born and continues around England, recalling works of our architects and craftsmen which have given me especial pleasure.

I have argued elsewhere that every voyage of exploration of Captain Cook's began and ended at Whitby where he was born. My journeys have been undertaken in idleness and to look at works of art, but they have brought me to many different parts of the world; and I could as well say that each and every one of them has started and had its end upon the Scarborough sands. For it was there, scrambling upon the rocks, that I first began to think, and hear, and see.

Sacheverell Sitwell
Weston, 15 May 1985

EDITOR'S FOREWORD

Throughout his life, Sacheverell Sitwell has been a traveller, and the countries he has visited, their people, their art and architecture have made up much of the subject-matter of his writings. His extraordinary eye, the breadth of his learning and the independence of his judgements make his books indispensable for anyone visiting places where his journeys have taken him, and this means many parts of Asia, Africa and the Americas as well as practically all of Europe. Since first getting to know Sacheverell Sitwell's books more than twenty years ago, I have seldom travelled without consulting them when planning a journey. I can recollect no real disappointments, but time and again I have experienced the intense pleasure of discovering in its physical presence some building or picture or sculpture known to me only from a description in the pages of a Sitwell book.

In fact, on my most recent visit to Sacheverell Sitwell to discuss with him the planning of this book, I made a detour to visit the church at Gayhurst, in the northern corner of Buckinghamshire right by the M1. I knew of it only from a brief reference to the monument to Mr Speaker Wright and his son in *British Architects and Craftsmen*, but I found a marvellous Georgian estate church, decorated like a ballroom, and a remarkable monument (whether or not Roubiliac's first work in England), with a blank slab where there should be an inscription – thanks to an undutiful son who apparently resented being left to pay for his father's monument. I mention this visit because it is typical that one should always find something more than one expects when using Sacheverell Sitwell as a guide. And it was a similar experience, visiting the church at Harefield in Middlesex (which required some perseverance), that suggested the idea for the present book.

However, Sitwell's writings do much more than provide a list of places to visit, for they open up ways of approaching and looking at art and architecture (or listening to music), and it is perhaps this quality that has made him such a notable influence on British taste since the 1920s. But there is something else which sets Sacheverell Sitwell apart from the distinguished tradition of English travel writers: he writes, always, as a poet, and whatever the subject-matter, his theme is always a human one. Works of art or literature or music – or the planting of a

8

garden, or the breeding of a new fruit or flower, or the image on a tomb, or the report of some past mystery – are evidence of the hand of man, a survival beyond physical survival, evidence of human fears and joys and pain and love. No other poet has approached human experience so exclusively through the medium of others' creations; but in doing this not only does he seem, paradoxically, to make the experience in some way more immediate, but at the same time he enriches the works he has chosen as the themes on which to play his variations.

In planning this book, I found many more passages from Sitwell's 'imaginative' prose works – a remarkable series of books from *The Gothick North* (1929) to *For Want of the Golden City* (1975) – that I would like to have included, but which for reasons of balance or length had to be left out. Nevertheless, I hope that many readers will find in the material that has been chosen not only suggestions for places to visit and descriptions to recall things seen or to evoke others that are unknown, but behind these a sense, always, of the author's consciousness of the meaning and significance of works that betray the hand of man.

Although there are books by Sitwell on a number of individual countries – Spain, Portugal, the Netherlands, Rumania, Japan, Morocco and others – his writings on England are scattered in many different works written over the whole span of his long career. This book has been compiled to bring together a selection of these, organised in the form of a journey through the country. It lays no claim to completeness (indeed, the author has never been in Devon or Cornwall), and it reflects his own tastes and interests.

The journey starts in Scarborough in Yorkshire,[1] where the author was born, and explores Yorkshire and the north-east before moving southwards, through Derbyshire, where he spent much of his childhood, and down the eastern side of England towards London. Here, before entering the modern city, we are taken down the Strand as seen by George Scharf in the Regency period, a reminder of the city that had changed comparatively little when the author first visited it at the turn of the century, but which has been so utterly devastated in war and peace during his lifetime. The journey onwards through the south and

---

[1] The old county names have been retained, since so much that has been written on English architecture that the reader may wish to refer to, in particular the *Buildings of England* series edited by Sir Nikolaus Pevsner, dates from before the local government reorganisation.

west is a briefer one, and we move up the western side of the country, finally to cross to the east coast again and end where we began.

Maps have been included at the start of each chapter, since many of the places mentioned are hidden away and difficult to find. Those whose names appear in Roman type can normally be visited by the public (subject, of course, to opening hours and seasons and, occasionally to prior appointment; details of these can always be found in the current edition of *Historic Houses, Castles and Gardens*), although churches – unfortunately, often with good reason – may frequently be kept closed, and it is a matter of finding whoever keeps the key. Those places in italic type are either included on the maps for orientation or are places described which are not open to the public.

The selection of passages (for which full bibliographic details are given at the end of the book) is my own, but I am indebted to Sir Sacheverell Sitwell himself for the support and advice he has given me in the course of the preparation of the book. Alison Cathie's help and encouragement in its planning were invaluable, and Francis Sitwell kindly read much of the long original selection of passages and made very useful suggestions. Madeline Edmead undertook to read the proofs and made many extremely helpful comments in the light of more recent scholarship. Finally, special thanks are due to Olive Cook, who helped me make the selection of photographs by her late husband, Edwin Smith, one of the rare people whose eye and hand matched those of the author himself.

PROLOGUE:
ON SCARBOROUGH SANDS

I have only to bend down, at any time or place, to pick a stem of wallflower, and its smell, as I draw a breath, carries me straight away till, in the space of a flash of light, I am again in the town, where I was born, with my old tutor, the 'Colonel Fantock' of my sister's poem, just above, and in the full yellow furnace-heat of, the massy bed of these same flowers that is like the pylon, the electric tower, that receives my message and gives me my answer. It is one of those huge, thickly filled beds which are only found in Corporation gardens, and so brimming with its own fullness that it makes one think of a spoonful of jam, or of the thick cream that one eats with summer fruit; while that massy splendour I have commented upon shows a survival of the taste of a hundred years ago, when they loved to encase precious stones as though in a solidified aura of the sun's rather brassy gold, which they were, even then, not content to leave alone but felt constrained to enhance its loudness of tone by as much pinching and twisting of the metal as their skill could contrive.

The hot summer air was faintly quivering a few inches above the ground, and over this deep bed of flowers it had become merged into and drenched by the yellow blossom, so that it could clearly be seen coiling into little spiral waves, or tingling like a held vibrato in music; indeed, your hand put down into this loud interval between earth and air felt chafed against and rubbed by the moving heat. This flower-bed grew right up to the edge of the asphalt path, that winding molten river through the grass, and it had an abrupt edge, a kind of sudden cessation of colour, for the green sea of grass started off sheer from its four sides and flowed without a pause up to another island in this archipelago, in this case a sister-like alternation, of the same affinities, for it was a bed of the dark, vinous wallflower which has a deeper and cooler scent and suggests a world with a near horizon of red garden walls. Along the asphalt path, by each of these islands, stood a black and brown seat which was hot to touch and the brown woodwork of which was blistered and swollen by the sun, and Colonel Fantock chose one of these because of its nearness to the flowers, and sat down taking its central division as a rest for his arm. I sat down, too, for a few moments, because our walk had been hot and tiring, but the Colonel was so warm that he could not talk for a while and so we held a monotonous silence.

Somehow it made one feel cool to look along, past the side of the flower-bed, down the wide, level grass, and so, after a time, I got up from our seat and started to walk across, noticing, at that moment, in what a curious manner the grass seemed to run straight into the sky as if the limit of vision was only a very few feet in front. I seemed to have become possessed of the insect's faculty of walking up a wall as though it is a flat, level floor, for no sooner had I gone a few feet further than I could suddenly see something the other side of it, the horizon somehow took a vast leap away from me, and I suddenly realised that the sea lay there below me, tumbling in an idle way as though to keep itself awake in the drowsy heat. I had now only to get my shoulders above the wall to have more and more of its surface unrolled before my eyes, and in another moment I was standing on the edge, the very brink of this wall, and there was a huge surging bay, a kind of immense amphitheatre, in which I occupied the highest seat, while the sea was playing to us with a listless and very tired enthusiasm.

I had hardly time to look once up and down this wide sweep when there came a brave burst of music from below, and one realised that, down at the bottom there, a great crowd of people were walking to and fro listening to the band. This was, indeed, the only sound that rose up to me from the huge, hollow shore, except when, during its softer strains, the sea had the more telling tone and its waxing, waning chords could be heard above the band that was now reiterating, and softly arguing out some question that must be settled before all the instruments could unite again and sound forth the charge, when they would drop their differences and thrill the air with a vast crescendo. It was a comic opera they were playing down below, and the cornet and the flute, taking place on this occasion for the tenor and the soprano, sounded out in long, rather wearying phrases, but, before long, the hero and heroine got lost in the noisy crowd, and the loud, vulgar measures of a chorus came along, reaching me up here just about a beat later than their birth below. So it was, that when this banal music ended in a magnificent, scroll-like flourish, the last reverberations were as if thrown back by the sea, and one was still involved, delight-fully, in this heavy foliage, though, really, it was already lifted away from one, dying with the waves.

Colonel Fantock had evidently appreciated the music; per-haps he remembered it, new and glistening, many years before, for now it was finished he stood up and came towards me, staying on the brink a moment and looking rather longingly, I thought, at the crowd below, as though he envied them being able to walk up and down while the band, like a living animal, performed to them. He had made up his mind to go and join them, and he proposed that we should walk down the gardens, bribing me with a promise that I could climb about on the rocks. So we turned our backs on the Esplanade, with its long line of stuccoed houses, and took the asphalt path which went down like a railway cutting between high, green banks and came out presently into a small valley, once, no doubt, a river-bed, though it had long been bridged over and cemented down. Under a municipal order this valley had been converted into a kind of distended rockery, and in an effort to authenticate this falsehood, a little rustic bridge of untrimmed logs was built across and embarked upon at either end by a nervous, wavering path which wound about and hesitated before it would trust itself on the shaking, perhaps snapping, timbers; but we came steadily down the broad asphalt of the valley-bed and walked under the bridge, which looked like the frail, wind-blown work of some insect, reaching immediately after this what must have once been the river-delta, though now it was kept back and blockaded by a high cement sea-wall.

This was a continuous line of fortification that ran the whole way round the town, joining on to the foreshore and the harbour, though the actual part of it that we had reached was the most distant defence, the very end of the line of ramparts, and beyond this the cliffs disappeared out of sight, armed with their own rough bulwarks and battlements, which fortifications they had to defend by themselves, without the help of man. At this spot it was a wall some thirty feet high and, in proportion to its scale, one had to walk some distance to find the steps leading down to the sands, and even then, so uneven and precipitous were the stairs, that, in order to make them safe, a heavy iron railing had to be embedded in the cement; while the fearful strength of the winter sea was proved by the rusting of the iron supports, for they had even stained the hard cement with this sign of their agony, and the discolouring grew more and more marked as one climbed down towards the beach where the waves had easier access to the railing, when they came running in from low tide under a strong wind.

In another moment we were treading on yielding sand, for the sea was very far out down at the bottom of the bay, though, just near the cliff, the shore was littered with pellet-like pieces of clay and with small pebbles; indeed, fine sand only began some distance out, and one noticed this particularly because if one wanted to throw a stone into the water there were never any to be found near the edge of the sea. This was, however, but a small deficiency compared with the other manifold pleasures of the sands, and so one lost no time in heading straight out towards the rocks. On our way there, we passed a whole armament of footprints; first of all the tracks of galloping horses, with sometimes the smaller marks of a dog running by the side, and then, when we had come nearer to the sea, almost to its very edge indeed, there were the curious angular prints made by the feet of the sea-birds, and so fresh and receptive was the sand that if you stooped to pick up a piece of seaweed, the leaf-like strands left a mark where you had lifted them from the shore. The sea had been over here very recently, for there were a few shells half embedded in the sand that were still full of water, and they gleamed and shone as if perfectly new, with the kind of freshness possessed by the flowers, and even the very earth, in some Pacific island never before reached by man.

We might almost have stepped out of a boat on to the sands, for the rocks rose a little above them and ran straight out into the water, just as an island might do, for it would only have one or two beaches on which one could land, and, for the rest, would come out of the sea with a broken and ragged sharpness that made it difficult to approach. But it showed here, low, and fairly level above the sand, and so we got easily on to its surface, and even Colonel Fantock, except for an occasional slipperiness, could see no dangers before him. When we had scrambled out as far as the rocks went, one had to turn round, of course, to come back, and then one saw the town sweeping right round the bay with as many windows looking on to the sea as possible; with, first of all, the long stuccoed lines of houses, then the great bridge that joined the new town to the old across a deep ravine, and beyond that the old town, much smaller in scale and creeping low down to the sea so as to be near the harbour, while right above this was the towering Castle Hill with the ruins on it coming out above a gaunt green hillside that looked like green baize. These ruins had been built in the time of King Stephen, so I had been told, but he seemed, like all his generation, too far away to have ever existed, and his castle lay up there, high on the skyline, looking as small as a child's fort, while one quite expected the King's armoured ghost to come, glittering, through the portcullis, where he would seem tall as the walls he had built to protect him. It was no use, though, waiting for this to happen, and so one looked down, away from the Castle, towards the near cliffs, or on to the sand.

Or up again to the bridge, behind which the huge mass of the Grand Hotel, with its peculiar French floridity of detail, for it had been built like the hotels in Northumberland Avenue, in the sixties, when François Premier and Henri Deux, or Quatre, were well studied and admired epochs, stood up like an enormous natural bluff or headland above the town. In fact its size almost rivalled the bulk of the Castle Hill, and it looked like a great lion lying with its paws stretched out towards the sands below. The Spa buildings, nearer at hand, were built, on a smaller scale, in the same bastard style, and from the rocks one could see very clearly the crowded promenade, the thronged terrace, where people were having tea, and that strange tower, built for no reason or purpose, up which there climbed every day, on its thin metal spiral stair, our only local alpinist, a young man suspected, not without just cause, of being perilously near the border-line of insanity – in fact he has now, long ago, crossed into the tropics, where one may hope that he is happier. Above the Spa, gardens ran right up to the cliff above, with many winding paths through the different groves of trees and shrubs. On certain grassy knolls, left bare for this purpose, there were hundreds of coloured lamps inlaid into the grass, in preparation for tonight's firework display, and they were arranged like beds of very metallic flowers, or like the stars, and rayed suns, that distinguished personages wear across their breasts.

We had come, by now, to the edge of a kind of inland sea, which spread out over quite a considerable area among the rocks, and to which I always made a point of coming whenever I walked on the shore because of the extraordinary beauty of the sea-plants to be seen growing out of its shallow depths. There were long palm-like fronds that floated, serpent-wise, upon its surface, for, until the wind was so completely silent that you could see the long tree-stems on which these fronds were supported, they seemed, in very fact, to be moving, slow and serpent-wise, across a glass world. Sometimes one of the little ripples that the wind made would tower up into a miniature wave, and it was astonishing how this appeared to be charged and concentrated with the violent blue of the deep sea out beyond the rocks. Indeed the continual force of the wind, so strong that it was like a great host of people running past you and all of them heading for the same direction, together with its salt, stinging smell, had the power of transporting one altogether, till the fronds of sea-weed became real palms, gliding and shaking themselves in the grasp of one of those blue tropical winds. At the same time, the sea glittered all over its huge mass for as far as one could see, and the sands showed themselves, for once, as a likely ingredient in the making of glass, for they were shining with a crackling, transparent fire.

The fishing boats in the bay were caught up and transfused in the sunlight, so that while any polished or metallic surface was thrown back violently on a golden line that flashed into your eyes, the universal and fathomless blue of the air had penetrated into every corner and crevice that it could reach. In this way the hulls and even the complicated web of rigging became ingredients of, and not objects in, the atmosphere. The hull seemed a blue body converted into the substance in which it lay, much as insects turn to amber within that sweet and cloying matrix; and the rigging seemed to climb through tubes of blue air; the ropes, in fact, were so many glass rods sparkling with blue, electric fires, and as the boats moved slowly through the ethereal brightness they had the force and the majestic movement of stars, for one can well imagine them tacking with the same freedom across their blue plain, with sails like a snow mountain to cool them, and firm rudders that beat down steadily the ripe-haired fields of foam, leaving a temporary destruction in their wake. This pool in the rocks, by which we were standing, had exactly the same blue intensity as the sea, for that colour came out of the sky with equal violence, however small the surface on which it fell. When an edge of water was lifted a little by the wind it would splash upon the rocks and leave, for a moment, some little trace of its colour till this was quickly devoured and taken up again by the hot sky.

In just the same way, the salt began to die out of the sea air, and the band far back at the cliff's foot never seemed to reach us now upon the wind, so that some of the machinery of memory must be failing, some contact must have been severed and disconnected. Sure enough, in a moment or two the whole scene had faded and vanished into thin air, taken up again as had been the fate of the edges of water on the rocks, and in very fact the only thing common to both these worlds was the hot sky, under whose influence I had been dozing through part of the summer afternoon.

YORKSHIRE
AND THE NORTH-EAST

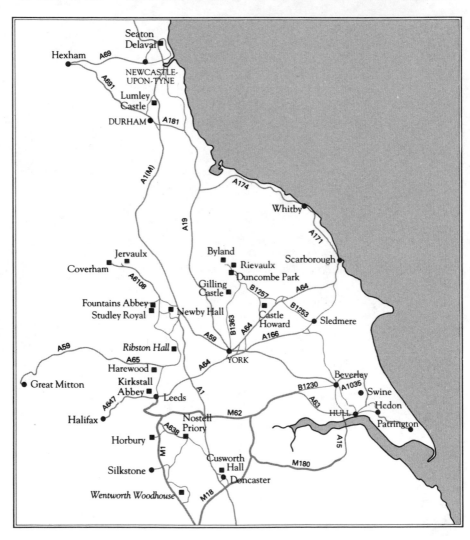

Seaton
Delaval

Hexham   A69

NEWCASTLE-
UPON-TYNE

A691

Lumley
Castle

DURHAM   A181

A1(M)

A174

A19

Whitby

A171

Jervaulx   Byland

Coverham   Rievaulx

A6108   Duncombe Park   Scarborough

Gilling
Castle   B1257   A64

Fountains Abbey   B1253
Studley Royal   Newby Hall   Castle   Sledmere
Howard

B1363   A64   A166

A59

Ribston Hall   YORK

A59   A65

Harewood   A64   Beverley

Great Mitton   Kirkstall   B1230   A1035
Abbey   Leeds   A63   Swine
A647   A1   Hedon
HULL
Halifax   M62   Patrington

Horbury   Nostell
Priory   A15

M1   A639

Cusworth   M180
Silkstone   Hall

Doncaster

Wentworth Woodhouse   M18

The gaunt appearance of Whitby Abbey on its cliff, as much and as often in the teeth of the wind as its neighbour Scarborough Castle, suggests abandonment long ago, and it comes as a surprise to know that there were monks here until 1539. It has been suggested that the choice of Whitby as a monastic site was due to Benedictine monks from Northumbria who had known the Scoto-Irish foundations on islands and exposed places like Lindisfarne and Iona. It was the monks of Lindisfarne or Holy Island who began to build the abbey at Durham in the tenth century, leaving their sea-gull'd fastness off the Northumbrian coast for fear of the Northmen. That this interior with Cyclopean columns of more than Roman solidity and permanence should result from the sea-serpent haunted minds of the monks of Lindisfarne, to judge from the snake-finials and basket-convolutions of their Gospel, is the marvel of Durham, which on opening any atlas we must agree to be the wonder of the north, for there is, in fact, no building on such a scale to the north of it anywhere in Europe or in Asia.

No view of Durham could better that seen from the window of the railway train. Nearer approach but adds to the majesty of the first impression and induces a feeling of respect and awe. All is on the Babylonian, the Ninevean scale, knowing the while that it far surpasses any building those satraps of the ancient world could put up of mud or clay that must be mixed with straw. The central tower of Durham, alone and in itself, is a stupendous relic surviving out of the ancient night of darkness, while the sternness and grimness of the interior are only relieved and carried from the major into the minor scale at the reredos of the high altar, or 'Neville' screen, a work of 1380, of lance-like fragility and pointedness, now lacking, of course, its alabaster figures that were painted and gilded. Of the same period are Bishop Hatfield's chantry chapel and throne, of nearly theatrical effect and presentation. Perhaps the chapel with the tomb and effigy are sacrificed to gain effect, for a stone stair mounts over it from one side and leads straight through the wall to his throne and the two seats for his chaplains to either side of him under high canopies reaching to the top of the arch. This stair is very much 'back stage' and invokes curiosity as to the mysteries playing at the other side near to the high altar. This is an early work of its kind, for Bishop Hatfield died in 1381. Another note, in almost an Oriental scale, sounds from the Galilee Porch, a building of the late twelfth century which more than one commentator has likened to the round-arched vessel of a mosque, its purport being to shelter pilgrims from the wind and rain.

Let us think now of the monastery itself,[1] which seems to have been upon the same scale as the Cathedral Priory, to judge from descriptions in *The Rites of Durham*, a book by an anonymous sixteenth-century author who may have been one of the monks.

> There was a famouse house of hospitallitie called the geste haule with in the abbey garth of Durham on the weste syde towards the water . . . ther interteynment not being inferior to any place in England, both for the goodness of ther diete, the sweete and daintie furneture of there Lodginges, and generally all thinges necessarie for traveillers – this haule is a goodly brave place much like into the body of a church with verey fair pillers supporting yt on ether syde and in mydest of the haule a most large Raunge for the fyer.
>
> On the right hand as your goe out of the cloysters in to the jermery was the commone house and a Maister thereof, the house being to this end, to have a fyre keapt in yt all wynter for the Mounkes to cume and warme them at, being allowed no fyre but that onely. Except the Maisters and officers of the house who had there severall fyres. There was belonging to the common house a garding and a bowlinge allie . . . for the Nouyces Sume tymes to recreat themselves.

And he concludes with the feast day 'when ther Banquett was of figes and reysinghes ails and caikes and thereof no superfluitie or excesse but a scholasticall and moderat congratulacy on amonges them selves'. With which brave words one cannot but contrast the cold days and nights of Durham, where the monks dressed by the light of cressets – bowls filled with oil and floating wicks, and set in hollows in square stones at either end of the dorter. And one fire only at which to warm themselves in the *calefactorium*! But where, on the other hand, the monks were coal-owners; the bursar of Durham spent £7 to winners of coal, '*lucracio carbonarum*', and another sum for '*exasperacione* [i.e. sharpening] le pykkes'.

HEXHAM North-west of Durham, toward the Scottish border, is the ancient priory of Hexham, where six out of the twenty canons

---

[1] In the cloister at Durham, though tampered with in the eighteenth century, there are still some thirty of the monks' carrels, half as many more of them as at Gloucester, and not so well preserved as those; but at Durham they were wainscoted, and entered by doors, the tops of which were pierced so that each monk could be under survey as he worked.

had to be hung because of the Pilgrimage of Grace. The church preserves the night stair of the monks, an architectural feature of a haunting nature, with worn steps but still with stone parapet in place. Impossible not to people this stone stair with monks – they were Augustinians or Black Canons – coming down it into the dark cold church, though at least the wooden choirstalls, thirty-six in number, argue some screening from the draughts. Here at Hexham, in his chantry chapel, is the late fifteenth-century effigy of Prior Rowland Leschman, lying in long woollen robe, and hooded, which we would describe as being in the sheepfold style.

YORK   York had been the centre of fertile land whether for crops or grazing in Roman times, which is why they made it their capital, and the Anglo-Saxons built a cathedral on the site of the present Minster in 627. The church which stands was begun in the time of King John, on an enormous scale, though it is in no way grander in aspiration than Ely, Lincoln, Durham, those wonders of eastern England, to all three of which it ranks lower as a work of art. I find its west front, the tracery of the great west window apart, and its pinnacled pair of towers, unexceptional in this kingdom of beautiful towers, often in mere parish churches; and the reassembled glass of its windows lacking in their vaunted beauty.

On a quite different scale from the Minster, and a reminder of the remoteness of this part of the country, is the graceful, open octagonal lantern of the church of All Saints, Pavement, in the city, where a lamp was kept burning at night to light travellers, who cannot have been more than six to eight miles away, through the forest of Gueldres.

FOUNTAINS   The colonising schemes of the Normans where this part of the north of England was concerned coincided with the arrival of Cistercian monks from France, and within a generation of the Conquest they had established themselves at Byland, Fountains, Rievaulx, their chief monasteries in Yorkshire. It was the policy of the Cistercians to retire to secluded places chosen for their remoteness and to make them into monkish paradises, though a strict simplicity was inculcated, which became relaxed during their four centuries of existence. They chose, too, sites beautiful in themselves, as witness the names of their monasteries not only in England; Clairfontaine, Froidefontaine, being an improvement upon mere Fountains, or 'Fontes' as they called it, with the six springs still rising within its precincts. That it is a beautiful site, none could deny, naturally beautiful, that is to say, without and before any improvement by the hand of man. The eventual plan of the building was brought over from Clairvaux by the third abbot, who was a friend of St Bernard, reformer of the Benedictine Order and founder of the Cistercians, and it is therefore of direct Cistercian inspiration and a part of their great architectural innovation all over Europe, which could be seen more clearly if only there was still a roof on the building and it could be studied in anything better than its bare plan. However, with the aid of that the complete disposition of this twelfth-century monastery can be made out in all kinds of minor detail, such as the long arcaded trough in the cloister near the fratery doorway where the monks washed their hands at mealtimes and combed their beards, and even the special kitchen where more delicate food, '*cibi subtiliores*', was cooked for the infirm monks and for those who had undergone the periodical bleeding. To give the ruin further life there is the nearly perfect and unruined Perpendicular tower built by Abbot Marmaduke Huby; the refectory can be seen, at least on the ground plan with a row of marble columns down its middle; and there is a good deal more than the foundations of the dormitory, where forty monks slept, as at a boys' school, in cells made into partitions by wooden walls. There is even a crypt that may have been the stable where the abbot kept his six white horses, '*sex equi ad bigam*', horses, as we shall know later, of monastic breed. Such was this great religious house, the walled close of which alone held eighty acres, and the boundaries of whose estates extended over an uninterrupted space of thirty miles; while in addition to 'many other wide domains, its lands in Craven held in a ring fence, a hundred square miles, or sixty thousand acres on a moderate computation.'

Other great Cistercian abbeys, Rievaulx, Byland, Jervaulx, BYLAND Kirkstall, were not far away. Of Byland little is left, though its church was three hundred and thirty feet long, the length of a cathedral of stone, but of not much more substance now than the strong wind which arose for no reason as late as 1820 when the bones of its Crusader founder Sir Roger de Mowbray were discovered and taken elsewhere for burial, a wind 'raised' by the RIEVAULX discovery of his grave. Rievaulx was in its day the largest and most famous monastery in England, although the present ruins give little idea of its original size, except for the huge refectory, but Rievaulx lies in an exceedingly beautiful valley which was made the 'theme' of one of the greatest feats of English land-scape gardening. Its terrace with a pavilion at either end, laid out by Mr Duncombe about the middle of the eighteenth century, with the garden at Stourhead and the lake and hanging wood in the park at Blenheim, is the supreme achievement of the landscape gardener.[1]

JERVAULX
Of Jervaulx there is really nothing left at all, or, at least, nothing that is alive. There is even less in a sense than what 'Old Jenkins', who lived to be 169 (older than Old Parr who was only 152) has to say of it, which is that remembering perfectly well, as he did, the Dissolution of the Monasteries and the mustering before Flodden Field when as a boy of twelve he was sent to Northallerton with a horseload of arrows, he re-membered seeing the dole at the gate of Jervaulx, of bread and red and white herrings, to 'poor persons, hermits and children'. And that is all. 'Old Jenkins' has no more to say. The monks of Jervaulx were famous for their cheese, which is still made to this day in Wensleydale, and for their white horses. The Commis-sioners recommended Jervaulx to the King for their horses: 'Surely the breed of Gervaix for horse was the tried breed in the North. I think in no realm should be found the like to them; for there is hardy and high grounds for the summer, and in winter woods and low grounds to fire them.' At Coverham, also, a Premonstratensian abbey a mile or two away, white horses were bred, and probably the white horses of the abbot of Fountains
KIRKSTALL
came from there. Kirkstall, near Leeds, a smaller and blackened Fountains, was a fourth Cistercian house; and the roll of the great Yorkshire abbeys is made complete with the addition of Nostell Priory of the Black Canons with twenty-eight priest-monks at the time of the Surrender.

The monks of this part of England, and the Cistercians in particular, were engaging in new activities. The small slag heaps and the pieces of charcoal still found in the ground at Rievaulx show that iron was worked here. Other monasteries further north in Durham and Lancashire were coal-owners. But their great wealth was in flocks of sheep. It is here that a pleasant and pastoral picture emerges which, even if it only affected a few of the monks in any one monastery, may be taken in palliation of the undoubted rigours of the Cistercian rule. It

[1] The pleasure grounds of Studley Royal, laid out by Mr Aislabie, another country gentleman, at the back of Fountains, and not making any play of the ruins, are perhaps equally beautiful, but they belong to another school of gardening, nearer to the fountains and clipped hedge of Belœil and Versailles.

entails for one thing the residence of those few of the monks in the monastic granges which would be built near the sheep walks. The shepherding was done in early days by the lay-brothers or *conversi* until the diminishment of their number consequent on the Black Death, after which it was the work of hired labourers. There were sheep walks over the Lincolnshire wolds – and one wonders at what date the traditional green smocks of those local farm labourers came in – and, also, there were sheep walks on the flat lands of Holderness along the Humber, and many more upon the Yorkshire Moors.

The monks sold the wool and ate the cheeses made from the ewes' milk. Flemish and even Italian merchants from Florence and Lucca came to buy the wool, and two lists for 1280 and 1315 survive, giving the names of the religious houses and the number of sacks of wool delivered, mixed and in bulk by the Benedictine monks, but graded into *bona, grossa et lacei* by Cistercians and Augustinians. It is curious to reflect on a merchant from Florence arriving at Rievaulx or Fountains on an early autumn evening at the season of the sheep shearing, at about a date which was still twenty years before Giotto's Tower was built. What would this Italian, who had been through Lincolnshire on his way, think of these great English abbeys? There was nothing like them in Italy. Just at this time Siena and Lucca were ahead of Florence, which had not quite reached the flowering of its genius. It would have been interesting to talk to him, and ask if it was not his opinion that this was the richest land in Europe. Dom David Knowles, who writes with such absorbed interest of all concerning our religious houses,[1] concludes, with a phrase of which a poet must envy him, that 'the northern houses of monks and nuns were the best wool-growers save for the small knot of sheepowners in Shropshire who clipped the finest wool of all – the famed "Lemster ore".' Other themes no less fruitful come in his pages, as of the abbey of Meaux, cruelly devastated by the Black Death, which had its sheep walks in Holderness and owned the grange of Croo, 'so named it would seem, from the most vocal of its tenants, in the open wind-swept country by Beeforth [Beeford] near the sea'. A thick grove of trees lay round it where nested a large colony of rooks. The villein who administered the estate, complained of the crying and 'crooing' of the birds, sought the abbot's permission, and cut down every tree on the place.

---

[1] In *The Monastic Order in England*, Cambridge, 1963, and elsewhere. His books have provided much valuable material for this work.

BEVERLEY Holderness (now the northern part of Humberside) is reached by way of Beverley, and it would be interesting to know how many foreigners have penetrated to this remote corner of the East Riding which has two of the finest mediaeval churches in all Europe, St Mary[1] and the Minster, the latter with no less than five storeys of blind panelling framing in a huge west window; huge soaring, engaged, not flying buttresses, richly cusped and canopied; and then the leap of twin towers that are exactly, perhaps unimaginatively alike in every detail. Inside is the Percy Shrine, the most glorious in imaginative conception of all the mediaeval chantry chapels, but the monumental effigy has long disappeared, so that it is a shrine without a tomb. The choir has stalls for sixty, and the complexity of detail is more than sensational, and one could be lying in the bracken looking up into the trees, lime trees it could be, that have taken on mullions and minor castellations among their leaves and then, as with a change of focus, we see the spires of ferns again.

We are close now to our destination in Holderness, the village of Patrington near the mouth of the Humber, but there SWINE are two churches to detain us on our way. At Swine, in the church that was once part of a priory of Cistercian nuns, there is the effigy of a knight of the Hilton family, a splendid study of military costume in the time of Edward III; his mail has three curious hexagonal ornaments at breast and stomach, he wears a tight-fitting belt, and there is a double chain fastened to his HEDON chest to secure his helm. Closer to the river, at Hedon, the church has a fine tower which, had it been a fifteenth-century minaret, would have been more written of and better known. There is a solidity about the tower of Hedon that puts it a little apart among Perpendicular towers, and does not detract from the tapering graces of its engaged buttresses; but the double-tiered parapet guarding the platform on its roof may suggest that for once the view from it was not the object and that it is a bell-tower, pure and simple.

PATRINGTON It is in the personal comparing of their results that one is most curious about the mediaeval spire builders, no one of whom can have achieved more than two or three steeples in his lifetime. How did they set about it, these aerial architects, who worked at such a height? Could they continue with their building in the winter? How did they put up the scaffolding? And who climbed

---

[1] 'That St Mary at Beverley is one of the most beautiful parish churches of England is universal knowledge,' writes Dr Nikolaus Pevsner confidently (*Yorkshire: York and the East Riding*, Harmondsworth, 1972, p. 179).

to the top at Salisbury, four hundred feet above the plain? For how long must they have stared up into the air at other steeples, shading their eyes with a hand? How was it possible without going all over England to build such a spire as that of Patrington, which makes a landmark for much of north Lincolnshire and all of Holderness. This, of closed lantern type, and of intent to cheer the souls of departing or returning seamen, has a sixteen-sided pinnacled arcade, above cusped obelisks at the corners, and from it springs the tapering octagon piercing the 'sea-rauks' or fogs of winter. In order to experience Patrington and its beautiful, unspoilt interior, it is necessary to make a special, laborious and otherwise pointless journey.

GREAT MITTON   The same is true of Great Mitton, at the opposite, western, extreme of the county (now absorbed into Lancashire), close by Pendle Hill and Malkin Tower, a region still haunted, we would hope, by Mother Demdike, Old Chattox, and the entire coven of the Lancashire witches. For Great Mitton church contains the Shirburne chapel with effigies by the Stanton family, three generations of sculptors, from 1610 to 1734, but the Shirburne tombs are by William and his son Edward, and it is noticeable of the Stantons as a whole that, their family style once established, and it was essentially the milder or secondary Baroque, they did not change much but continued in their ways.[1] The Great Mitton monuments consist of recumbent statues in white marble on black bases, two Richard Shirburnes and their wives and a third Richard, with a mural monument to yet another Richard Shirburne, a child, which is a work without precedent, showing a little figure, walking, and rapt in horror at the skull and crossbones at his feet. Above is a nimbus of angels' heads.

CASTLE HOWARD   English Baroque is at its grandest at Castle Howard. We would delay, therefore, no further but transport our readers immediately to the scene, using as vehicle the famous passage from Walpole: 'Nobody had informed me that I should at one view see a palace, a town, a fortified city, temples on high places, woods worthy of being each a metropolis of the Druids, the noblest lawn in the world fenced by half the horizon, and a mausoleum that would tempt one to be buried alive; in short, I

---

[1] The disentangling of the different works by members of this family, and their identification, is entirely the work of Mrs Katharine A. Esdaile and her son, without whose efforts the renown of these prolific sculptors, *in toto*, would amount to no more than the mere mention of their names. Cf. 'The Stantons of Holborn', in *The Archæological Journal*, LXXX, 1928; and *English Church Monuments 1510-1840*, London, 1946.

have seen gigantic palaces before, but never a sublime one.' That this is true of Castle Howard with its temples and avenues no one would contest who has had the good fortune to see this fantastic building, or even only studied it in the perspective views in the third volume of *Vitruvius Britannicus*. Let us preface our remarks on Castle Howard with the statement that it stands in one of the most beautiful parts of England, unblackened, as yet, by industry, near the green woods and terraces of Rievaulx Abbey.

Castle Howard is the work of Sir John Vanbrugh. That Vanbrugh had genius for architecture is plainly evident. He was the master of effects that no other architect has achieved. But we feel of him, as we do of Berlioz, that it is of no use when he sets out to be ordinary or little. The op. 14 of Berlioz is the *Symphonie Fantastique*, surely the orchestral masterpiece of Romantic music. The op. 1 of Vanbrugh, in architecture, is Castle Howard. Vanbrugh was thirty-five years old: this was his first building.

The plans were ready in 1699, and by the year following, or soon after, Hawksmoor had been appointed clerk of the works, and building had begun. It has been remarked of Castle Howard, as of Blenheim, that the eye cannot grasp it in its entirety, but this, curiously enough, is true of the eye of the camera, but not the human eye. The huge masses of this heroic architecture can only be photographed from too far away to do them justice. But the human eye can range from point to point. We can look from Castle Howard, down the green avenue of lime and beech to the great obelisk with its inscription in honour of Marlborough, the hero in periwig and armour who haunts all Vanbrugh's architecture, and turn in another direction over the trees to Vanbrugh's Temple, with Hawksmoor's Mausoleum behind it. We can move from front to front of Castle Howard and compare its architecture. We shall find the grand façade is French, and neither Italian, nor English, in feeling; that is to say, it is like no actual building in France, or Italy, or England, but that, in treatment, and this is typical of the whole Vanbrugh problem, there is a reminiscence of the Condé stables at Chantilly, for two hundred horses, by Germain Boffrand, built *after* Castle Howard. At Castle Howard, we opine, Vanbrugh intended a French château, but it came out otherwise. Great artists in their immaturity, and this applies particularly to Vanbrugh, who was of the obsessed and not the learned kind, have often achieved remarkable works which have emerged differently from their intention. In the case of Vanbrugh, the extreme competence of his workmen in this, the great epoch of the English craftsman, together with superlative help and interpretation on the part of Hawksmoor, his *régisseur* or assistant manager, have resulted in this deflection or extension being carried to its extreme limits. But it is precisely when artists of this calibre divagate from their original conception and can be studied in the wanderings of their instinct that we recognise and learn their persons. With Vanbrugh especially, it is by his aberrations, not his conformity, that we know him.

The perspective views of Castle Howard from *Vitruvius Britannicus* show the vastness of his original scheme. For it was not completed. Sir Thomas Robinson, the Palladian, altered it, left out the little domes at one end, and never built the stables. The forecourt was not enclosed, as it seems to be in the engraving; while the great entrance arch of four obelisks, like ancient Egypt, that were to carry a cupola, was not erected. But the huge body and high dome are there, and the entrance wings with their colonnades and shallow steps. Such is the essential Vanbrugh planning, to be repeated at Blenheim and at Seaton Delaval. There are the two fronts, for pomp and pleasure, while we shall recognise Vanbrugh instantly, as we step inside, from the stone hall seventy feet high with its huge fluted pilasters, and from the mouldings of the huge fireplace that becomes Italian Baroque above, perhaps to match the frescoes of Pellegrini upon the higher walls and ceiling.[1] A fine composition is formed by a round arched door frame of dressed stone set between pairs of recessed and engaged pilasters, with a balcony of splendid ironwork running across above it, backed by a higher door upon the passage, of similar design, the whole framed in by the arch that arises from the inmost pair of pilasters. What are yet more characteristic of Vanbrugh are the corridors of naked stone with their smooth surfaces.

We have said that Vanbrugh never excelled in little, and this is contradicted, apparently, in the erections in the park at Castle Howard, but only to be proved true. There is a point in the park from which the whole of the great building can be seen lying magnificently in the distance, fulfilling all that Walpole wrote of it. Vanbrugh's Bridge is in the foreground and, to the right, his Temple lies among the trees. We may have seen his

---

[1] Pellegrini's fresco on the dome was destroyed in a fire in 1940 and has been replaced by a modern reconstruction.

Satyr Gate in the walled garden and been prepared, by that, for the grotesque mask on the keystone above the shallow water. The original of this bridge can be traced to Palladio, but Vanbrugh altered its meaning by his rustication.[1] To say that he rendered it bucolic is not true, for this bridge is not pastoral in image. It consists of three arches, rising in the middle, and a balustrade, with a long ramp to it on either hand. The two piers, in the water, have empty niches like the doors of tombs above them. If it be not pastoral, we could call it, in Walpole's phrase, Druidic, leading from one grove or metropolis of beech trees to another. But, in fact, its only equivalent is in Vignola's enchanted world of Caprarola, where we would find river gods and moss-grown giants in plenty. But Vanbrugh is the master of these bridges that cross over nothing, and are only trodden in the imagination. Castle Howard as a domain, with its trees and waters, is as though the poetry in Vanbrugh which had no outlet in his plays, has found its expression in another art.

His Temple of the Four Winds is a little masterpiece, raised on steps, with four Ionic porticoes. Each porch, of four pillars, has its pediment that carries vases, while the square body of the Temple, with urns at its corners, rises into a cupola and lantern. This little building is entirely useless, and a waste of money, but nothing in our Classical architecture is more beautiful, or more correct. This is a strange contradiction, coming from the hand of Vanbrugh. The secret is that the Temple is an intrinsic part of Castle Howard, and arising out of that, when his inspiration was already working smoothly. It is subsidiary to the whole domain of stones and trees.

We would propose that this Temple, Vanbrugh's last work, and Hawksmoor's Mausoleum at Castle Howard are greater works of art than many of our cathedrals. They belong to the class of landscape buildings, and probably, of their kind, they are as beautiful as anything in Europe. From Mr Geoffrey Webb we learn that Castle Howard cost £35,000; the garden works, including the Temple or Belvedere, another £24,000; and the Mausoleum, £19,000.[2] And he observes that in fact the Mausoleum was a major architectural work, comparable in size and architectural importance with, say, one of Wren's more ambitious City churches. As much must be stated, in order that

---

[1] The Bridge, so much in the style of Vanbrugh, was not in fact erected until some fifteen or more years after the architect's death.

[2] In an essay embodying Hawksmoor's letters to Lord Carlisle concerning the Mausoleum (*Walpole Society*, xix, 1931).

neither Vanbrugh's Temple nor Hawksmoor's Mausoleum should be classed as summer houses or pavilions.

The Mausoleum is approached by long flights of balustraded steps, and stands, itself, upon a huge stone platform. It is a circular domed building, with disengaged Doric columns. In the interior there is a vault, up to the level of the platform, and above that is the chapel, with Corinthian columns that uphold a rich and splendid frieze of stone. The domed roof, of stone, is high above. The whole of the Mausoleum is ideally Roman, even Virgilian, in grandeur. Here Hawksmoor is altogether exceptional. No longer Baroque; or, indeed, anything else than Roman, but in the poetical, not the correct meaning of that term, for it applies only to the high dome and the drum of columns as we catch a sight of them from far away, through the trees or across the landscaped waters. In that setting the Mausoleum of Castle Howard is one of the poetical beauties of the Kingdom.

SEATON DELAVAL   Built by Vanbrugh in the same years as the Temple at Castle Howard is Seaton Delaval, stranded in extraordinary and unpremeditated circumstances close to the Northumbrian seashore, but in a web of colliery lines, close to a mining village, and set in a landscape of clinker heaps that, by night, are lit up by flares. Everything to do with this house and its history is dramatically romantic and extreme; not least the Delavals themselves, their lives of debauchery and the violence of their ends. The males of the family drank to excess and fell down dead, but never died in bed, while the daughters were renowned for their beauty, among their number being Lady Tyrconnel, who had hair so long and luxuriant that it floated behind her, upon her saddle, when she rode. The entire family, one night, with Garrick's authority, took the boards at Drury Lane; and it needs little imagination, knowing the history of the family, to feel certain that Seaton Delaval, their home, would be burnt out in a fire, caused, in actual fact, because the jackdaws had built their nests in the neglected chimneys. Such was the family of the Delavals, and Vanbrugh devised the appropriate setting for their beauty and folly, building this huge house with three rooms only on the ground floor facing the entrance side, and one other room to extend the whole length of the garden front. This garden front has an immense Ionic portico, but the drama is interior, and plays its effects upon the forecourt side. Here we have a rusticated Doric front of Cyclopean scale, a flat entrance arch, and another, above and echoing it, in gigantic keystones, and at the corners ringed columns grouped in fours, flanked by octagonal towers. This front is lifted on a high flight of steps, so that the massive foundation piers, as it were, of the towers and columns are to be seen.

But the peculiarity of the plan of Seaton Delaval is the depth of this forecourt, or in other words, the extreme length of its wings, each with its façade to match. The axis of the forecourt is different, thus, from those at Blenheim or Castle Howard, for their treatment does not open or curve towards the spectator, but faces directly inward at right angles to the main building. These wings, with the central block between them, give an effect that is magnificent, and to which none of the same criticisms can be applied that form the disparagement, to some minds, of the other principal buildings due to Vanbrugh.[1] Seaton Delaval did not cost, altogether, an excessive sum of money; it is huge in scale and in purpose, more than in actual fact. It is a huge stone scene, of sculpture, not of painting, and as remote from the eighteenth century that gave it birth as are the temples of Angkor from their inhabitants, of whom there are no traces. In point of drama, Seaton Delaval may impress more than any other building in England.

Vanbrugh, it seems, had a particular following in the North, probably because his 'castle' style – seen best in his conversions of Lumley Castle in Durham for Lord Scarborough and of Kimbolton Castle in Huntingdon for Lord Manchester – was suited to the Yorkshire scene. Vanbrugh writes from York in 1721: 'I return'd but last night from the North (for here you must know we are in the South). . . . If I had had good weather in this Expedition, I shou'd have been well enough diverted in it; there being many more Valluable and Agreeable things and Places to be seen, than in the Tame Sneaking South of England.' In this context we should consider the obscure architect, William Wakefield, to whom, according to an old inscription in a church in York, and upon the authority of Campbell in *Vitruvius Britannicus*, Duncombe and Gilling, two houses near Castle Howard, must be attributed. Both houses are in the Vanbrugh-Hawksmoor style; Gilling Castle, where the

[1] The endless arches, in perspective, of the wings of Seaton Delaval resemble nothing so much as a view of the ruined stables and granaries of Moulay Ismail, at Meknes, in Morocco. It was this dusky tyrant who aspired to the hand of an illegitimate daughter of Louis XIV. Here, in the Dar-el-Makhzen, he kept his twelve thousand mules and horses; his ostriches from the Sahara; and the tawny nurseries in which he raised his Black Guard. But Seaton Delaval was completely restored twenty-five years ago and is lived in once more.

GILLING CASTLE

new work was on one front only, being an essay entirely in the Kimbolton-Lumley manner.[1] Gilling, the home of the Fairfax family, goes back to the fourteenth century, and it also preserves perhaps the most complete Elizabethan interior of all, save only that at Hardwick, which we shall shortly visit. The dining-room has a plain ceiling, crowded with pendant stalactites, and with only small moulded figures in the compartments; and below that a frieze of what was known as 'forest-work', giving the arms of the gentry of the different wapentakes of Yorkshire in the year 1585. It has three windows, too, filled with shields of the Fairfaxes, Stapyltons, and Constables, painted by a German, Barnard Dininckhoff; a splendid wooden mantelpiece; and most beautiful panelling upon the walls.

WENTWORTH
WOODHOUSE

Wentworth Woodhouse, in south Yorkshire, is a house whose scale at least derives from Vanbrugh. It was built by Henry Flitcroft, who was also responsible for the main part of Woburn Abbey, a house much more wonderful for its contents than as an edifice. Wentworth Woodhouse, the largest house in England, and six hundred feet long, it is difficult to admire. There are many absurdities in the spun out façade which may have been less ponderous when the air was brighter and before the mine came up to the park gates and the slag heaps rose like pyramids in the distance, but the huge portico has dwarfed and crushed down the entire range of the ground floor, and the long wings are flat and empty with their balancing frontispieces and the square pavilions at the ends. But the consolation is the 'Whistlejacket' Room with its splendid horse paintings, great works of art in their kind by Stubbs.[2]

YORK

Lord Burlington himself, whose amateur talents are insufficiently appreciated, is to be seen and admired at York in the splendid pillared interior of the Assembly Rooms, and his influence is evident in the Mansion House, which has at least one magnificent interior. The local school of architects at York is as yet comparatively unstudied, but attention may be drawn, among many other beauties, to the interior and splendid stair of the old Fairfax House, probably the finest of the old York

[1] Wakefield is said, also, to have designed Atherton, in Lancashire, where an old guide book says that 'the Atherton family built an enormous house, but it was never finished, and eventually was taken down by Lord Lilford'.

[2] In the nearby church at Silkstone, there is a noble effigy of Sir Thomas Wentworth, a helmeted marble figure with breastplate and great riding-boots, which seems to echo the bronze technique of Hubert Le Sueur, sculptor of the equestrian Charles I at Charing Cross and the superb effigy of the Earl of Portland in Winchester Cathedral, which the sculptor of Sir Thomas Wentworth, Claudius René, so nearly repeats.

houses. York was also a centre of the Rococo in the north,[1] while one of the liveliest and most beautiful specimens of the Rococo in England is Somerset House, Halifax. It has an elaborate stucco ceiling, festoons upon the walls, and a panel over the fireplace of a hero in Roman armour, holding an olive branch, and surrounded in the approved style by flags and drums and cannon. Perhaps the improbable Rococo of Halifax is further illustrated by the information, in an old edition of Murray's *Yorkshire*, 1874, that 'fancy alpacas' were made here, 'varying with varying fashions, and distinguished by all sorts of fantastic names', and that the traveller Pennant, passing through Halifax about 1770, says that rugs 'of a blue colour' were manufactured here expressly for Guinea, and were packed in pieces of 12½ yards, and wrapped in an oilcloth painted with negroes and elephants 'in order to captivate the natives'.

Carr of York is another architect of local fame, working mainly in the North of England, and almost always in the correct Palladian manner. Various little edifices in York itself are due to him, the Castle Museum and the Court House, dating from a period when the town was like a little Northern capital, and the local families spent their winters there. Carr neither made mistakes, nor showed originality, for the set rules allowed but few departures from the orthodox. The Royal Crescent, at Buxton, shows Carr working in the style of Bath.

He was the architect of Horbury church, Yorkshire, where the spire surmounts a circular drum after the fashion of Nash's later All Souls', Langham Place. But his country houses, Tabley in Cheshire, Lytham in Lancashire, and numerous instances in Yorkshire, only prove that the example of Vanbrugh had been forgotten. There are no traces of the 'Castle' style of Gilling or of Lumley. The northern school of Romantic building was carried no further. Carr was a local architect, but with no regional peculiarities. His buildings could stand, as well, in any part of England.

Architecture, being set in its forms, was at this time in the hands of the most prolific of composers. James Paine is an instance, who must have built as many houses as Boccherini wrote quintets, or as the operas of Cimarosa. Yet his level of accomplishment is astonishingly high. He never falters, never hesitates; it was not necessary for Paine to wait to be inspired.

---

[1] Stucco ceilings from various houses are illustrated in George P. Bankart, *The Art of the Plasterer*, London, 1908. Wilberforce House, Hull, belongs, we could say ethnically, to the same group of Rococo.

His ideas must have come quickly on the drawing board. His early practice was in Yorkshire, beginning with the Mansion

DONCASTER

House at Doncaster, of which, for some reason, he published a book of more than twenty views, for a far more interesting work

CUSWORTH PARK

is Cusworth Park, a mile or two away, with its rusticated base, fine doors and windows, and Palladian pavilions to either hand. Cusworth is now the Museum of South Yorkshire Life.

NOSTELL PRIORY

Nostell Priory, Wakefield, is another work by Paine. The dining-room with its Baroque stucco frames, redolent of Italy, may be a relic of his decoration, but we would stop at Nostell rather for the sake of its tapestry room with a ceiling by Robert Adam contrived out of an eight-pointed star, and as many painted lunettes to match, with a border of little painted cameos set in gilded scrollwork. Joseph Rose, the plasterer who worked with Adam at Syon, was employed upon this, and upon the saloon ceiling, which is worked out in another style, with pink, green, and white for colours, actual modelled cameos in white plaster being set on a blue ground, while the flat panel of the cove has a great cameo in the centre between rayed parhelions or heads of waterlilies, with ornaments of open fans spread in the corners.

NEWBY HALL

Newby Hall, Ripon, contains the same collaboration of Joseph Rose and Robert Adam.[1] The front hall has a pair of military trophies, like those in the ante-room at Syon, only here they are in plain white stucco, and are not gilded. A sculpture gallery, and a rotunda in the centre, were added in order to house the sculptures brought back from Rome by William Weddell, but the decoration is too stiff and dead, the red of the walls is too dead and ugly. Probably a gallery of Roman sculptures could not be otherwise; but how great is the contrast when we come to the Boucher tapestries in the drawing-room! These are roundels of Cupid and Psyche, by Boucher, on a rose-red ground with flowers and birds by Neilson. The needlework chairs and sofas match the tapestries; there is a fine, but not obtrusive, ceiling; and an Adam carpet in green, and pink, and brown, upon a ground of cream. This whole room is a vision of the age of leisure, and one look at it will tell us that this can never be again.[2]

[1] Joseph Rose, working on his own, carried out the splendid library at Sledmere, near Malton, occupying the whole length of the house on the upper floor, a hundred and fifty feet in length, and rivalling Adam's library at Luton Hoo. This Sledmere library was burnt down in 1911, but has been restored.

[2] Adam was the architect, too, of the stables at Nostell, and of those – a less elaborate version, without the balustraded roof – at Newby.

HAREWOOD

Harewood, near Leeds, is Adam at his most typical, hard and emotionless at times, and then superb and on the grandest scale. The entrance hall, for instance, is just Adam, and no more than that. Not so the magnificent gallery, which has window pelmets and valances carved in wood from the hand of Thomas Chippendale. Between the windows there are console tables and high, festooned mirrors over them. The finest of the Reynolds portraits on the walls have special Adam frames; while the ceiling, in many colours and most exact and minute in execution, is again by Joseph Rose, to the design of Adam. It could be argued, though, that the little panels of painting in the ceiling are aggravating and distracting, for in order to examine them it is necessary to turn the head this way and that, or if we ignore them they are of no purpose. But this is beside the point. The wonder of Harewood is the furniture by Adam, some pieces of it made by Chippendale; these include the superb sideboard with urned pedestals and wine cooler in the dining-room, carried out in rosewood, satinwood, tulipwood, and ormolu, as well as sidetables with tops of marquetry, and a magnificent inlaid satinwood commode, with concave ends, and ormolu mounts, to which the companion piece exists at Renishaw.

RIBSTON HALL

As a last example of decorative architecture in the north, there is Ribston Hall, only a few miles distant from Harewood, a name made famous by one of the most delicious of all eating apples. The saloon there is a magnificent room that much resembles the work of James Wyatt, but its designer is not known for certain. Ribston was the old home of the Goodricke family. The saloon has splendid doors and overdoors, there are paintings magnificently framed and spaced upon the walls, and a polychrome ceiling that is one of the richest specimens of the 'harlequin' or coloured manner. It is a flat ceiling, with a cove, and has the characteristic fans of Wyatt, groups of musical instruments, and his paired white sphinxes. It is much in the style of Wyatt, yet not entirely, and it would be interesting to know who was responsible for this very brilliant work of art.

THE EAST MIDLANDS

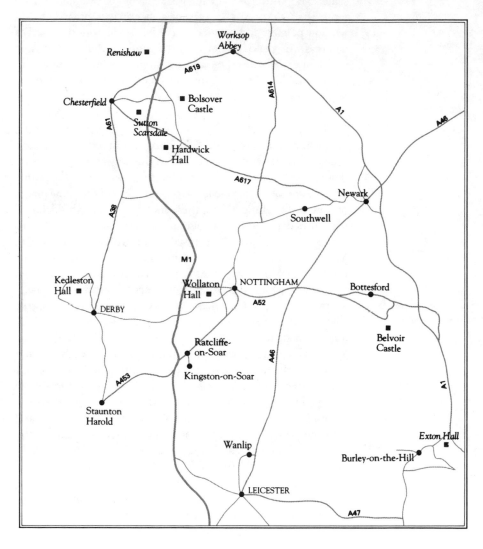

Renishaw
Worksop Abbey
A619
A614
Bolsover Castle
A1
A46
Chesterfield
A61
Sutton Scarsdale
Hardwick Hall
A617
Newark
Southwell
A38
M1
Kedleston Hall
Wollaton Hall
NOTTINGHAM
Bottesford
A52
DERBY
Ratcliffe-on-Soar
A46
Belvoir Castle
Kingston-on-Soar
A453
A1
Staunton Harold
Wanlip
Exton Hall
Burley-on-the-Hill
LEICESTER
A47

DERBYSHIRE

I would remember my old home, in Derbyshire, in early September, at blackberrying time. It seems misty and cloud-bound all the year among the Derbyshire hills, and this actual month is the dimmest and most distance-hiding of the seasons. No statue can be seen, let alone a passing human figure — gardener or woodsman — at a further distance than ten yards before you. There were the few remaining trees of a lime and elm avenue, in front and to the right of the house; and their old and splintered masts still towered a dizzying height into the air, too far for the eye to follow them, these autumn mornings. My bedroom faced due north down a hollow valley, out of the park, to a line of hills a mile or two away which rose up into a series of moors that divided, and hid us, even when it was clear, from the smoky stacks of Sheffield. This side of the house had a gloomy, Sunday-like outlook, as do most houses which face that particular cardinal-point of the compass. It had a long, stretched-out front that consisted of two great wings starting on either side from a recess into which the centre, or as it were heart of the house, advanced in the form of a pentagon of three storeys to which the porch and front door were attached. My room was in one of these long wings, and looking from the window you could see nothing of the building except its long straight front and the three storeys of windows all hidden by dark and smoky leaves of ivy. Mine was but one of this line of portholes giving on to the grey seas of winter sky.

There were luckily a few pictures in the house to rebut a despairing mood and supply some ground for optimism. A large family group painted by Copley about 1780 carried a kind of personal authority with it, as though one's great-great-grand-father had been able to speak out of the picture and tell one everything was all right and that one could go on hoping. It was painted with that convincing reality that Zoffany managed to give to his interiors, and being on a larger scale and less fussy in detail than is usual with the latter painter, this picture carried a deeper degree of conviction with it, though it perhaps lacked by this very reason the play-scene appearance that Zoffany's predilection gave to every picture he painted.

There were, besides, various other family portraits of more or less merit, with a few Italian pictures bought and brought home by my father. None of these latter were able to satisfy any really deep feeling; but this deficiency was filled and made good by what I can only consider as the fabulous beauty residing in five great panels of Brussels tapestry bought by an ancestor from the sale of the Philippe Egalité collection in London. They portrayed five triumphs, of such abstract qualities as justice and commerce; but it was a world of Indian suavity and opulence, and Indian in the poetic not the geographic sense, for it was the East before artists had learned the difference between India, China, and the El Dorados of America, and so it contained subtle exaggerations on what the designer considered as the mean level of this trebly-distilled land of beauty. There were elephants and black slaves, bell-hung pagodas and clipped hornbeams; in the background were clouds tacking like fleets of sailing ships, and, lower down, terraces with pots of orange-trees upon their balustrades, and continual fountain jets that gave a cool note to the hot summer portrayed in every other symbol. Some great folios lie open upon the stone steps, as though the lady in her plumed headdress who sits above them had lately been read to by one of the slaves who is waiting upon her. She has had them put to ground, for a horn far away in the distance must be the prelude to some new procession that will come out of the distance, slowly climbing one terrace after another till they come almost to her side. I have never yet been able to discover who designed these tapestries, and I still consider them some of the most beautiful products of human genius.

Two of the panels were hanging in the drawing-room, one of them very dark and faded, and the other curiously light and 'cleaned' in colour – probably because it was over the fireplace and had profited to this extent by winter fires. This room had seven great windows coming right down to the floor, and two more of them at the end of the room; while, as though to stress the importance that the builder of this drawing-room attached to his creations being sufficiently lighted, there hung down from the middle of the Adam ceiling a great ormolu chandelier which spoke to one at once of George IV and the Brighton Pavilion, while the glass shades of those numerous oil lamps contained, as do so many unconscious details in decoration, a true confirmation of their date, for they had exactly the silhouette of the dress of fashionable women of that period. A tall Georgian mantelpiece lay in front as one walked down the room and on each side of it there were two mahogany doors of great height, tallying with two equal doors on the wall opposite that flow of windows; the walls themselves being occupied by the huge panels of tapestry.

Going through one of these doors, one turned the corner into an ante-room, beyond which the ballroom could be seen stretched out to great length between the opened double-folds of another tall mahogany door. This room was even longer and higher than that through which one had passed, and the far-off ceiling had a stucco design of a rare and cloud-like lightness, which made the heavy structure really appear to float above one's head. Here, the other three panels of tapestry were upon the walls, and indeed these tapestries exerted an extraordinary fascination upon us children.

In another season, we would walk in the bluebell wood, across the colliery line, while all the time the colliery engine pants behind us. They will be magically beautiful again, for a few days or a week or more, long before the pale barley ripens, pale as the hair of the little girl whom we saw coming down by the gasworks, past the Domesday mill, into the haunted shadows. The Derbyshire woods are dark, dark, and have 'Alpine' grass (I do not know the botanical name) growing upon banks and in dark corners, a straight, lank, dark green grass, like a Nereid's hair. If you find a stone or pebble on the ground it is, as likely as not, a piece of clinker from the mine, and a seam of coal may come to the surface upon the side of any hill. But I have been told that an older and paler form of bluebell grows here. The whole wood is dyed blue with them and their honey breath brings poetry and the sharp-shadowed image. When I think of them, now, I remember the Venus of the bluebell wood, which was what I called the stone fountain of Bolsover Castle when I was little more than twenty years old.

BOLSOVER CASTLE   Bolsover is troubled and stormy. It excites, and does not lull, imagination. It stands on a spur of land above a precipice, where the land breaks and falls, two hundred or three hundred feet, on to another level. You have to climb to it and come along the ridge; or the land drops, and the northern corner of Derbyshire lies below you with the moors and high hills in the distance. At its foot there grew tall trees, reaching to the keep, but they have been cut down, the Castle stands gaunt and empty on its crag, abandoned to the weather and shaken and riven by the mines beneath, but its romantic fire must touch and heat the blood of all who see it.

The gateway to the Castle has something grandiose and theatrical in its air, and takes us immediately to the masques and horsemanship of the Cavaliers. The moment it opens we are on enchanted ground, for there is nothing like Bolsover. To one side, as we enter, lies the Riding House where the Cavalier Marquis, and later, Duke of Newcastle, trained his horses, his barbs and Neapolitans and mares of noble Spanish strain, in the cabriol, the *jetée*, and the other figures of the *haute école*. This Riding House is in a style of architecture that is unique so far as England is concerned, with a great Italian doorway, gigantic in proportion, and gable after gable, of Dutch influence, but like nothing ever built in Holland.[1] In front are the huge rooms, ruined and roofless, in Italian style, built for the entertainment of Charles I and his court when Ben Jonson's masque of *Love's Welcome* was performed, in 1634, with dresses and stage setting by Inigo Jones, the architect being John Smythson. We shall walk later through those rooms, in admiration of their stone doorways.

The keep lies to the right, with its forecourt and two lodges, and with the battlemented roof common to this part of Derby-shire. It was built by the same John Smythson, but had been begun by his father Robert Smythson around 1610, hence the difference in style. Most beautiful are the vaulted ceilings, of the hall particularly, and of another room, the Star Chamber, which has saints and patriarchs, not remote from Titian, on the walls; beside which there are the earliest instances in England of lacquer painting on the panelling of certain rooms, and other rooms have Flemish paintings on their ceilings. The kitchen is a wonderful and fearful hall, with deep stone sinks, given over to the rats and ghosts of scullions. But the chief beauty of the keep of Bolsover is the chimneypieces of local stone and Derbyshire marble, some of them fitted into the corners of the rooms, wonderfully varied in design, and the work, probably, of French craftsmen.

At the foot of the keep a terrace has been contrived along the top of the wall, above the precipice. It was wonderful to walk here before the trees were felled, with no parapet, and on a level with the topmost boughs, and look down the steep fall on to the land below, mysterious with mines and collieries, with the parks of Renishaw and Sutton Scarsdale sloping in the distance with their woods, dark green and almost black, and in the

---

[1] Bolsover Castle itself was built by Sir Charles Cavendish, younger son of Bess of Hardwick. His son was the Cavalier Marquis, and later Duke of Newcastle, and this is the place to mention his book on Horsemanship which contains many views of Bolsover Castle as the background for the *haute école*.

feeling that this is the beginning of the North, that the accent is northern, and that we can see the Peak and the Derbyshire Moors upon a clear, late afternoon. But on the enchanted ground of Bolsover we must look within, and in an inner enclosure, below the keep, we see the Venus fountain, a stone Venus who combs her hair, set on a pedestal above a stone basin, dug deep into the soil, and furnished with niches and ledges that could be garden seats, while in the surrounding wall there are strange little rooms with fireplaces, and the whole feeling is that this is the court of love. The Venus fountain, so far as we know, is unique in England. Nothing else, like this, keeps the love songs of the Cavaliers and their ladies, and still echoes, to our imagination, with the trembling of the lute string.

It is sad but wonderful after this to walk through the roofless rooms of the great gallery, marvelling at their huge stone doorways. It may be that the forgotten architect, John Smythson, is freakish and too large in scale, but we would remember nothing else than that the court of the Cavaliers came here for a night or two, that these great rooms were put up for that purpose, and that the masque was given here. But there is still the terrace below the long gallery, and running so far along the hill, that is not so steep upon this side, that its surface has been wrecked and shattered by the mines beneath, as though by artillery, and it is not possible to walk down to its end. And, turning back, we see the curious architecture of the façade, with stone stays or buttresses, for they cannot be mere ornament, that resemble guns or cannon set upright into the wall; and we see a splendid stone door above a flight of steps; and the shivered, rooky battlements, black as rooks, and the whole building, Bolsover Castle, entire, dead, dead, as the Mayan ruins of Uxmal or Chichen Itza, and as remote from us, but with a ghostly poetry that fires the imagination, that can never be forgotten, and that never cools.

The palace-dwellers of Bolsover had travelled beyond their native land and fenced themselves in here with a huge girdle of walls and gates, so that the summer evenings seemed to live HARDWICK HALL longer while the lute echoes lasted. Hardwick, built by the same family, was a yet safer retreat, for it lies in a huge park the very trees and rocks of which seem to suggest, in their fantastic forms, the antlers and the distant belling of the herds of deer. When you arrive up actually at the house, it seems very far removed from the world, both of this day and of the Elizabethans, as though it had always been remote and silent. The windows, indeed, at the back of the house, where there is the long gallery always to be found in the great Elizabethan houses, give on to a wide, misty waste of grass which stretches away as far as the eyes can see; so that any noise you hear in the silence of the evening, or the early morning, must come out of these heights and hollows. But it is a language of sound as dead as a dead speech, so that none can understand, or need, indeed, bother as to its meaning; it is like the Latin words, half-effaced, below a statue, which none but a scholar can decipher, and none but he would wish to understand.

It is the towers of Hardwick that rise up before us as we enter the park. They have the habit of grouping curiously, according to which angle they are seen from, sometimes spread out to a great extent, with the six towers at the corners, or, from this approach, all four close together, as though the building is shaped like the diamond on a playing card, more still, like the ace of clubs, so that the fourth tower is hidden, almost, behind the other three.

But the towers sink back again behind a wall, till the wall itself becomes more elaborate, with a battlemented ornament like a halberd head upon it, and we come to the porch or gatehouse into the walled court, and our breath is taken away at the high and immense building that lies within. We see the six towers, now, at their right interval, two to a side, and one flanking, or behind, the other. But what seems incredible is the huge height of Hardwick, and its enormous windows. There is more glass than wall. The scale is gigantic, and the six towers bear a stone parapet that is perforated with the letters E and S, which initials are repeated in the flowerbeds to each side of the stone flagged pathway; but in fact these battlements look more romantic still from the distance, when, as Mrs Ratcliffe writes, they look as though splintered by the lances of the tournament.

The house was built by Bess of Hardwick, who was born here, in the Old Hall, in 1520, and who had four husbands, Sir William Cavendish and the Earl of Shrewsbury among them; and she died at Hardwick on a day when snow prevented the builders from climbing into their scaffolding, and so work was brought to a standstill. It was erected, therefore, during the last years of Queen Elizabeth and the early years of James I, but the name of the architect is unknown. It is anonymous, like mediaeval building, and we shall see how, according to mood, it can be the last and belated masterpiece of the Perpendicular;

a great house of the Renaissance; or the lesson and precursor of much modern architecture.[1]

We enter Hardwick by the doorway in its long plain pillared porch, and are in the hall, a high room with a splendid fireplace carved with stag supporters for the Hardwick coat-of-arms. There is here some needlework on a black ground, of heroines and the Virtues, once thought to be by the hand of Mary, Queen of Scots. So we come to the first floor of low ceilinged rooms, full of portraits and old furniture, but with little promise of what lies above, the first inkling of which is the stone staircase hung with tapestries of Hero and Leander, with older 'verdures' higher up, and a landing, and 'millefleur' tapestries, and then a doorway with an elaborate iron lock. It is the great chamber or state room, in our opinion the most beautiful room, not in England alone, but in the whole of Europe, with a great frieze of parget work, ten or twelve feet deep, of coloured plaster, representing a stag hunt, and a boar hunt, the court of Diana, and the story of Orpheus. There are forest scenes of men and dogs hunting under the trees; and, in a corner, Diana and her court. Above the window bays are panels of Spring and Summer. Spring is whipping Cupid with a birch of flowers; while Summer, crowned with corn, sits naked on a heap of corn stooks to watch the harvest. This noble room – but the plaster frieze is so beautiful it dwarfs all else – has a magnificent and plain fireplace, set flat, so that it does not interrupt the eye, and the floor has the Hardwick or rush matting laid upon it.

There are some French cabinets in the room that belong to the Renaissance of Henri II and Henri IV, with grotesque masks, but of the richest workmanship, and a marquetry table which has its entire surface inlaid with figures of musical instruments, guitars and mandolines, with chessmen and backgammon boards, with playing cards, as on the coat of Harlequin, and in the midst that beautiful and mysterious poem:

> *The redolent smelle of eglantine*
> *We stagges exalt to the Divine*

---

[1] It is likely that plans for the new house were provided by Robert Smythson, and although 'the evidence ... is not absolutely conclusive ... it is extremely strong.... On the other hand there is no evidence or likelihood that Smythson closely supervised the building of Hardwick. It was probably the case, as often happened with Elizabethan houses, of a "surveyor" providing plans and elevations, leaving the detailing to the workmen on the spot, who made alterations to suit their own convenience or as dictated by the client while work was in progress.' M. Girouard, *Hardwick Hall*, London, 1976.

that might be part of a madrigal by Roberto Greene, the 'stagges' being, no doubt, the stags of the Cavendish arms.

The remainder of the house is no less fascinating. One room has a stone relief of the Muses, mandoline in hand, above the fireplace; and nearly every room has plaster decoration, sometimes of nude figures for the elements, Fire, Wind, and Water, part gilded;[1] but, particularly, there is wonderful needlework. Some small panels are, it seems, authentically by Mary, Queen of Scots. These were brought from other houses – probably Chatsworth and the old Hardwick Hall, as the new house was not built until after her death. There are some velvet chairs, too, with their backs worked, one with Sir Walter Raleigh driving in his coach, according to the tradition of the house, and the other with a pool of hounds with their red tongues hanging out, and the kill taking place at the foot of a tree with jewelled fruits. There are delightful and indescribable tapestries of giants and bearded heroes in the Roman costume of the time of the Emperor Charles V, deeply engaged in lost histories and forgotten legends. The beds of state are wonderful, but hanging, as Walpole saw them, 'in costly golden tatters'; curtains of black and silver, Venetian velvets and damascenes, hangings rayed with gold, or of baudekyn powdered with flowers, or worked with gold and silver wires and threads. No other house possesses such needlework.

But we come at last to the great gallery, all but two hundred feet in length, hung with tapestry from end to end, and with portraits hung upon the tapestry. Not so many years ago, the tapestries were three or four deep on top of one another. Among them were the fragments of the hunting tapestries, now sewn together, and at Chatsworth, which were brought here when Lord Burlington's old house at Londesborough, in Yorkshire, was burnt down. They are among the most beautiful Gothic tapestries in existence. And here, in this long gallery, hangs the portrait of Queen Elizabeth, in an enormous farthingale, stiffer and more elaborate than any crinoline of the Second Empire, not plain black, like the hooped skirts of the Infanta in portraits by Velasquez, but patterned, incredibly, with birds and fishes,

---

[1] Much of this plasterwork and parts, doubtless, of the great hunting scenes were the work of Abraham Smith, remains of whose work are to be seen also in the ruins of the Old Hall at Hardwick. Some of the figures, those, for instance, of Spring and Summer, are proved by Miss Margaret Jourdain to have been adapted from engravings by Martin de Vos, and others from Crispin van de Passe, yet one can but think of them as original, so transformed are they by the poetry and inspiration of the craftsman.

a sea horse, or serpent, and even a spouting whale. We can look out, from the windows in the long bays, upon the park and the stag-antlered trees.

We can come out of the house and wander as far as the ruins of the Old Hall near by, where Bess of Hardwick was born, and in which Mary, Queen of Scots, was lodged, for she never inhabited the new building. It is in ruin, like Bolsover and Kirby Hall; but we can look up at the remains of coloured plasterwork; at the forest chamber and its hunting scenes; at the giants' chamber, with little left of the pair of giants, the Gog and Magog in Roman armour over the mantelpiece; at a limb in plaster, here or there, or part of a figure, or a coat of arms; and in one place there used to be, it may still be there, that mysterious inscription again, which is worked upon the table, among the mandolines and playing cards:

The redolent smelle of eglantine
We stagges exalt to the Divine.

We turn round and there Hardwick stands before us at another angle, and we see the lead statues and yew alleys of its haunted garden.

SUTTON SCARSDALE   Under the shadow of the great cliff of Bolsover was yet another great house, and we would recount here our own experience of Sutton Scarsdale, lying only a few miles from my old home. This story is in fact an extraordinary instance of what has been allowed to happen under our eyes, by way of destruction of our national heritage of works of art, with no redress, and no means of prevention. While we were spending the autumn at my old home, in 1920, or soon after, word was brought to us that there had been a sale at Sutton Scarsdale, and that my brother and myself had better go there. I was recovering from a long illness, and having just turned writer, had in mind a book on the wonderful spectacle of eighteenth-century Venice, during the phase of late Baroque and Rococo. This subject gave place, eventually, to *Southern Baroque Art*, my first prose book, but at the time of which I am speaking, I could think of nothing else but the paintings of Tiepolo, and can still taste the rare intoxication of his brush upon the plaster. The spell lasted for many months; and in this mood I set out for Sutton Scarsdale.

This was the house, according to local legend, of the rake in *The Rake's Progress*. A large colliery village, with rows of outside lavatories, lies to the side of it. But when we got there the harm had been done already, and it was too late. Sutton Scarsdale is a long low building with a Corinthian, stone façade, of supreme elegance by Smith of Warwick, architect of Stoneleigh Abbey. No purchaser would even buy the stone, and, later, it was proposed to blow it up with gunpowder. The interior was gutted, and a ruin. It contained a stair, with twisted balusters, and some splendid panelled rooms which have been removed, now, to an American museum. But the glory of Sutton Scarsdale was in the pair of Venetian saloons, on two floors, one above another, with fireplaces at each end; all, fireplaces, walls, and ceilings, the work of Vassalli, and of Artari, 'gentleman plasterer', as he is called by Gibbs. When we saw it, the ceiling of the lower room had fallen in, so that there was the extraordinary spectacle of four Venetian mantelpieces, all of the richest work imaginable, richer, far, than anything in a Venetian palace, hanging in the air, with the remains of the coloured stucco in panels and niches upon the walls, and some fragments of the figures on the higher stucco ceiling. One of the mantelpieces, only, in the upper saloon was still perfect, and we were told that an offer of ten shillings would be accepted for it. But some days went by before a farm cart could be sent over to fetch it, and during that interval it had collapsed entirely and lay in little pieces on the floor. Such was the fate of what was, certainly, the finest work of Artari or of any of the Italians in England, for in other houses, at Houghton or at Mereworth, they had to show restraint and work up to the Palladian solemnity of their setting. Only at Sutton Scarsdale was it the full Venetian Rococo, and here, perhaps, at greater outlay than any Venetian family of the *settecento* could afford. The violent force of this revelation of the Venetian eighteenth century may be imagined. Probably, if it had to declare itself, it could have found no more willing audience.[1]

KEDLESTON How different the furniture in the 'Venetian' manner at Kedleston, all by Adam, but unlike him and totally unlike any furniture to be seen in Venice: the State bed with branching palm trees, the palm mirror, and gilt dolphin sofa with its tritons. But at Kedleston Adam is inimitable and at his best, though the exterior and the planning of the house was largely the work of Matthew Brettingham and Paine. Adam was called in early on, but only the south front of Kedleston is due entirely

[1] The ruin of Sutton Scarsdale was bought by Sir Osbert Sitwell in the 1950s and, thanks to the efforts of Mr Reresby Sitwell, is now in the hands of the Department of the Environment [ed.].

to him. This is coldly Roman, by a Lowland Scot, and like a triumphal arch with a dome above it in the middle of a square block of building; but, then, we would never admire Adam as an exterior architect. The great north portico is due to Paine, and as bleak and chilly as his portico at Nostell. But the interior of Kedleston has one room, by Adam, of truly Roman grandeur. This is the hall, with its twenty fluted columns of Derbyshire alabaster from a neighbouring quarry.[1] Adam has lavished the utmost refinements of his skill upon the two fireplaces and upon the compositions of white stucco figures that are above them; but more so still upon the grates of burnished brass and steel, the fenders and the fire irons. These grates and fenders are real show pieces. Their technical perfection is that of the Japanese lacquerers and swordsmiths, and it would not be surprising if, like the columns of Derbyshire alabaster, they are a local product, for steel or iron grates of superb workmanship are often found in Derbyshire. Before we leave Kedleston we may admire these grates more than anything else in its interior. For the domed rotunda behind this, with its cast iron stoves and delicate wall lights, is a serious and grim apartment. But what can be done with the hall and rotunda? For they are quite unsuited to a private house, and we may find ourselves agreeing with Dr Johnson, on leaving, that 'the house would do excellently well for a town hall; the large room with the pillars would do for the judges to sit in at the assizes; the circular room for a jury chamber; and the room above for prisoners.' Adam, indeed, like many architects before, and after him, has made the house into a costly prison for its inhabitants. But the hall, for all that, is Roman in magnificence.

DERBY   Close to Kedleston is Derby, where the church of All Saints, now the Cathedral, is by Adam's fellow Scot, James Gibbs, who himself studied in Rome under Carlo Fontana. Here, there is individual and beautiful ironwork by Robert Bakewell, which, anywhere but in our land of understatement, would be as famous as the grilles and balconies of Jean Lamour in the Place Stanislas at Nancy.[2] The other glory is the Perpendicular tower, retained when Gibbs rebuilt the church. This rises in

---

[1] 'The hall is very stately ... it has two rows of marble pillars, dug as I hear, from Langley, a quarry in Northamptonshire; the pillars are very large and massy, they take up too much room, they were better away,' Dr Johnson's *Diary*. Langley is in fact in Derbyshire, only a mile or two from Kedleston.

[2] The entrance gates at Staunton Harold, the home of the Ferrers family, nearby in Leicestershire and the screen in the church there may also be by Robert Bakewell.

three perfectly proportioned storeys: doorway, with west window above that, neither of them excessive in size; then, a storey most beautifully latticed and ornamented with blind tracery and arcading; last, the bell-chamber of large window surface to let out the sound; then, pinnacled and parapeted roof-platform, all the metal pennons flying from the four corner pinnacles. But who would want to stand up there to look down on the china works and engine yards? Once, as can be seen in a 'primitive' painting of Queen Anne's time at my old home, Derby was a red brick town of fine houses – but how subtly differenced from a Dutch town of the same date! – with the tower of All Saints, even then, rising over it as though it had stood there for ages.

NOTTINGHAMSHIRE

SOUTHWELL   The chapter house of Southwell Minster I have known since childhood. It is polygonal but with no central column. An extraordinary and fantastic floral profusion, or blossoming and leafing in stone, characterises this chapter house and its approaches, but more especially the entrance to it; the columns of which are of Purbeck marble with beautiful floral capitals and floral mouldings in stone above them, the entrance itself being through and under a double archway of an airy elegance with delicate tracery in the opening above it. Dr Pevsner, who has devoted a small volume to the chapter house, remarks wisely that 'it will never be possible to determine how far they [the flowers and leaves] were copied from sketches in notebooks made during French apprenticeships or journeys and how far from nature. Both methods were no doubt used.'[1] Maple, oak, hawthorn, ranunculus, potentilla, vine, ivy, and hop have been identified among other plants. This floral persistence has almost an obsessional character in the chapter house at Southwell, and it may have been a fever which lasted but a few years in the minds and hands of its creators, probably a single master-sculptor and his pupils.

NEWARK   Newark, which I have also known well since childhood on the way north to my old home, has its parish church with tower to be looked up at and admired, and, as in many town churches in the Midlands, with a spire which is the adjunct of the tower.

[1] Dr Nikolaus Pevsner, *The Leaves of Southwell*, London, 1945, p. 31.

The spire of Newark resembles that of Grantham, not many miles away in Lincolnshire, and both are good; but one must award the palm to Newark because of the glorious statement of the bell-chamber on the fourth storey of its tower; canopied double lights on each face with statues in little niches at the foot of them to each side, and a crocket-less spire with corner turrets and more storeys of spire-lights than at Grantham, where the two sets of spire-lights are banded together boringly instead of being given an intriguing spacing. But the church at Newark has not been entered as often as it could have been. For in this unlikely Midland town are two chantry chapels, the Meyring and the Markham, so alike as to be interchangeable and mistaken for each other, except that the latter has thinner, taller window-lights and a crested, not a battlemented cornice. Both have the look of ancient, but portable stone cages.

KINGSTON-ON-SOAR

The reign of curiosities is at hand. It can be embarked upon at Kingston-on-Soar, in the chased and lozenged pillars of another chantry chapel, late in date (1547) and suggestive of a temple of Golconda reported by mariners at second hand through the Portuguese, until we remember the century earlier Manoelino of Roslin Chapel, near Edinburgh. Persons familiar with Alcobaça or Belem will be unable to dismiss from their minds that there is somewhat of Portuguese-Indian influence in this church upon a tributary of the river Trent. The decoration of the chantry includes the motif of a child in a barrel repeated over and over again, this 'babe-in-tun' being a rebus for the Babington family. In the same church is also a curious kneeling figure in the Scrope tomb, a middle-aged son, this time, with long hair and beard, cloak and ruff of Spanish fashion, and armoured breeks, kneeling, reading a book. But his parents are too 'dressed up'.

RATCLIFFE-ON-SOAR

In the next village, Ratcliffe-on-Soar,[1] are the alabaster tombs of the Sacheverells, double tombs, a few of them, that is to say, knights lying with their wives and children innumerable, but the church is small and inconspicuous, the floor is often two or three inches deep in water, and many, if not most, lovers of art, in ignorance, would neglect it and pass by.

WOLLATON HALL

Good and bad taste existed, side by side, in the reign of Queen Elizabeth. Wollaton Hall, sunk in Nottingham, is ugly now, and must have always been, built under bastard Dutch or German influence, like the worst excesses of the German

---

[1] One of the Nottinghamshire alabaster quarries was at Ratcliffe-on-Soar.

Renaissance, and even then, at second hand, for its ornament is copied from German drawing-books. Wollaton Hall was designed by Robert Smythson, who was master-mason at Longleat and may have partly designed that, too. His son was John Smythson, to whom the glorious and romantic Bolsover Castle is due.

WORKSOP MANOR   In the north of the county, just across the border from Bolsover, are the remains of Worksop Manor, which, had it been completed, was to have been the most considerable of all the works of that master of fluency, James Paine. This tremendous scheme, for the Duke of Norfolk, provided for a quadrangle with sides three hundred feet in length, and two interior courts. The interior wing between them was to contain the Egyptian Hall, a hundred and forty feet long and fifty-five feet high, approached through an outer hall and a Tribune, which was to be circular with a peristyle of eight columns, while from the wing on the far side of the Egyptian Hall the grand staircase was to rise. A vista led right through the building, somewhat after the example of Vanvitelli at Caserta. But the Duke of Norfolk's son died, and work was discontinued when only one wing had been completed. The foundations are on the site of the previous Worksop Manor, with five hundred rooms, that was burnt down, and the whole area, though a subsequent owner, the Duke of Newcastle, cleared the ground, still contains stretches of wall and other traces of Paine's plan.

LEICESTERSHIRE AND RUTLAND

And now we go farther into the country with destination the White Ladies of Grace Dieu, a priory of Augustinian Canonesses, a journey into bucolic regions of the monks and nuns with halts and stops upon the way. As we get deeper and deeper into the country and into the leafy silence unbroken by engine of any kind, we hear of harvesting and haymaking, and LEICESTER   the like, and even of hunting and hawking. Leicester Abbey, where Wolsey came to die; where, so it was said, the sanctuary lamp hung by a plait of the hair of Petronilla, daughter-in-law of Robert de Bellomont, known as le Bossu, Earl of Leicester, founder of this rich monastery of Black Canons in 1143; where Henry VIII's Commissioner Layton, finding the abbot and monks difficult and contumacious, proposed to accuse them of the grossest vices in order to induce them to surrender, and succeeded in his object; it was here in this classical land of the chase that there was monastic hunting across the flat fields and over the hedges. The canons started out early, often before daybreak (cubbing?), this was in 1528, and the abbot seldom made an appearance in choir, and when he did, brought his fool with him who made the Black Canons laugh with his jokes and tag-ends of song. The vicar-general of the diocese, visiting them a few years before the Surrender, had tried to improve things by his order in the original dog-Latin that none of the canons should keep 'ultra iii brase de lez greyhounds et nulli alii canes nisi ii or iii cowple off Spanyells pro le haris'.[1] And at

ULVERSCROFT Ulverscroft, founded for Augustinian hermits by Robert Blanchemain, another Earl of Leicester, which even the Commissioners write, 'standith in a wildernesse in the fforeste of Charnewood and refressith many pore people and waye farying people', the priors kept their hounds and hawks, and had a ranger, a huntsman, a falconer, and seven woodmen employed in cutting firewood for the house. It was indeed but a mile or two from the White Ladies of Grace Dieu

GRACE DIEU   Here, from the account books of one of the nuns, Dame Petronilla, for the years 1414-18, an impression, as of even the sounds of pastoral life so long ago, is to be gathered in. She gives minute details as to the number of calves and pigs or the sale of wattles and hurdles. The villeins, men and women (some Irish among them, who came here for the harvesting), this in 1415 the year of Agincourt, had each a pair of gloves given to them for weeding the barley. The nuns of St Michael's, Stamford, in this same context, who always recorded the day 'when we began to reap', gave eight pairs of gloves at a penny-halfpenny each to the hired reapers to shield them from the thistles. According to their sub-prioress, the nuns at Grace Dieu themselves 'sometimes help secular folk in garnering their grain during the autumn season.' And it is complained to the bishop in 1449, concerning Margaret Belers, the cellaress, that 'she goes out to work in autumn alone with Sir Henry [the chaplain], he reaping the harvest and she binding the sheaves, and at evening she comes riding behind him on the same horse. She is over friendly with him and has been since the doings aforesaid.' Here, too, with a feeling of the days drawing in, there is the autumn visit of the candlemaker and the buying of tallow and mutton fat for the making of cressets and rush lights. How dismal and dark

---

[1] 'More than three brace of greyhounds, and no other dogs except two or three couple of spaniels to hunt the hares.'

the long evenings must have been! Made no more cheerful by
the age or madness or eccentricity of some of the inmates; the
(only) six monks of Owston, an Augustinian priory not far
away, where 'relygion is not very duly kepte for lake of numbers
and for because one of them is a very aged man and a nother
not havying his wytt very well but fantastycall and more than
halfe ffrantyke'; or another complaint of a prior, 'aliquando
lunatica . . . ideota . . . furiosam . . . decrepita et non abilis ad
equitandum'.[1]

LANGLEY   At Langley, another Leicestershire nunnery of Benedictines,
there are indications in an inventory of 1485 of a whole sacristy
full of embroideries, pieces of that *opus Anglicanum* for which
the English nuns were famous, though in fact these are of a late
date in this art that had greater association with the early
Middle Ages. Four altar frontals are listed of green damask
powdered with swans and eagles; and three of black powdered
with swans and roses; a vestment of black damask broidered
with roses and stars; a complete vestment of white worked with
'rede trewlyps' though, astonishingly, true lovers-knots are
intended by this and not, as one might surmise, 'red tulips'.
Those had not yet been brought here from Turkey. A great
cloth (banner) the inventory goes on, of red powdered with
'bects beds and boturfleys'; a large coverlet of 'blew and better
blewe with swans and cocks', and 'a tapet of ye same'; a coverlet
of 'ostrych fydyrs'; one of 'grene and yowlowe with vynys and
roses'; of red and white with a trellis of birds; of 'grene and
yowlowe with eyes and swannys', and so on. Also, in a smaller
way, the nuns of Langley Priory made 'blood-bands' or silk
bandages to be worn during the *minutio* or blood-letting.

BELVOIR CASTLE   Treasures of another age are to be found in the Duke of
Rutland's collection of Charles II silver at Belvoir Castle, while
BOTTESFORD   nearby, in the church at Bottesford, a *locus classicus* of English
sculpture, are the tombs of the seventh and eighth Earls of
Rutland, whether by C. G. Cibber or Grinling Gibbons, re-
spectable, but in no way portentous monuments. Gibbons is
certainly to be seen in the monument to Baptist Noel, Viscount
EXTON   Campden, at Exton, in Rutland, though above all else Gibbons
was a woodcarver and not at his best in stone or marble, and,
here, his bas-reliefs of the children are more successful than the
marble statues. He was paid a thousand pounds for Lord
Campden's monument, and, even in its mutilated state, we can

---

[1] 'More or less lunatic . . . idiotic . . . raving . . . decrepit and unable to get
on a horse.'

still admire the two kneeling figures at an altar and the pair of winged cupids, poor memorial though this be, in numbers, to a nobleman who had four wives and nineteen children. Near to him, in wig and lace cravat, lies his fifth son, who died at eighteen, 'free from the age's grand debaucherys'. Nearby, at BURLEY-ON-THE-HILL Burley-on-the-Hill, is the later monument to Lady Charlotte Finch, with the statue of the young kneeling girl by Sir Francis Chantrey, a beautiful example of this sculptor's tact and skill.

And before leaving Leicestershire we should notice the headstones in many of the churchyards there. Loveliest of all are the purple, green, or blue slate headstones from the WANLIP Charnwood Forest quarries, particularly at Wanlip, with incised urns and vine tendrils and formal foliage, designs that are ultra-Adam in delicacy and refinement, to be ranked as works of art with the finest Sheffield plate, and arguing an extraordinary contentment of mind and pleasure in his work on the part of the humble stonemason who sketched out and carved them.

LINCOLNSHIRE

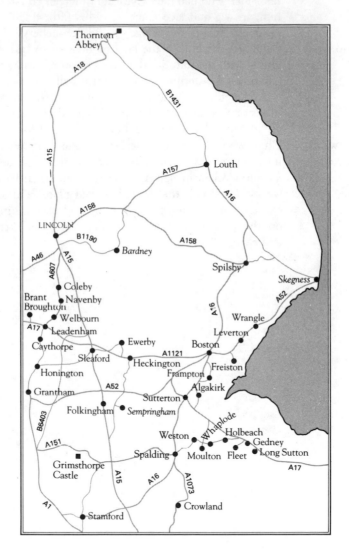

Let us suppose ourselves for a few moments of time on a rainy morning or afternoon in Lincoln. It is to be a wet day, raining all day long from the beginning, but with intervals so that one can go out with raincoat and umbrella, walk round the outside of the cathedral, look up at the towers, and then take refuge inside the building. There are strong gusts of wind and the jackdaws that fly out from the towers are soon blown back, wheeling and complaining, into their eyries. Likewise, back into the White Hart, too, when raincoat and umbrella are wringing wet, but out again and on the same round in another half-an-hour for there is nothing else to do. This is the way to see it and live with it, never for too long at a time, and let the extreme and extraordinary nature of the cathedral make its impression on one's mind.

First of all it is its whiteness against the rainy sky, and the black caps of its turrets, and an affinity in time and origin to the White Tower of the Tower of London. They are of the same blood and language, if of a different purpose. Then, the huge scale of the undertaking with the west towers coming up and shielding behind the Romanesque west façade; and something curious about the corner turrets to either end of this west façade, which is that they recall the French pottery jars of childhood shaped like beehives, and which when you lifted off their lids had honey inside them. That association with honeycombs at the corners of its west front is a thing that clings to the stone like a swarm of bees, that one cannot dismiss from one's mind, and that adds a flowery fragrance to the rainy day. It does not rain here in Lincolnshire any more than in Holland that is just across the North Sea; and yet the wonder of Lincoln Cathedral is that it was built, less in sunshine than in rain. There are no buildings on this scale across the Dogger Bank; no Ely, Lincoln, York, or Durham. They are only found on this side of the North Sea, along our east coast. The inconceivable energy they display is what is interesting about them, and that it was a display of strength inseparable from those other qualities that make a great work of art.

It could be argued that fine architecture is only suited to the rigours of either heat or cold. There is little good building in lands of eternal spring. Art does not follow climate but exists despite of it. That is why it is found in unsuitable places and in unsuited families. It can come unexpectedly and without warning so that we do not know where to look for it. Lincoln Cathedral may in itself come as no surprise because of the huge number of beautiful village churches in every direction, one of them for instance 'at about every mile' along 'The Cliff', 'the steep western face of a long wold range' that leads from Honington to Lincoln.[1] One or two of these, Navenby for instance, are remarkable enough; not that this string of churches is comparable to those further south in the county in that exceedingly unpicturesque part of Lincolnshire, except when the corn is ripe and ready for harvest, lying between Spalding and Boston; or to the even more remarkable line of churches in the other direction, eight of them in the twelve miles between Spalding and Long Sutton; with others again no less beautiful and extraordinary across into Norfolk and ending at King's Lynn. These are in excuse, it could be said, but not in full explanation; though it makes it less unnatural that this stone monument worthy in terms of labour alone of the Pharaohs or the Khmer Emperors of Angkor should rise on its hill in the midst of the marshlands and the fens, the very name of the city it is thought being of the same derivation with that of London, meaning 'the hill-fort of the pool', and signifying a time 'when all the part below the hill was a stagnant mere'. These village churches, to which it is a hopeless and perhaps unworthy ambition to drag visitors from abroad because of the inhospitable nature of the locality and the uncertain weather, are extraordinary enough in themselves without the crowning wonder of the cathedral, but anywhere else, except where they are, they would certainly have aroused wonder and world-wide admiration. But so it is, and so they will remain, more of private interest than of public acclamation.

And out into the rain again to look up at the towers. We cannot envisage ant-like masses of workers removing baskets of earth, or carrying hods of stone or mortar. This is not the Orient where buildings go up behind lattices of bamboo or screens of matting, and armies of men and women work indiscriminately as beasts of burden and for tools use little more than their bare hands. Here they worked to careful drawings and only a few men at a time were on the towers, to which the ladders would be firmer and more substantial than those of poles and lianas up which the workers of another skin-colour swarmed with naked feet. Not did they cook their meals and sleep at the foot of the cathedral but lived in town houses, however humble, built of wood or brick. They were skilled

[1] Caythorpe, Leadenham, Brant Broughton, Navenby, Welbourn, Coleby among them.

workers organised into guilds and having served long appren-
ticeship, not conscripted and pressed into service like a gang of
slaves. There were master-sculptors and mass relief-carvers on
the temples and long corridors of Angkor. At their best they
were great artists; at their worst stylised and archaic strip-
cartoonists. They have an exhausting and telling monotony
that no Gothic master-of-the-works would have countenanced
or allowed to pass. For above all the Gothic craftsmen were
adept at changing or varying the subject, introducing new
themes, and were prime inventors and perfectors of the gim-
mick. The play on words was a mere pastime for them in all
their fondness for another meaning or a rebus, games into
which they entered with the spirit of the acrostical, double-
meaning comic scenes in Shakespeare's plays. No hundred
heads of the Buddha, all with the identical, mysterious and
benign smile, as at the Bayon of Angkor, for the builders and
sculptors of our thirteenth-century cathedrals! Their individuality, their personal identity would not have allowed of this.
They could not have sunk their humour into the same mould.
Even in their anonymity they were irrepressible. As for example
the seated figures of kings – to judge from their crowns – all
seated on thrones under canopies just over the Romanesque
central porch of Lincoln. They are fourteenth-century figures,
all in different attitudes as though seated in the stalls of a
chapter house, and it is only surprising that more difference has
not been wrought into the stone canopies above their heads.

Or take an isolated figure such as the statue of Queen
Margaret on the outside of the Angel Choir, that is to say, at
the far corner of Bishop Russell's chantry chapel, the right-
hand one of the two chapels flanking the south or Judgement
Porch of Lincoln.[1] One wonders what she is doing there,
standing in her niche, no other carved figures near her, at the
foot of a buttress above the cresting of the Perpendicular chantry chapel! Standing out there through seven hundred winters,
indifferent to sunshine or rain! Her face, which is that of a
beautiful woman, is the sculptor's idea of a queen, for it is too
early to be a portrait. She holds the hem of her robe in one

[1] These two chapels, the three-windowed, self-contained tomb-apartments
of Bishops Longland and Russell, exactly similar in exterior, suggest that the
custom of the chantry chapel, had it continued a little further and not been
damped down and extinguished by the Reformation, could well have culmi-
nated in the provision of creature comforts such as they were used to in life, as in
burials in Ancient Egypt, for the occupants of the tomb. They were reserved
apartments in perpetuity, with staff of priests who were servants almost as much
as they were intercessors or remembrancers.

hand, and our eyes go up the buttress above her to where the rain drips down on her, or, in fact, just misses her on this day at least, from a pair of stone gargoyles, which jut out perhaps thirty feet above her head. There they are, those necessary and inevitable, those almost obligatory parts of the baggage train of all Gothic cathedrals, in pairs at the foot of the gabled roof to every buttress all along the south front, and doubtless all round the building, carrying the rainwater in the hollowed troughs of their stone bodies and spurting it down; and behind each gable we see the arc of a flying buttress joining it like a stalk to the shell or vessel of the main building; one could say pressing its foot to keep its balance against the buttress, rather as an acrobat leaning perilously outwards presses the sole of his foot against his mast or pole to keep his balance.

And we have come round the back of Lincoln, past the outside of the Lady Chapel, to the decagon of the chapter house, inside and out more like a celestial kitchen, with its high conical roof and of an extra fascination because of its buttresses like tie-posts, eight of them, no less, standing a little apart from the building and stretching their stone arms out to keep it steady. It seems even then on the point of ascent, but has been tied down these centuries with the stone columns and tall pinnacles at all its angles. Or is it some kind of stone mother and her litter, each of them umbilically connected or strung on to the parent? And there is another of the stone beehive buildings high up, near the entrance to the chapter house, and this could be of honeyed import to either or both the stone parent and her offspring. This is a chapter house with a central shaft or pillar and a star vault of some twenty or so radiating ribs which of custom make it like the corolla of a clematis or passion flower, over a chamber that gives an impression of masculine strength with more in reserve, and could be the council chamber of warrior monks, if not active militarists, at least of some of their Buddhist *confrères* far off in China who were famous for their boxing.

But the interior of Lincoln is of moment for its Angel Choir which is of unequalled beauty and in ultra-perfection of the early Gothic, mid-thirteenth-century style. It is not so much the lower as the upper or clerestory which is so beautiful, and of an Oriental moving or marching elaboration towards the high altar, which is Eastern in idea but of which no Oriental architect has been capable. It is masculine in intent and most emphatic and vigorous of effect; a gallery of paired arches, two

of them at a time between the larger buttresses from which flow
the stone ribs of the ceiling. These paired arches have a central
column of clustered pillars of black Purbeck marble; half-
quatrefoils of stone to either side of these, and a full quatrefoil
above all enclosed in the pointed arch. And it is in or on the
spandrels between these arches that are to be seen the angel-
musicians that give the Angel Choir of Lincoln its name. There
are twenty-eight of them, in whose faces and figures Dr
Nikolaus Pevsner distinguishes 'more than two hands, but only
two masters', to judge by 'round faces and stronger limbs'.[1]
There is room, but no more than that, for the angel-musicians
in the spandrels between the arches; but those apart it is the
wonderful vigour of that arched gallery to both sides of the
choir, and the simplicity of the huge trefoils, only, in the
spandrels below the gallery. There is no call for detail in this
splendour of attack, though it is to be found in abundance in the
stone roof bosses whereon have been identified 'leaves of the
English countryside – oak, vine, maple, ranunculus', and
according to one authority, 'the yellow waterlily', which carries
with it the promise of slow summer afternoons passing with the
punt-pole through whole water-meadows of the lilies, when
most of Lincolnshire was fen and water and the fens were not
always frozen. Below those ceiling bosses the majesty of the
Angel Choir of Lincoln is unsurpassable, if echoed with brass
band orchestration in mid-Victorian town halls of the industrial North and Midlands, but without the yellow waterlilies!

The other interior glory of Lincoln Cathedral is its spired
choirstalls, in double storeys topped with cusped spires and high
pinnacled standards. The misericords at Lincoln, i.e. the
underneath of the stalls which, when turned up, were the
support of the canons while they were standing – and many of
them would be aged – are of extraordinary variety, including
the well-known Fall of Pride, an armoured knight falling from
his stumbling or wounded horse. The stalls, with seating space
for one hundred and eight, and volume of sound, musical or
other, commensurate to that number, tower up like spired
headdresses and are suggestive of cold matins and colder
evensong, as though they were in fanciful protection against fog
and sleet. They are of wholly English invention, far removed
indeed from the spikiness of German Gothic although they may
be seething and pricking with their points. But it is difficult to

[1] *Lincolnshire*, Harmondsworth, 1964, pp. 106-8.

admire them without thinking of the agonies of cold their occupants must have suffered during perhaps seven months of every year. The cold was indeed a strong suit in the ritual. If the stalls at Lincoln are compared with those of Gloucester it will be noticed that the stalls at the latter place are of flat contrivance with only a symbolic hood or canopy, no more than that, over the head of each occupant of a stall. But, and one must be cautious about climatic changes and conditions, it was the county of Gloucester, not Lincoln, that was famous during the Middle Ages for sweet red wine.

Whatever the monotony of landscape, mediaeval monks were particularly enamoured of the marshlands and the fens. The learned monastic historian Dom David Knowles extols the 'paradisiacal fertility of the fenland with its lofty timber and blossoming fruit trees, and the sacred isolation of the monasteries'. Other writers praise 'the park-like meadows and beautiful wealth of red and white chestnut bloom, the remains of ancient manors', but it was surely the isolation and the security this conferred which was the attraction. They, also, liked it for its far horizons, pleasant aspect, and for its eels and wild fowl, a permitted addition to their strict diet.

CROWLAND   If the derivation of Crowland is really, as it sounds, 'the land of crows', it would lend colour to the legend of 'lofty timbers' upon the islands of the fenlands. This was a rich monastery and contained the shrine of St Guthlac, an eighth-century saint who sought refuge here as an anchorite on St Bartholomew's day, in memory of which event little knives were given away on St Bartholomew's feast day, each year, emblematic of his martyrdom by flaying. This custom continued through the Middle Ages until 1476, and these little blades are still occasionally found or dug up. But the church of Crowland is a melancholy ruin, and shares what little is left of the past with the triangular bridge – a 'dry' bridge for no water runs under it – though once there were three streams – and it is in honour of the Trinity, or else it symbolises the borders of three counties which meet each other nearby. But the water-history of Crowland is even more visually interesting than the ruin of its once splendid church when we know that Henry VI came by water to Crowland, and that Edward IV embarked at the wharf just below the bridge for Fotheringhay, two and twenty miles away by water. Moreover there is even a kind of picturesque memory of its bird life, and of some parallel between it and the young

Thames above Windsor where 'swan-upping' still continues among the eyots – it has just begun, and is expected to last for a week or ten days as this is written – when we read of a roll of parchment at the Record office which has a double column of swans' heads, the bills painted in red and showing the names of the different owners for the years 1497-1504, the abbot of Crowland among them, and the monks or the rectors of several churches subject to the monastery.

The swan-marks are in proof of the aqueous lands of the fen monasteries. Crowland is in fact just within the border of Lincolnshire, and the Holland division of this county is full of churches built in rivalry with each other by the abbots of Crowland, Spalding, and Ramsey. They indeed out-rival the churches of the Nene valley built by the abbots of Peterborough and must always in every case have been much too large for the population. The abbots can only have been competing in magnificence.[1] It is a strange part of the country, completely flat, and where you cannot look in any direction without seeing a church tower or spire, whose bells were for comfort in the flat expanse of meres and fields, as the countryman an hour's trudge out in the damp wild knew the voices of the bells and from what steeples they were sounding.

LONG SUTTON

Coming from King's Lynn out of Norfolk the first of the Lincolnshire churches is at Long Sutton, which owes its splendour to its being the property of Castle Acre Priory and which was built in clear rivalry with Whaplode that belonged to Crowland; continuing with Gedney, also in possession by Crowland, Fleet, Holbeach, Whaplode, Moulton (see p. 69), Weston, eight churches in all between Long Sutton and

HOLBEACH

Spalding. At Holbeach is a monument with one of the most perfect of knights in armour: Sir Humphrey Littlebury, in freestone, lies clad in mail with hands clasped, his head resting on a helmet on which is a woman's head in a net, his shield with two lions upon it at his side. Somehow the light freestone, being less funereal than alabaster, gives us the vision of this knight, armed cap-à-pié, dismounted, walking in a green field

---

[1] Opinion is not unanimous upon this point. 'It has been stated in several historical notices of the parish that Holbeach church was built by the monks of Crowland Abbey. This was most certainly not the case since monks never built or repaired parish churches unless forced to do ... The frequently repeated story that the magnificence of the row of churches from Long Sutton to Spalding is due to the rivalry of the monasteries of Spalding, Crowland and Castle Acre is entirely without foundation and is based on a totally false conception of the relationship of religious houses to parish churches.' Kathleen Major, M.A., B.LITT., F.S.A., in a booklet on All Saints Church, Holbeach.

with heavy step, the white tents with their bright banners and
pennons not far away, and with one of the brand-new castles of
Edward I, triumphs of the military, toy-fort architecture,
shining white before our eyes.

Between Spalding and Boston there are Algakirk, Sutterton
and Frampton; or going on from Boston towards Skegness the
chain of churches which includes Freiston, once a priory,
Leverton and Wrangle. There is yet another group of churches
around Sleaford, one of which, standing on a hill in the old
FOLKINGHAM   market town of Folkingham, has a Perpendicular tower that,
though more bucolic, could be by the same hand as the
pinnacled tower at St Neots in Huntingdonshire, not far away
across the fens and willowed streams.

There are, too, the big town churches of Boston, Grantham,
STAMFORD   Stamford; this last town is of justifiable pretension to be among
the most pleasing in the Kingdom, and only a solemn greyness
of the fine old houses, as of nearing more northern regions,
deflects comparison with the radiance of the Cotswold stone at
Broadway or other of the stone towns of the golden west.
Stamford is conspicuous for its spires, and for two of them in
particular, St Mary's and All Saints. St Mary's has five storeys of
arcading in its tower. The broach spire, rising from that without
pinnacles, plays fancifully and delightfully with its spire-lights
(or spire windows), repeating the same game on all four sides of
its octagon so that no two lights are next to each other on the
same storey, and giving their canopies bold vertical projection
from the slanting body of the octagon, and on the four storeys
varying each pair of them in size in quasi-humorous, nearly
playful fashion. All Saints, across the stream and up the hill
opposite, has a Perpendicular tower with octagonal turrets and
a crocketed spire with three storeys of spire-lights, neat and
compact if not much more remarkable than that. In another
Stamford church, St Martin's, are the tombs of the Cecils,
which, while they form no part of the architecture, are delightful in themselves. The Lord Treasurer Burghley lies wearing
armour and the red robes and star of the Garter, with in his left
hand the wand of his office; while the tomb of Lord Exeter,
carved in Rome by Pierre Monnot, shows Lord Exeter and his
lady leaning on a sarcophagus, with female virtues in attendance, and a pyramid behind them. William Palmer was employed to set the monument in place, and Palmer cut the
lettering, as he cut the enchanting canopied statue of the Hon.
Margaret Watson at Rockingham nearby.

GRIMSTHORPE
CASTLE

Near Stamford is the last major work by Vanbrugh, and it is peculiar and unexpected that this should be the most habitable of all his houses. Grimsthorpe Castle, for the Duke of Ancaster, was to have been rebuilt entirely. Vanbrugh's designs were published in *Vitruvius Britannicus*; the mediaeval and Tudor house was to have been destroyed, and nothing kept of it but the courtyard of its plan, with new buildings round that. But in the end only one front was built, comprising the forecourt and the entrance. Nevertheless, Grimsthorpe must be, humanly, the most considerate of Vanbrugh's houses for it imposes no burdens that are difficult or even impossible to bear. His front of the house consists of a pair of two-storeyed towers with Cyclopean blank windows on their ground floors, a low curtain wall with an iron railing, and a court enclosed by walls with recessed arches in them, that run back from the towers to the house. The façade itself is composed of a pair of three-storeyed towers, the big brothers of that smaller pair, with augmentation of a full Palladian window on their middle floors. Between them lies the fabric or main body of the front; two floors of massive, rounded windows, a balustrade with urns and statues, and for the corners of this frontispiece pairs of plain ringed columns supporting heavy pedestals for sculptured figures. It is a compound of Vanbrugh's Cyclopean style with a deference to the new Palladians of the coming years. At the same time, the main body with its statues and balustrades, with identical balustrades and urns at the four corners of all four towers, is Baroque architecture. Inside, lies the two-storeyed hall with its round arcades that are blank, or frame ancestral portraits. This is the most splendid and simple of Vanbrugh's interiors, with its monolith of a mantelpiece and the plain mouldings of the ceiling. Perhaps this one room and the staircases are enough. Probably it is to the good that Vanbrugh built this much, and no more, at Grimsthorpe.

BOSTON

And soon we will have sight of Boston 'Stump', which is said to be seen from forty miles away on the Norfolk coast. Boston 'Stump' which, at least, is well known from association across the Atlantic, being less English than Flemish or Netherlandish of appearance, a huge giant of a tower of purpose to be seen from miles around and out to sea, with high bell-chamber where the beacon burned till the octagonal lantern was added for that purpose; a gaunt tower, then, topped by a conceit.

SPILSBY

North from Boston is Spilsby, where the tomb of Katherine, Duchess of Suffolk, a daughter of Maria de Salinas who had been maid of honour to Catherine of Aragon, has caryatids of a hermit, a Saracen, and a savage, in the manner of the early travellers' tales. And, continuing northwards, there is Louth, a bucolic market town which is on the way to nowhere, and even now quite a way away over the wolds on a summer day with larks singing, red poppies in their ragged companies and battalions, and ominous aeroplanes forever overhead – Louth with that giant crocketed spire three hundred feet high, two-thirds as high as the Pyramid of Cheops, rising at an angle as you come to it down the 'somnolent' July street. This spire and tower, built of the local and flashing white limestone, is one of the last, if local triumphs of the Perpendicular, built between 1501 and 1515. The tower is in three stages; doorway and much larger west window; a second storey of coupled lights; and more ornate bell-chamber with larger double lights under crocketed canopies; from which spring the fifty-foot pinnacles and the flying buttresses that uphold the tower. As to the spire itself there is some difficulty. It is now 294 feet tall; but was originally, so it is said, 360 feet high; partly blown down twice, in 1587 and again in 1634, rebuilt but shortened in the process. All that can be said is praise for its splendid and appropriate proportion. The first moment of seeing Louth spire from far off, and on nearer approach down the narrow street in front of it with the huge white pyramid holding itself up above the town, is among the architectural and aesthetic sensations of this country, of a different order, it is true, but of comparable intensity to the exterior and interior of Hardwick Hall, and the first view of Stourhead across the lake to the temple under the hanging wood.

By which time we are in Lindsey, that third division of Lincolnshire, and in fact have been out upon the wolds where there are far fewer churches than in Holland or Kesteven. Thornton Abbey, of the White Canons, is at the extreme end of this district (now part of Humberside), and only a few miles from the Humber. More is left of this than of most religious houses in this part of England; the splendid Perpendicular stone gateway, an arch with an oriel window above it, flanked by two pairs of octagonal towers, a bigger and a smaller, like a stone version of the brick gateway to a Cambridge college; and two walls only of what must from its traceries have been a beautiful octagonal chapter house. These both, and the legend of an abbot who was walled up alive, for the abbey seems to have had a sinister reputation, the culprit being either one who died in

LOUTH

THORNTON ABBEY

1385, or another, in 1443. A MS. account of the abbey, now in the Bodleian, says of the former that his record has been mutilated 'to prevent scandal to the church'; and of the other, that 'he died, but by what death I know not. He hath no *obit*, as other abbots have, and the place of his burial hath not been found.' Further to which, Dr William Stukeley, the eighteenth-century antiquary, tells of a wall being taken down at Thornton in his time and a sitting skeleton being found inside it, with a lamp.

SEMPRINGHAM   Coming back once more to Kesteven we must be delayed at Sempringham, near Sleaford, by the Gilbertines, the only order founded in England, and which was for both monks and nuns. They lived under the same roof, divided by a wall even at mass, and might, as one writer has commented, just as well have been in separate buildings. The Gilbertines, even in St Gilbert of Sempringham's lifetime (he died in 1189 aged, we are to believe, 106!), numbered fifteen hundred nuns and canons, the latter in black cassocks with white hoods, and with beards, but of the head house of the order nothing is left, a high church tower and two cloisters having disappeared entirely.

HECKINGTON   In compensation, Heckington nearby has one of the most lovely of all the Lincolnshire churches. This is the perfection of the Decorated style, dating from about 1345, its exterior as marvellously and delicately executed as is the interior of Patrington, that other distant and remote church across the Humber. On the strength of long detours undertaken on two occasions only to see Heckington, the writer would express his admiration for this wonderful work of art, considered in every exterior detail and emerging as almost more of a sculpture to be admired from every angle than as a piece of architecture. Its modest size, and the marvellous reticulation of its buttresses with their receding planes and edges, the beautiful crocketing, the delicate tracery of its seven-light east window, all are admirable at this village church which is one of the beauties, not only of Lincolnshire, but of England. Perhaps this tribute to it will be accepted from one who has admired such a piece of technical virtuosity as the red chapels of Banteai Srei far away in the Cambodian jungles, near to Angkor. And, as there, the problem is who was the architect? Who were the carvers?

The exterior must be due to the master-mason responsible for the delicate stone plinth of the building, the buttresses, and the window traceries of the church at Sleaford. A mason and his men would make their lifework out of two or three nearby churches not many more than that number of miles apart from each other; at Bloxham, Geddington, King's Sutton, in the part of England the writer lives in; and as with the Perpendicular church towers of Somerset which fall into groups, and yet reveal that their designers must have gone from group to group, looking up and taking note, and criticising. It is the general opinion that Heckington owes this lavish magnificence in detail to its having been taken over by royal licence by the Abbey of Bardney, after which work on it was begun at once and continued over some thirty years. But another reliable authority would not have it so, and describes the monks of Bardney as impoverished and fortunate in this instance to take over a brand new fabric. Thinking over which problem, there EWERBY will be time to go on to see the church at Ewerby, only two or three miles away, where there is a beautiful spire; the details of light and shade and recession of the exterior have been considered and carved with exquisite care, and throughout there are signs of the master-mason who worked at Heckington.

NORTHAMPTONSHIRE

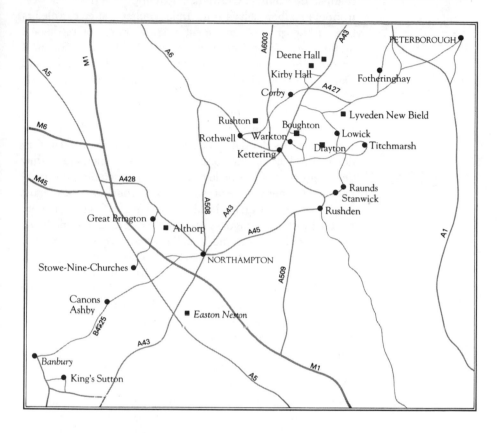

Peterborough (now moved to Cambridgeshire) is the next among the great Benedictine abbeys of the fens, of which number are Ramsey, Crowland, Spalding, Thorney. The west front of Peterborough with its triple porches is often extolled as one of the greatest and most original works of mediaeval architecture, an opinion with which it is difficult to concur if one admires, as does the writer, the wonders of Lincoln, Ely and Durham. As to its interior, there is no fair comment because it was so thoroughly destroyed or 'put to rights' by Cromwell's troops, a privilege it owed to a personal visit to the city from this second instalment of that, where all or any of the arts were concerned, pestilential and destroying family. His soldiers tore down the chapter house and destroyed every monument they could either shoot at or lay hands upon, including the cata-falque of Catherine of Aragon, which it would have been most curious to see here on the borders of the fens of England, a tomb covered with the arms of Castile and Aragon, Catherine being daughter to Ferdinand and Isabella, who drove out the Moors, conquered Granada, and united Spain. Cromwell's troops who, as long as they remained in the town, drilled in the nave of the Cathedral, also pulled down the cloisters, destroyed all the stained glass, burnt all papers and documents, and broke to pieces the reredos, which was of carved stone, painted and gilded, and inlaid with plates of silver. But it is possible to admire still the Eastern Chapels or New Building with its fan vaulting, a combination or hybrid of the palm tree and the fan. The fans or trimmed palm fronds, whichever we prefer to call them, are large in scale and touch each other in their circum-ference across the ceiling, with no need for any ornament in particular in between them. They are palm trees, it could be in fallacious theory, of a couple of years of growth, trimmed twice over until their outer edges meet. And it has been suggested, probably with good reason, that the same master mason designed the fan vault of King's College Chapel, Cambridge.[1]

The last abbot of Peterborough became the first bishop under Henry VIII, who by some quirk of kindness in his merciless nature left it as his first wife's burial place. But it had many associations with the Plantagenet kings, his ancestors, and the influence of this great fane, whose abbot in the early Middle Ages was Legate of Rome all over England, and at the outer gate of which all and sundry as at some eastern mosque took off their

[1] Mr John H. Harvey, in *Gothic England*, 1947, suggests John Wastell as his name.

shoes, spread far and wide into the surrounding country. It was the abbots of Peterborough who built the village churches along the Nene Valley, churches that were later to become the paradise and pilgrimage route of the mid-Victorian ecclesiologist. The church at Stanwick, and more still that at Raunds with its white, white tower and spire filling the background – which in its curious pallor is as the white tent or pyramid above the sheep pens in a shepherd kingdom belonging to that world of the long gowned effigy of Edward III in Westminster Abbey and to the pastoral subjects of William Blake – for it is of the early thirteenth century, and, therefore, of that primitive simplicity which was his birthright and which he had neither to affect nor learn – these and other churches along that river valley were under the mother-wing of that great abbey. And the Nene at that period it would seem was navigable. Barnack 'rag' was transported along it, and 'thus conveyed easily into the heart of the country', but that was before the draining of the fens when this whole part of England was of another, or, of the same, only more pronounced and accentuated character; this local stone being, it would seem, excuse and *raison d'être* for the spate of building from quarries which have now lain exhausted for many centuries.[1]

KETTERING   Kettering, close by, has a spire familiar to the point of dullness, and most often when I have passed it, rain or fine, pushed aside in my mind, I have to confess, for thinking of some façade in Italy or Spain, some temple in India, or pagoda in Japan, but splendid none the less with the turrets at its corners; it resembles, when one gets down to examining it, All Saints, Stamford, in Lincolnshire. All Saints has larger two-lighted windows to its bell-chamber and more interesting and varied stone panelling below that, but their spires are so nearly alike that they may well be from the hand of the same architect. The spire at Rushden can be paired with another Lincolnshire church, that of Moulton, both being crocketed and with four storeys in their towers; but their two steeples, compared to-gether, offer the greatest differences in agreement with each other, that is to say, one octagonal tower is capped with battle-ments, and the other with a cornice or parapet formed of quatrefoils, while the windows run at different levels up and down the spires, three on one face of the octagon and none at all on its neighbours, or, in the other instance, the windows on

RAUNDS (margin, at "The church at Stanwick" paragraph)

RUSHDEN (margin, at "spire at Rushden")

---

[1] 'The strangely broken and tossed ground near the village, which marks their site, is known as the "Hills and Holes".' Murray, 1878.

the lower floor 'start fair', but alternate upon the higher faces, where the spire is a thin attenuated steeple. Those are witches' hats rising out of the cornfields if you can get them at this angle.

KING'S SUTTON

King's Sutton, within sight of its companion spire at Bloxham across the border into Oxfordshire, is a minor miracle of the imagination at work in stone, at which ingenuity of design I have never ceased to wonder though I have had it before my eyes nearly every week I have lived at home for more than fifty years of my life. How is it done? It has a cusped pinnacle rising at each corner of the parapet, and set back from that, at each angle of the squinch, where, in fact, the broach begins, another taller pinnacle; each pair of them, the one behind the other, joined by a flying buttress that pierces, or so it seems, the taller one at the back and continues, allowing for an airy quatrefoil, into the body of the steeple. In addition, the spire has the most fanciful lights or openings worked into it, windows they may be and, of course, are, but from wherever you look at it, from the low meadows leading to it from the main road, the train window whence you see it high among the rooky trees, or scrambling round the foot of it on a windy day, looking up at the daws flying in and out of its pierced apertures, the spire of King's Sutton is of an incomparable lightness, more like some holy vessel of wood or metal than a church steeple built of stone. For how long must the nameless designer of King's Sutton steeple have altered and remade his drawing until he knew he had reached utmost perfection! How far afield had he been? Had he seen the spires of the fens? He cannot have spent all of his life in this village on the edge of the Cotswolds.

GREAT BRINGTON

In the church at Great Brington are the tombs of the Spencer family of neighbouring Althorp. These works, unparalleled and magnificent of their sort, comprise the tombs of two Sir John Spencers and their wives and that of Robert, Lord Spencer and his wife. The first knight is in armour, bareheaded, in a robe of bright scarlet lined with green, while his wife wears sleeves worked after a honeycomb manner, a ruff, and a large hood like the Maltese faldetta, the folds of which fall below her waist. The tomb is framed by obelisks and a solid canopy, and there is lavish display of heraldry upon the knight's tabard, by shields hung on a heraldic tree, and by heraldic shields below the cornice of the tomb itself. The second Sir John and his lady, ornamentally, is the most sober of the three tombs; but she wears a fluted hood and the same ruff and honeycombing of the sleeves. The third of the tombs is surmounted by three obelisks, but what is peculiar in the sculpture is the still more tremendous hood of Lady Spencer, her ruff, her pleated woollen sleeves, and more than all else, her counterpane or coverlet, worked with heraldic motifs and pulled up, stiffly, to her waist, a feature which is unique and unknown elsewhere. There is, in fact, even to persons more than passingly familiar with Tudor tombs, something memorable and peculiar in the wives of the Spencers, with their ruffs and sleeves and tremendous head-dresses. These tombs are ascribed[1] to the Dutchman, Joseph Hollemans, as is the Spencer tomb (1609) at Yarnton, Oxfordshire, and the beautiful wall-tomb of Sir George Fermor and his wife at Easton Neston, here in Northamptonshire, with the identical or characteristic hood of Hollemans, and at the back, under an arch, a fan or peacock's tail formed by the staves of a number of pennons, the slabs of the tail being filled in with tulips and conventional flowers, and then the banners flutter-ing out over the ribs of the tail to fill the arch.

Another of the Spencer tombs at Great Brington, in black and white marble, is by the great sculptor Nicholas Stone (1586-1647), though not entirely by his hand. Working in London, he sent forth his monuments to the far ends of England, there being more than a hundred churches that contain his sculptures. He married the daughter of Hendrik de Keyser who carved the tomb in the Nieuwe Kerk, at Delft, for William the Silent, and it is proper, therefore, to expect a Dutch or Flemish influence in his early works. No praise could

STOWE-NINE-CHURCHES

be too high for his monument to Lady Elizabeth Carey at Stowe-Nine-Churches, which is made of white marble and of black touchstone.

WARKTON

At Warkton, the monuments to the second Duke and Duchess of Montagu are by Louis François Roubiliac, the Huguenot sculptor from Lyons, who had studied as a youth under Balthasar Permoser, court sculptor to the King of Saxony. It was Permoser who carved the apotheosis of Prince Eugene of Savoy, at Vienna, and worked on the fantastic decorations of the Zwinger at Dresden. The Montagu tombs are among Roubiliac's great set pieces and exhibit him in what different schools of opinion would call his best or worst. The execution is impeccable, but conception and imagery may not be dissimilar from that of the gilt French clock. Such, alas! are the monuments of this age in the last and final meaning of the

[1] By Mrs Kathleen Esdaile, *English Church Monuments 1510-1840*, London, 1946, p. 49. According to her researches, he had settled at Burton-on-Trent.

word. It may be that the beliefs and emblems of mortality are changing. They are altering to set figures and to stock-in-trade. The next act in the drama, and even the most rabid partisans of sham-Gothic will find it impossible to show evidence to the contrary, will be the last one, and it will be based upon the Attic tomb-relief or stele. An example of this mode at Warkton is that minor triumph of architecture, the monument to the third Duchess, figures by Van Gelder, but the pillared hemicycle by Robert Adam.

LOWICK

But near at hand, in the church at Lowick, is one of the most beautiful and unexpected of English monuments, the tomb (1419) of Ralph Greene, Esquire, of Chellaston marble, lying beneath a head canopy which, in miniature, is not less elaborately worked and fretted than the roof of a chantry chapel with its pinnacles and fan vaulting. Here he lies, side by side, with his wife, Katherine Malley, and holds her by the hand; his, in the words of the indenture, being 'the counterfeit of an esquire armed at all points', while we learn, further, from the contract that 'gablettes' was the name used for the canopies or tabernacles at their heads. The carvers were Robert Sutton and Thomas Prentys, both of Chellaston in Derbyshire. The tower of the church at Lowick, like that at Fotheringhay in this same county,[1] has an octagonal lantern chamber of beautiful fantasy. But it is true there is a plenitude; there are, indeed, too many pinnacles.

TITCHMARSH

Monuments of another kind are the set of painted wall-memorials at Titchmarsh. These are the work of Mrs Creed, an amateur artist, and are almost alone of their kind in England. Mrs Creed was a first cousin of John Dryden, whose mother came from Titchmarsh. Dryden often visited her; she composed, as well, long dedications and inscriptions; and an old guide book says that there are few churches in the neighbourhood which could not at one time boast of a painted cloth, a table of the Commandments, or a monument, designed and painted by Mrs Creed. These monuments are in the style, exactly, of a painted cloth, but they have merits, and we may regret the vanishing of most of her works and of the portraits and frescoes by Mrs Steward, her daughter. At Titchmarsh, also, there is a perfect model of a Perpendicular village tower. But why here, where it seems rather out of its place because it looks of provenance from the Cotswolds or the West Country?

[1] It has been suggested, not improbably, that the octagon on Wyatt's tower at Fonthill Abbey was inspired from Fotheringhay.

CANONS ASHBY   The Dryden family house is also in Northamptonshire, at Canons Ashby, where the garden was laid out in the poet's lifetime. There is, perhaps, no example in England of a seventeenth-century garden that has come down to us in its original planting, with the scheme of flowers undisturbed and unchanged. It is too long ago for such immutability to be possible. The nearest approximation may be in a garden like this one, where the old plan of planting flowers and vegetables together in·formal beds, flowers in front and at the back and vegetables in the middle, has never been altered since the end of the seventeenth century. It is, thus, a harmonious whole, entirely in keeping with the contemporary gate pillars and stone finials of bold design that make the beauty of this old garden. For these ornaments, like statues, form the population of a garden. They are the human interest of the scene.

EASTON NESTON   At Easton Neston, where we have already seen the Fermor tomb, the house is by Nicholas Hawksmoor, the only important example of his domestic architecture, built for Lord Lempster, and its history is confused and puzzling. Wren is said to have added wings, at an earlier date, to a house that was later pulled down, and then rebuilt by Hawksmoor. Wren may in fact have given plans for Easton Neston. But the wings in any case are now pulled down, and the house is in Vanbrugh-Hawksmoor manner, not in that of Wren. The interior rooms are high and narrow, with long windows that should look out on formal canal and avenue, and fine stucco-work, including the beautiful ceiling panel of Venus and Adonis, one of the most beautiful of all works in stucco, and deserving to be given some better name than stucco decoration. This may be by the Anglo-Danish Charles Stanley. The History of Cyrus painted upon the stair at Easton Neston is by Sir James Thornhill, but like many greater, and less, artists Thornhill varies, and here he is dull.

The absence of other great houses built by Hawksmoor is the more to be regretted because he was an architect who arrived at originality by such painstaking thought and logic that the Baroque school in England might not have been driven out by the revived Palladian. Two houses of his period, but by lesser hands, are Drayton and Boughton. At the first, the interior

DRAYTON   screen and great doorway may be ascribed to William Talman, the architect of Chatsworth, and there is a delightful, but ridiculous, staircase painting by Lanscroon,[1] a pupil of the

[1] Lanscroon painted, also, at Powis Castle, Welshpool, and at Burley-on-the-Hill in Rutland.

BOUGHTON

frescoist Antonio Verrio and to be preferred to him. But who, we may ask, was the architect of Boughton, for the Duke of Montagu, one of only two English houses known to be of definitely French design? Boughton, it is certain, is under French influence, for the Duke of Montagu had been Ambassador at Versailles. Here we may admire the faded frescoes by Verrio, the flower pictures by Baptiste, and its furniture, while thinking of its former avenues.

ALTHORP

French influence a century later is to be seen in the work of Henry Holland for Lord Spencer at Althorp, although only the recasing of the exterior, and a few rooms of the interior are by him. The outside of Althorp is of white brick, and the effect of this, as at Holkham, in Norfolk, is to dwarf or minimise the scale. Holland was not a great architect so far as façades are concerned. He seems, indeed, to have been bored by a façade. The blue boudoir at Althorp, fitted up with what had been, formerly, the decorations of Lady Spencer's dressing-room, is a charming specimen of Holland in his French mood, and reflects the French taste of 1790. The painted panels are the work of a Frenchman, Pernotin, who was employed by Holland at Carlton House. All the detail is admirable in taste and thought; but architecture, we may feel, is nearly at an end.

But there is still time to turn aside into a curious architectural cul-de-sac. This consists in the buildings of the Papist, Sir Thomas Tresham, all in Northamptonshire, comprising the Rothwell market house, Lyveden New Bield, and the manor house and triangular lodge at Rushton, all nearby. Sir Thomas Tresham, who was by birth a Protestant, and who was knighted by Queen Elizabeth on her visit to Kenilworth, was converted by Campion and reconciled to the Church of Rome. With all the zeal of the convert, he was repeatedly fined and imprisoned for his faith. His buildings bear every mark of having been designed in detail by him, forming something absolutely apart and personal. Lyveden New Bield stands by itself in the fields,

LYVEDEN NEW BIELD

roofless and unfinished, a mile from any road. It is built on the plan of a Greek cross, with oriel windows on two floors at the termination of each limb of the cross. But the curiosity lies in the carved ornaments along the cornices, which are all emblems of the Passion; the purse, lanthorn, torches, spear, and sword; the cross, ladder, hammer, and nails; the seamless garment and dice; the crowing cock and the scourges. These are finely cut into the stone by skilled hands. In looking at Lyveden

New Bield, deserted, deep in the fields, we are haunted by a curious poetry, for this is the parallel, in architecture, to Vaughan or Crashaw. And in fact the buildings of Sir Thomas Tresham have a secure, if little, place in the history of the Renaissance. They are, in a sense, too obscure and mysterious to be forgotten. The triangular lodge at Rushton, more modest still in size, is the most curious of all, covered as it is with emblems, and even an emblem in itself,[1] but no description of it could better the narration of an incredible and unlikely scene during a meeting of the Mayor and burgesses of Rothwell in their market house, one of Tresham's buildings. It was the year 1822, and during their session, a panel in the wall above the mantelpiece fell out and clattered down, revealing a secret hiding-place in which was an old and faded manuscript, with the following statement:

> If it be demanded why I labour so much in the Trinity and Passion of Christ to depaint in this chamber, this is the principle instance thereof: that at my last being hither committed (in prison), and I usually having my servant here allowed me, to read nightly an hour to me after supper, it fortuned that Fulcis, my then servant, reading in the Christian Revelation, in the treatise of Proof there is a God, etc., there was upon a wainscot table at that instant, three loud knocks (as if it had been with an iron hammer) given; to the great amazing of me and my two servants, Fulcis and Nilkton.

For the triangular lodge we have, then, Sir Thomas Tresham's own evidence of his intention, delivered by what the superstitious might consider to be a supernatural means.

Sir Thomas Tresham's buildings are too 'nice', by the original meaning, to be mere mason's work. They must have been set forth and drawn in detail, according to his indications. It is only necessary to compare them with the 'Porta Honoris' at Caius College, Cambridge, to be sure of this, for that is a little, odd fantasy in German style, amateurish in design and finish, though pertaining in manner and intent of execution to these more serious buildings with their religious meanings.

---

[1] The triangular lodge is on the plan of an equilateral triangle, each side measuring 33 ft 3 in. There are three floors, three windows on each of three sides, and the windows are in three divisions. The inscriptions are in twice three couplets in three lines. Each of the Latin inscriptions is of thirty-three letters; and the single words below them are three sets of two letters. The Tresham arms are in a trefoil, and the roof is furnished with three gables.

Kirby Hall is a building as fine and magnificent as it is little known, and it is one of those buildings that have to be appreciated in their natural setting, in this case across the green and shadowed fields. For it is approached by a gated road, having left behind the lake and grey mass of Deene in its deer park, where Lord Cardigan lived who led the Hussars at Bala-clava, and having in front, only too visibly, the industrial wasteland of Corby. There are three gates, and little is seen of Kirby till it is near at hand. But little, and that hides itself again, till we turn a corner and stop at the forecourt of the house with a blank doorway, over to the left, contrived into the outer wall for mere magnificence, and bearing in its rustication the breath of the Italy of Vignola, and in the quality of its shell-like ornament the hand of Inigo Jones, for it could be none other. Only a blank doorway in a garden wall, but it recalls Caprarola or Villa d'Este, adapted to this green land, belonging, in fact, to what his later disciples called the Venetian manner, under the influence of the Palladian villas of the terra firma. It is an Italian doorway; but, at the same time, like a painted doorway in the scenery of a masque.

But we must enter the court of Kirby Hall, to find we are surrounded on all four sides by glorious architecture, and by a plan and symmetry that are too rare in Elizabethan building. The north façade that lies behind us, for long accepted as the work of Inigo Jones himself, is now known to have been by Kirby's master-mason, Nicholas Stone. The date 1640 is set clearly in the stonework. The exquisite ornament for this façade is in the full Renaissance of Urbino or Mantua, for it is not unworthy of those palaces. Nevertheless, what we have come to admire at Kirby is the Elizabethan building. We have before us the south front of the court, or banquet hall, dating from 1570, or soon after, with a splendid porch of three storeys and to either side great windows, immensely high, filling two storeys from floor to roof, with fluted pilasters in between. The ornament of the porch itself is unique, but with a later window and balcony by Inigo Jones on the first floor inserted into it, improving, and not spoiling, its magnificence. These long windows may remind us of Elizabethan virginal music and of the strict form and close harmony of Byrd and Bull. Not only in the elaboration, but in the actual handwriting. The reproduction of a page from the Fitzwilliam Virginal MS would explain our meaning. There are unimaginable harmony and peacefulness in those immense flights or staves of leaded panes and their stone casements, and looking round on the court where music and poetry linger, we must wonder, but be thankful, that Kirby has been so long deserted and is unspoilt because of that.[1]

Passing the banquet hall and other empty rooms we come out into the garden and walk to the far side of that, in order to have the full flight of the west front before us, across the newly planted beds of roses. It is the box or cabinet architecture of John Thorpe, in excelsis, and for this once, his mysterious hand may, perhaps, be responsible. The delightful gables and obelisks are quite typical of his drawing, and so are the chimney stacks which should show the smoke and flame he always added. But the house is a ruin and deserted, which makes more mysterious the neatness of its finish. For it is impersonal, and has no note of tragedy. But, in presence of this work of the great Elizabethan draughtsman, we are conscious of its beautiful and quiet restraint, so different in key from much of their flaunting architecture, and we begin to think this is the most beautiful in the whole of England. How satisfying is its simplicity, crowned with the gables and finials above the second storey! But this is not all. For walking to the far end, where the garden continues along a parapet, we look round again and see that the building ends in a great pair of twin bay windows, facing south, set side by side, like two huge galleons tied up at anchor. They are like the poops of two stone ships, never meant to sail, but only to catch the sunlight, and their gables in fact are like the ships floating and reflected, keel uppermost, but, certainly, they remind us of great vessels with their cabins made on the curve, and bound in, as it were, to the shaping of the hull. How English they are, those twin bay windows, side by side, upon two storeys! Those bow windows of Kirby are carpenter's work, made in stone; and looking back for the last time on the whole range of building, we decide we do not know which is more beautiful, that court of the Renaissance with its golden detail, or this quiet and grave beauty where gable and obelisk must once have matched the knots and yew pyramids of the Jacobean garden. We come away in the knowledge of having seen a building the like of which there is not in Italy, the land of architecture, for with all their genius they could not attain to this restraint and calm. Kirby Hall is in complete harmony with the green fields and ancient shades.

[1] Kirby Hall was partly inhabited as late as 1820. A few years before this it had been suggested as a retreat for George III and his court in the event of a Napoleonic invasion.

THAMES
AND CHILTERNS

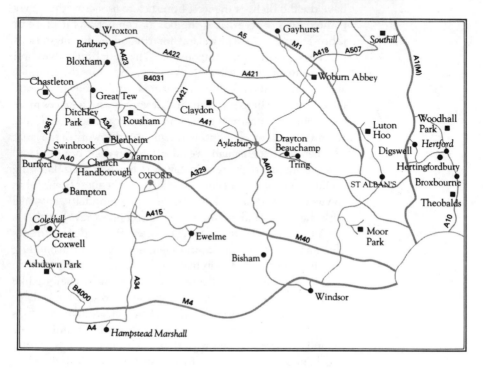

BLENHEIM PALACE   Let us arrive now at Blenheim Palace. We enter the park through the triumphal arch from Woodstock and are in the Mall, so called. The lake is below and Vanbrugh's enormous bridge near by, intended, as Reynolds understood it in his *Discourses*, for the tramp of Roman legions, for a ghostly army. *Pons Blenhimensis* is written on the plan, and by that name should be known this wonderful work of the dramatic imagination, for it leads into the home or shrine of the hero. Here the abused hand of Lancelot ('Capability') Brown takes up the water which, originally was but a trickle, makes it flow like a great river under the heroic arch, and carries it into the distance where, on the far side of Blenheim, its further bank is a high hanging wood, incredible in beauty during the autumn months. Well might 'Capability' Brown boast that 'the Thames would never forgive him for what he had done here'. The lake at Blenheim is the one great argument of the landscape gardener. There is nothing finer in Europe. In its way this is one of the wonders of the eighteenth century, when we hear the October guns firing in the far wood and the lights of an early sunset lie along the water. The place at which we are standing must be, more or less, where Sir Joshua Reynolds meant when he wrote of Blenheim in his *Discourses*. For in the distance, we catch our first sight of its walls and colonnades, its square towers, like stands of arms, and the ornaments like grenades upon the buttressed finials. We see the recessed centre, between the wings, the porch and pediment, the distant trophies, or so we imagine, and the statues.

But it hides back between the trees. The road turns, and there lies the enormous building at another angle. We come to a Doric doorway of yellow stone, set in a curtain wall of round arches with mock battlements above them, and walk through this into the courtyard; and out through another stone gate, of Vanbrugh's typical ringed columns, with lions above them, and find ourselves before the front of Blenheim. We will walk to the centre, watching how the building moves with us, and stand before the portico, but some distance from it. The head or body of the building is this portico; two pillars in the middle, two engaged pilasters to either hand, a sculptured pediment, and the body of the great hall set back behind it, three windows to either side upon two floors, with tall composite pilasters between. We watch, in Reynolds's phrase, the advance 'of the second and third group of masses', for the curtain wings spread outward to a pair of towers, with pillared colonnades below them that give light and shadow, and that end with fine sculptured trophies, or piled arms, upon the cornices, above their tube-like corridors. Turning round, we see the great bridge before us, and looking back, admire the graded levels and the shallow steps, for these levels, on this front of Blenheim, are important as the pedals in a piece of piano music. Its meaning or expression would be entirely lost without them. The isolation of its parts, which stand quite still, or move at will, depending on how we look at them, makes this entrance front of Blenheim, whether we think it beautiful or not, one of the most extraordinary feats in architecture.

But we will continue round the building, for it is architecture upon all four sides, looking first at the garden front of Blenheim. This faces, now, on to a bare expanse of lawn and cedar trees, for the great parterre was swept away in the craze for landscape gardening that destroyed the formal garden, but left the lake instead. The south façade is to be seen, therefore, under precisely the opposite conditions to those intended for it. A huge Corinthian order forms the centre, and together with the recessed pilasters to either hand it composes what could be termed a solid or static triumphal gateway, the monumental meaning of which is proved, when we examine it, by the colossal bust of Louis XIV upon the plinth, a trophy taken in battle from the gate of Tournai. An emblem of war and victory upon a building in the heroic manner. Within this façade the state rooms of the palace extend in a long line, and are hung with the tapestries of Marlborough's wars, woven in Flanders. The four towers at the corners of Blenheim are solid as guard rooms and are crowned with those curious buttresses that suggest stands of arms and that support, in fact, four flaming stone grenades to each. But we can walk to the two ends for the two lesser fronts. To the east there is a small garden, flanked by an orangery, and this garden was laid out again by the late Duke of Marlborough, who did much to restore the glories of the formal Blenheim. From this harmony of the elaborate 'broderie' of flowers and coloured pebbles with Vanbrugh's architecture, we may imagine for ourselves that colossal Corinthian order as it must have looked with the great parterre spread out before it. The windows of the great library take up the whole length of the remaining front of Blenheim, broken between the two towers, in the centre, by a protruding apse or bay which is continued on the upper floor with caryatids between the windows, that must be a reminiscence of the 'Persian' court of Inigo Jones, designed for Whitehall. Below this, the late Duke of Marlborough restored the fountain by Bernini, and laid out the garden and the shelves of water that lead down to the great lake and the hanging woods, beyond, of 'Capability' Brown. This is probably the most successful work of the formal gardener done in our time, and being conceived on the original lines is really in scale with the whole gigantic planning.[1]

In a book that deals more with architecture than the contents of houses we have only time to pass through the great hall, to note the typical corridors of Vanbrugh, admire the saloon with walls painted by Laguerre (a far better painter than Verrio), and with marble doorcases carved by Grinling Gibbons,[2] and traverse the state rooms, up and down, to either hand, lined with the tapestries of the French wars, ending with the library; and thence to the chapel to see Marlborough's tomb designed by Kent and executed by Rysbrack, a monument that shows him to be one of the great sculptors of the Baroque movement, especially in the exquisite details of his bas-reliefs, which compare almost to the early military scenes in Watteau's paintings.

The great architectural conception of Blenheim may be at its grandest and most magnificent in intimacy, as I have seen it upon a wet November evening, when the rain is splashing on the court and in the colonnades, when, looking out from a window in a corridor, we see a shadow like a level causeway in the distance, and know it must be the Roman bridge of Vanbrugh with its great arch and the square rooms within its piers,[3] and in imagination hear the clarions and watch the torches come nearer and throw their marching lights upon this heroic building. It is this, certainly. Not less, on such an occasion as the last summer before the War, when the whole of Blenheim was floodlit for the ball, from panoramic court and

---

[1] The French garden architect Duchêne was employed.

[2] In his *Blenheim Palace*, London, 1951, Mr David Green reveals that not only are the doorcases by Gibbons, but also several fireplaces in the house and the stone ornaments upon the roof.

[3] Sarah, Duchess of Marlborough, in one of her best letters, complains of being able to count thirty-three rooms in the bridge at Blenheim and a house at each of the four corners, and continues, despairingly, 'but that which makes it so much prettier than London Bridge is that you may sit in six rooms and look out of a window into the high arch, while the coaches are driving over your head.'

scenic portico to the dark cedars on the lawn and the bust of 'Le Roi Soleil', a prisoner, upon the pediment; from the powdered hair and 'Padua' scarlet of the state liveries, through the crowded ballrooms, down to the rooms hung with 'Indian' papers that look out upon Bernini's fountain; to the shelves of water and the deep lake that seemed to move and flow. That was a galaxy of light upon this theatrical, but heroic building, upon this private monument that is a Roman triumph and a public pantomime; and amid those lights it was possible to admire Vanbrugh's architecture as it may never be seen again.

ROUSHAM   After Vanbrugh and 'Capability' Brown, we can see the work of William Kent at Rousham in both the house and the gardens. All that many of us know of Kent is the phrase of Walpole that he 'first leapt the fence and saw all Nature was a garden'. Or the story, also in Walpole, of the two ladies for whom he designed birthday gowns: 'the one he dressed in a petticoat decorated with columns of the five orders; the other, like a bronze, in a copper coloured satin, with ornaments of gold.' Anecdotes, both of them, that might invite an appetite for more. In fact, this protean talent first saw the world at Bridlington, in 1684, where he was apprenticed before long to a coach painter, but after five years, 'feeling the emotions of genius,' ran away to London, and thence to Rome by easy stages. Here he studied and won a prize in painting. And, in Rome, he met Lord Burlington, who, when Kent returned to England in 1719, gave him rooms in Burlington House. A series of buildings then began in which the names of Kent and Lord Burlington are associated, as professional and amateur, the most important of which is the villa at Chiswick. At the same time Kent was kept busy as a painter, and among the most interesting of his decorations are his arabesque ceilings in bright blues and reds at Rousham in the style of Raphael's Loggie at the Vatican, which in their turn were modelled on the Roman excavations. This close attention to Classical detail will explain Kent's cornices and doorways, and proves the thoroughness of his Italian training.

These paintings apart, the house is not in Kent's most magnificent mood, and we find him making experiments in 'Gothick'. But, at Rousham, we may appreciate him as landscape gardener in the uses to which he put the infant Cherwell.

The greatest pleasure we had was in seeing Sir Chas. Cottrell's house at Rowsham; it reinstated Kent with me, he has nowhere shown so much taste. . . . The house is old, and was bad: he has improved it, stuck as close as he could to Gothick. . . . The garden is Daphne in little, the sweetest little groves, streams, glades, porticoes, cascades, and river imaginable; all the scenes are perfectly classic

writes Horace Walpole. This is one of the beginnings of the English landscape garden, but the control is still in the hands of a Classical composer. Had he not seen the lichen creeping over the stone giants of Villa Lante and Caprarola; and the Classic order and decay of Villa d'Este! 'Capability' Brown and Repton, for all their ingenuities, were barbarians compared with Kent. The Italian in Kent is eloquent in a wooden garden bench, at Rousham, which is no less than a masterpiece in garden furniture; while his sketch, in watercolour, of the cascade betrays the follower of Claude and Poussin.

DITCHLEY PARK The Italian training of James Gibbs is also evident in the most important of his surviving houses, at Ditchley Park nearby. This has fine rooms, and a good saloon with plasterwork by Artari, Vassalli, and Serena. But we feel at Ditchley that English interior architecture is drawing to its close.

GREAT TEW Which is the most beautiful village in England? There are at least two dozen; but among them is Great Tew, its houses built of golden-brown stone, with thatch nearly to the ground. These are the work of another great landscape gardener, John Claudius Loudun, who laid out the village early in the last century, during the first contagion of our modern wars. Great Tew, with its memories of the Cavalier Lucius Cary, Lord Falkland, is a pattern book of the picturesque. Coming down past the long church wall with its red flowering currants (*Ribes sanguineum*) we wind deeper and deeper among clipped yews and laurels, to find cottage after cottage in that descending valley with high-pitched roof and mullioned window. The thatched roofs become more fantastic as the valley narrows into a winding lane. Only the leaded windows give away the date; or golden stone and mouse-fur thatch could be timeless. This is a village of enchantment. We could wish that John Claudius Loudon had left other memorials than a row of books. Not far away across the fields of red plough and the rough stone walls, past Broughton Castle in its moat, by Gold Street and Silver Lane of Bloxham, now gone, with the spires of Adderbury and King's Sutton pointing in the larkfull summer sky, we could

WROXTON come to the old houses of Wroxton, of golden local stone, with purple clematis upon the walls and Madonna lilies in the little gardens.

BLOXHAM But we would stop first at Bloxham, where the spire is of dark golden stone; an octagon superimposed upon a square, altering into that above the bell-chamber, which has the richest possible fringed parapet, called the 'allis' by Bloxham people, whence the steeple rises, not crocketed up all its length, but with an occasional cusp left, here and there, for handhold to lift off the steeple, and see what is going on inside. And on certain days the spire and bell-chamber of Bloxham church can be darker still, almost as dark as 'black' Barbados sugar.

CHASTLETON Turning to the west towards the Cotswolds, we come to Chastleton, and, as the house comes into view, not far away, an intense delight is to be had from the grain and closeness of the stonework, for we know instinctively, as in Italy, that this is the Renaissance, that new images and poetry are at their birth in the stuccoed and mullioned rooms above. There is a topiary garden, with no less than a full-rigged galleon at sail, in box; while the interior and faded wonders end at the long gallery, than which nothing more romantic and forgotten could be imagined.

BURFORD Of the Arcadian Cotswold towns only Burford is in Oxfordshire, where, in the great church, is the Tanfield monument, a magnificent six-post tester, with painted alabaster effigies, and enchanting virtues on their little pedestals. This is the masterpiece of Gerard Christmas, an East Anglian of an ancient East Anglian family. His two sons were sculptors and like him Pageant Masters to the City and Carvers to the Royal Navy, working and gilding upon the high galleries of the *Sovereign of the Seas*. As is the case of so many Elizabethan tombs, with their roofs and testers, the Tanfield monument has become part of the furniture, or the interior fittings. Like a great bed or tabernacle, it has moved in and taken up residence within the late Gothic church.[1] On another scale, but beautifully harmonious in the balance of its parts, is the pillar tablet to Sarah Bartholomew, with two cupids' heads at the base, and above, winged but limbless cupids framing an inscription. It was attributed at one time, and not unworthily, to Grinling Gibbons, but is given, now, to Christopher Kempster, a mason

[1] By contrast, the obelisk supported on four swans from Bisham Church, Berkshire, is comparable to a poetical image become a garden ornament, and then solemnised and made funerary.

of Burford who became one of Wren's contractors for St Paul's.

SWINBROOK   In the next village, Swinbrook, are the tombs of the Fetti-
places, father and sons, in two sets of three, leaning in perpetuity on their cold, stone shelves. The earlier set, by another
Burford mason, lean their heads on one hand, and the other
hand is upon the hip of their baggy trunk-hose. The later set, by
William Byrd of Oxford, lean on an elbow, and have their other
hand resting on their raised-up knee. This series is in pink-
veined marble with black shelves and pillars, and gilt and tinted
YARNTON   heraldry. At Yarnton there is a Spencer monument by John
Nost, a standing father in heroic costume, and to either side
his son and daughter, all framed architecturally, but with no
pillars; while among the lesser memorials that form the delight
of nearly every parish church, there is the pillar tablet with four
BAMPTON   cupids and an inscribed cartouche at Bampton, and the flat
heraldic panel framed in pilasters and a base and cornice at
CHURCH   Church Handborough, but with the coat-of-arms so brightly
HANDBOROUGH   painted that it would persuade us to forget the dead.[1]
EWELME   Before coming to Oxford itself, we must still visit Ewelme, to
the south of the city, where lies buried Alice, Duchess of
Suffolk, the granddaughter of Chaucer, in one of the most
beautiful tombs in the kingdom – which has her effigy in
alabaster, coroneted, the Garter on her arm, and below angel-
weepers of alabaster, shield on arms, standing in niches, each
gilt-haired angel with a pair of long red wings from high above
his shoulder to down below his knees. For the details of the
sarcophagus were painted in bright colours: 'little alabaster
angel-weepers stood on a green ground flowered with daisies,
their wings red, with peacocks' eyes, their hair gilt, their robes
scarlet edged with gilt, against a golden background'.[2] Here,
too, is a spired font cover of singular beauty that can be raised
from its bowl by a pulley and counter-weight that are in the
shape of a Tudor rose, but at Ewelme we remember the figure of
the Duchess of Suffolk with her folded hands, the long lines of
her robe and skirt, her wimple and her widow's veil, which are
gravely and serenely beautiful.

OXFORD   It is on the top of Magdalen Tower that, 'in accordance to a
custom which is said to have originated in a requiem for Henry

[1] A still gayer specimen, probably by the same hand, with little recumbent
effigy in the middle is at Salford Priors in Warwickshire. It is a local type, but of
London origin, as an emblazoned pedigree on vellum by such a heraldic master
as Sylvanus Morgan may remind us.
[2] F. H. Crossley, *English Church Monuments*, 1150-1550, London, 1921.

VII, in commemoration of his visit in 1488, glees and madrigals were always sung at sunrise on May Morning to usher in the spring.... On this occasion the bells (the most tuneful and melodious in all these parts) are all rung, when the whole tower shakes and bends perceptibly,' to quote from a *Murray's Handbook* of more than a century ago. It is only a wonder there have not been more ceremonies on the top of towers; the Perpendicular towers which are one of the glories of the kingdom and 'the grand and truly distinctive offspring of our national architecture' (Charles Wickes). Not, antiphonally, atop the twin towers of Beverley Minster, for neither they nor the Angel Steeple, or Bell Harry Tower of Canterbury, under its other name, are intended for music. They are too tall for that. The proper venue for music of this sort must be a collegiate chapel tower like that of Magdalen, or any one of several dozen other Perpendicular towers in country towns and villages all over England. Into the secrets of campanology, alas! I cannot enter for they are unknown to me, but the music of the church bells was of course an integral part and consideration in tower building. Magdalen Tower, as it rises above the bridge, affords one of those classical scenes of England, like Warwick Castle seen from the bridge over the Avon, although it is by no means the most beautiful of the Perpendicular towers. Its three lower storeys, blank and of no interest, and bell-chamber above that, all are subordinated to the parapet and flat roof-top with its eight pinnacles which are more than twice lifesize. It was completed in the last years before the reign of Henry Tudor.

The Divinity School of Oxford, known to tens of thousands who have attended there in cap and gown, has a vaulted ceiling of stone from just these years; but could one honestly say that this is beautiful? They are dependent, not growing fans; and have the aspect of strengthened or reinforced umbrellas, placed upside down as would often be the case to dry off after a day and night of Oxford rain. Umbrellas, not with ferrules on their ends but carved and awkward-shaped bosses; while the stone ribs that arch across and carry the ceiling, separate, but do not show the fans to advantage among the thronged bosses and carved badges of the stone ceiling. As for the roof of Oxford Cathedral (the chapel of Christ Church), it is curious and complicated indeed, with at first glance a touch of the Manoelino, as though, below, there could be the twisting, the clasping or entwining columns of Setúbal, that 'are formed of three stems of stone that enrol and wind round one another'. But nothing of the kind. There is nothing else to disturb the calm. It is but the ceiling. And this, though interesting and certainly unusual in the extreme, cannot be said to be successful. As fan vaulting it is inferior in conception to the great fan vault springing from one central column over the stair leading to the hall of the college, though that was built in the delayed Gothic of the time of Charles I.

The entrance gate to Christ Church, Tom Tower, is by Wren, an architectural jumble or muddle, but it has endeared itself to many generations and no one sensible would have it otherwise than as it stands, with faults half committed but forgiven in advance, in harmony with the 'Laudian' Perpendicular of the hall staircase. Wren began his career at Oxford, as scientist, mathematician and astronomer, and although his first considerable work, as architect, was the chapel of Pembroke College, Cambridge, he soon returned to Oxford, and in 1663 the Sheldonian Theatre was begun, one of the most familiar and conspicuous buildings of the whole University. Not being intended for theatrical performances, but for the recitation of prize compositions and the conferring of honorary degrees, the interior galleries run right round the building, and it was the concern of the architect to adhere to the plan of a Roman theatre, while so arranging the windows that ceremonies might take place by the light of day. The plan was derived by Wren from the reconstruction of the Theatre of Marcellus in Serlio's book of architecture, which had been translated into English in 1611. The flat wooden roof of the interior, with a span of seventy feet, was considered a wonder in its day and was certainly ingenious as a piece of carpentry. But as the classic theatres of the ancients had no roof, this is disguised as a *velarium*, or, in fact, the ceiling represents a painted canvas stretched over golden cordage, and this, the first thing of its kind in England, was from the brush of Robert Streater, Sergeant-Painter to Charles II. So remarkable did this painted ceiling seem, that it drew forth a whole epic in its honour, a poem which it would be interesting but tiring to compare with that which greeted the no less curious Trasparente by Narciso Tomé in the Cathedral at Toledo.[1]

---

[1] *Urania: or a description of the Painting of the Top of the Theatre at Oxford as the artist laid out his design*, by Robert Whitehall, 1669. The title of the Spanish epic to the Churriguerresque, is *Il Trasparente*, by Francisco Xavier de Castañeda, Toledo, 1732; in midst of this 'fricassée of marble' San Rafael, head downwards, with his legs kicking out above him in the air, holds in his right hand a huge gilt fish.

While the Sheldonian was building Wren went to Paris, and it has been suggested that the terminal stone figures of the outside railing, Sages of Antiquity, the Twelve Caesars, or whoever they be, were suggested by figures of the same description at Vaux-le-Vicomte, near Paris. The magnificent château was brand new. It had been begun by Fouquet in 1657; though we must add that similar terminal busts or 'sportive masks' appear outside a building of the late sixteenth century at the University in Cracow, so that the clue to all three sets of them may be in a hint from Serlio.

This is the only time Wren went abroad, and upon his return to England in 1665, he went again to Cambridge, returning only much later to Oxford, for Tom Tower was erected in 1681-2. Ten years later he was consulted about the chapel of Trinity College, for which Dean Aldrich of Christ Church may have drawn up the plans. The earlier chapel of Trinity, it is pleasant to remember, had been the scene of much music when Charles I and the Cavaliers were in Oxford. We are told that 'my Lady Thynne and fine Mistress Fanshawe were wont to come, mornings, half-dressed, like angels', and that 'Trinity Grove was the Daphne for the ladies and gallants to walk in: and many times my Lady Isabella Thynne would make her entrys with a theorbo or a lute played before her'. This later chapel, whether by Dean Aldrich or by another, shows the influence of Wren, having magnificent plasterwork upon the ceiling, and a screen and altarpiece which are among the finest works of Grinling Gibbons. The altarpiece is carved in lime-wood; the screen and lattices are of cedar, for the screen has pierced panels which are different on the two sides, they are, indeed, incomparable, while a pair of angels sit on the pediments, both above the altar and over the doorway in the screen, and a sculptured vase in each case stands between the angels. These works by Grinling Gibbons are, in fact, so splendid and exuberant that Trinity Chapel remains in memory as carving more than architecture.

Our last view of Wren in Oxford must be his bust by Edward Pierce in the Ashmolean, a work worthy of Bernini, and a portrait of extraordinary interest of this great genius, giving, as is remarked by the only authority upon this sculptor, 'a Wren quite different from the thin-lipped mathematician in a heavy wig commonly painted'. Instead, we have a most vital personality, reminiscent, in the eyes and mouth, of Lord Nelson. By contrast, the bust of Nicholas Hawksmoor, Wren's pupil and assistant, at All Souls, shows him with close-cropped hair, not in the fashion of his age, for he had become eminent, not through fame or genius, but only from hard work.[1] Perhaps Hawksmoor's danger was that he could build in any style. He seems to have been a person who could work with equal determination on a good plan, or a bad; and with as much painstaking interest over the work of another man, as on his own. But in Oxford he excelled, and we may admire him at Queen's, and discover, to our surprise, his talents at All Souls

Queen's College had been begun before the end of the century, but Hawksmoor's screen on the High Street was completed only in 1736, the year of the architect's death. This is absolutely Baroque in spirit, and could appear, to some tastes, the most admirable building in Oxford. If the 'High' be, as it is often said, one of the most splendid streets in the world in point of architecture, then Queen's is, on the whole, the most successful building in its whole length. Hawksmoor drew up plans, too, for Brasenose[2] and for the Radcliffe Library, but these were rejected. His other venture, at Oxford, was the rebuilding of All Souls. This had been abused, indiscriminately, but besides being interesting, historically, as the earliest instance of all-over 'Gothick', its bastard spires and crockets are a definite part of the beauty of that group of buildings. Are they not in some sort of harmony with the serio-comical busts, with the curve of the Sheldonian, the late Gothic of the Divinity School, the Jacobean court of the Bodleian, and the Radcliffe Camera of Gibbs? Far from lamenting the work of Hawksmoor at Oxford, we could wish that he had been allowed his hand at Cambridge. For he was no Vandal. He pleaded for the preservation of the old buildings at All Souls. His plan for the 'reforming' of Cambridge will have contained more good than bad; while, if we are to consider Hawksmoor as an eclectic, it is remarkable, to say the least of it, that the hall of All Souls, with its Thornhill portraits, should be contemporaneous with the High Street front of Queen's, and with the Mausoleum at Castle Howard.

It must be only in the natural order of events that Gibbs

[1] This bust 'is the only known portrait of Hawksmoor and shows him at the end of his life. Made of plaster painted black to simulate bronze, it was no doubt modelled by Sir Henry Cheere, who worked at All Souls in 1732. An interesting possibility is that Roubiliac, who was working in Cheere's workshop at the time, may have had a hand in the bust.' Ian Lowe, in F. Markham, *Oxford*, London, 1967.

[2] Plans for Brasenose, of monumental character, are in *Vitruvius Britannicus*.

should have worked at Oxford, too. But the Radcliffe Camera, though the most monumental of his works, is not the most successful. In its position in that group of buildings of which the Sheldonian and the Bodleian form part, we may pass it often, but it leaves no particular impression. It is a domed building that is a library, but no more than that. Hawksmoor, as so often at Oxford, had made the first design; but Gibbs's library, as completed, consists of a rusticated plinth or ground floor, above which comes the rotunda with sixteen pairs of engaged Corinthian columns, capped with a balustrade and urns, and a dome above that. The defect of the Radcliffe Camera, the design of which may have been suggested by Wren's sketches for a mausoleum for Charles I (at Windsor), is that the plinth is so low and dull. The rotunda, thus, starts from too near the level of our eyes, and is so tall itself that it conceals the dome. This is, of course, the obvious difficulty in a domed building unsupported by wings and aisles, as at St Paul's; and, indeed, domed rotundas have only been achieved by the very greatest masters, as all will agree who have seen the still more beautiful, octagonal, ninth-century Dome of the Rock at Jerusalem, or have but admired its image in the background of Raphael's *Sposalizio*, in the Brera at Milan, or again in the fresco by Perugino in the Sistine Chapel. In that divine company Gibbs's Radcliffe Camera burns with a little light, but does not shine.

COLESHILL   Towards the Wiltshire border (in the north-west part of Berkshire which is now transferred to Oxfordshire) were two great houses of the seventeenth century, but one of them has perished. Coleshill was the work of Sir Roger Pratt, a Norfolk country gentleman who studied the art in France, Italy, and the Netherlands, and built Clarendon House, in London, and Horseheath in Cambridgeshire. It was built for his relative, Sir George Pratt, and was in the style of the Venetian villa, with a difference. For, although the architect consulted with Inigo Jones at the time he was beginning Coleshill,[1] it was not slavishly Palladian, like the villas built later for Lord Burlington and other amateurs. It had English individuality of its own, from the plain but imaginative exterior with its simple pilasters, to the staircase, and to the stucco ceiling of the hall, which was particularly fine and original. But Coleshill was terribly damaged by fire some years ago, and even the shell of it is now demolished.

[1] Cf. R. T. Gunther, *The Architecture of Sir Roger Pratt*, Oxford, 1928, p. 5.

ASHDOWN More divergent from the work of Inigo Jones is Ashdown, a
house in a most lonely situation below the downs, under the
White Horse upon the pagan hillside. It is an unforgettable
experience to pass Ashdown upon an autumn evening, for it
stands up so tall against the sky, among the naked trees. Some
thread of memory connects it in our minds with the ancient dew
ponds, near by. The 'property' swans of *Le Lac des Cygnes* should
be drawn across, before our eyes. For this curious high house, so
solitary and undisturbed, with its dormer roof ending in a
balustrade and cupola, with its formal layout, the little low
rooms flanking at each side, and the pair of pavilions in front,
recalls a 'slott' in Sweden or Denmark. This is the castle to
which the prince and his companions will return in the evening
after hunting, and we see in imagination the 'spangled' bed got
ready for Odile and the silver mirrors in her room, and hear that
haunted, nostalgic air with which the ballet opens. Ashdown,
built at the beginning of Charles II's reign, was long thought to
be a work of Webb. More like a Restoration house than any
work by Webb, Ashdown may be in part the work of William
Winde, who was largely responsible for Lord Craven's other
HAMPSTEAD houses, Combe Abbey and Hampstead Marshall, of which last
MARSHALL only the kitchen garden and eight splendid pairs of gate piers
now remain.

WINDSOR At St George's Chapel, Windsor, which is just where the fan
vaulting should be at its finest height of refinement and invention, one might be inclined to think it fails. This, although it is
attributed to William Vertue, one of the two brother master-
masons who worked the ceiling of Henry VII's chapel at Westminster Abbey. At St George's Chapel the roof errs on the
side of simplicity. For a chapel not a large church, and with
its infinite possibilities for expenditure on a great scale, it is
disappointing. They are palm pillars of ordinary proportion,
neatly trimmed and arranged so as to make room for a triple
row of carved bosses that proceed in straight line along the
ceiling. But the choir aisle ceiling has a different and more
subtle treatment. Here, the fans spring in authentic manner
from the capitals of slender columns; their trimmed and un-
frayed edges meet in the middle and enclose octagonal panels
with carved bosses in their centre. Nevertheless, for the writer
St George's Chapel was an inspiring place of release from
school, and it is full of chantry chapels. Coming in at the west
door, on the right-hand side and polygonal in shape, there is

the Beaufort chapel or chantry of Charles, Earl of Worcester, who in view of his origin, though illegitimate of descent, was lucky to be left alive by Henry VIII; but all else in St George's Chapel must pale beside the Garter Chapel, which is among the masterpieces of the national or Perpendicular style, and the stalls of the Knights, which are no less than a goldmine of chivalry and poetry. Among the ninety stall-plates decorated in coloured enamels we meet with such heraldic triumphs as the red mantling powdered with golden lozenges of the romantically named Sir Sanchet Dabrichecourt and his crest formed of a bunch of feathers; the black mantlings of Sir Thomas Banastre and the Captal de Buch; black mantlings, but red lined for the Soudan de la Trau; and purple mantle sown with golden hanging locks for Lord Lovel. And as we depart from this palladium of heraldic art we may look up at the 'King's beasts' upon the pinnacles that fringe the roof-line.

The town of Windsor, which, otherwise, would centre wholly on the Castle, is given character by the red brick and white Portland stone Town Hall, with its statues at either end of Queen Anne and of Prince George of Denmark. At first glance the Town Hall is Dutch in style, till we remember that we have never seen anything that resembles it in Holland. It was designed by Sir Thomas Fitch, and Wren was called in to supervise the completion, but Wren's proposed mausoleum for Charles I at Windsor proceeded no further than the sketches, though money was voted for it. Two drawings are preserved in All Souls by Grinling Gibbons of the proposed sculptures, one of which, according to the *Parentalia*, was 'adapted for Brass work, the other for marble'. In both of them the King stands, crowned in one, and uncrowned in the other, upon a flat disk, by which a shield is intended. Cherubs are flying down with laurel wreaths, and the shield is upheld by 'Heroick Virtues', who stand on a stone that crushes evil, shown by figures crouching. Neither mausoleum nor statue was erected. Instead, the equestrian statue of Charles I by Le Sueur was set up in Charing Cross, where it stands today, and Wren may have designed the pedestal, which was carved by Joshua Marshall.

HERTFORDSHIRE

ST ALBAN'S A learned authority has spoken of the red tower and walls of St Alban's, lending to the ancient Benedictine abbey something

of that distant view of the Alhambra seen from below its hill,
which if it gives over-emphasis to the picturesqueness is at least
introduction to the men of learning and the treasures, now lost,
that it once held. Matthew Paris and his school of sculptors and
painters worked here. The high altar of St Alban's was their
work, and the shrine of Becket at Canterbury, which may have
surpassed all things of its kind except for Byzantine Constantinople. But not a vestige is left. Alike, the work at St Alban's
and the shrine of Becket are all perished. The fabric of St
Alban's is left, but shorn of its original adornment, in the
absence of which it is impossible to judge of their handiwork,
and even that of Matthew Paris, his chronicles apart. The
Abbey Church is conspicuous from far off for its immense
length and bulk, like indeed a great giant's body; early in style
as to its interior of Norman-Romanesque, with Roman bricks
and tiles from Verulamium, the biggest Roman settlement after
York, pressed into service, but marred by the amateur efforts of
the mid-Victorian Lord Grimthorpe, who spent his fortune in
restoring it and giving it a hideous new painted wooden ceiling,
which could be the handiwork of the local Women's Institute.
In compensation are two chantry chapels. That of Duke
Humphrey of Gloucester, brother of Henry V, is in two storeys;
an open chamber where the tomb should have been (his coffin
was found elsewhere in the Abbey) and three arches above that
which are open without supporting pilasters, and then the
upper storey with four traceried windows in double stages and
niches, now statueless, between them. It is a little uninteresting
in fantasy and composition. More beautiful is the chapel of
Abbot Thomas Ramryge, who died in 1521, so that in date it is
very late indeed. Again it is in two storeys, and of the 'stone-
cage' form which was one of the minor if special inventions of
the Perpendicular. In fact, an openwork stone screen of three-
light windows, unglazed of course, a little conventional perhaps, but redeemed out of the ordinary by the imaginative
delicacy of the work above where the stone cage-work is reinforced and made more interesting by the canopied niches,
again without statues, that alternate the three-light windows;
or, in this storey it more resembles a stone grille. And the
fan-vault below within the tomb-chamber brings that taste of
Andalusian-Moorish, almost of the *medersas* of Fez and
Marrakesh, that is the culminating and unexpected, indeed the
un-English, yet ultra-English, and departing delight of the
Perpendicular style.

Something of the same imagination is found in the costumes on the monumental brasses of the fifteenth century. At St Alban's itself the utmost extravagances of armour are shown by the elbow pieces or coudières of fantastic shape and size worn by

DIGSWELL   Sir Anthony Grey,[1] while Lady Peryent, at Digswell, has most curious plaited hair, a collar of SS, a swan embroidered, mysteriously, on the left side of her outer collar, and a small hedgehog at her feet. There are many instances of the crespine

BROXBOURNE   or caul of network for the hair; Lady Say, at Broxbourne, is notable for her heavy necklace or carcanet of gems and for her butterfly headdress of gauze extended upon wires.

THEOBALDS   Theobalds, one of the houses built by William Cecil to honour Queen Elizabeth, 'ranking among the greatest palaces ever built in this country',[2] was demolished under the Commonwealth, but we can read of the ceiling of the hall, which was decorated with the signs of the Zodiac, and in which the sun, by some mechanism, ran its course across the ceiling, and the stars came out at night. And there was another room at Theobalds, painted with designs of the towns, mountains, and rivers of England; and the other ceilings which were painted 'byse' or light blue, with gilt roses.

Two Hertfordshire churches have eighteenth-century memorials in which we may admire particularly the attitudes of

TRING   the 'sitters'. An otherwise dull memorial at Tring, carved in 1707 by John Nost, shows Sir William Gore and his wife, he in an immense periwig, comfortably settled as though picnicking, upon either side of an urn under the inevitable canopy. While, in the mid-century, Roubiliac carved Lord Chief Justice

HERTINGFORDBURY   Spencer-Cowper at Hertingfordbury, a small and most exquisite marble panel showing the judge in robes and great full-bottomed wig, sitting enthroned, head on hand, as though listening intently to counsel's argument, between two standing, emblematic figures, a panel with some of the elements in it of terracotta sculpture, built up, as it were, not carved down, and with the graces of the French eighteenth century added to it.

MOOR PARK   At Moor Park the influence is rather from Italy, so much so

[1] Knights also wore their long moustaches protruding from their helmets, and studded mail, consisting of knobs or studs riveted to a lining of cuirbouilli, a prepared leather, a variety of armour which appears in the brasses to Sir Thomas Cheyne and his son at Drayton Beauchamp, in neighbouring Buckinghamshire, the latter of whom is wearing laminated sollerets formed of scales or small shingles of steel.

[2] J. Summerson, *Architecture in Britain 1530-1830*, Harmondsworth, 1970, pp. 73-4.

that the house was long thought to have been built by the
Venetian, Giacomo Leoni, the Italian member of Lord Burlington's Palladian circle, who built Lyme Hall and Lathom Hall in
Lancashire. Moor Park now appears to have been designed by
Sir James Thornhill, the painter. This building, without its
wings and colonnades, and now become a golf club house, is
still wonderful by reason of its hall, with marble doorcases,
superb stucco-work, and paintings by Amigoni. In the white
drawing-room there is a ceiling panel of Bacchus and Ceres,
probably by Bagutti, with fauns playing pipes, and a cupid with
a load of corn. The frame of this stucco panel has festoons of
vines tied into sheaves of corn. There is, also, one of the most
beautiful of imported Chinese wallpapers, done with birds and
flowers upon a ground of blue. These painted Chinese wallpapers are among the delights of the eighteenth century, and in
their finest examples are almost peculiar to this island. Trade
with the Celestial Kingdom being chiefly in our hands, we may
read in Mrs Montagu's letters, of her closet in her London
house, 'lined with painted paper of Pekin, and furnished with
the choicest moveables of China'. There are the two types,
with and without the human figure. The former may have, for
subject, the cultivation of tea, or the pleasures of the Chinese.
They may contain hundreds of figures variously occupied,
though we prefer for our taste those that have for subject birds
and flowers. These painted papers were sent back as presents by
merchants and ambassadors, and we may picture to ourselves
the long voyage through the Indian seas, past the turtle isles of
St Helena and Ascension, up the great Atlantic to the white
cliffs of England, and then the pleasures of unpacking. So
intense was the romance and poetry from these distant lands
that we shall find it perpetuated down to the middle of the
nineteenth century, in the chinoiserie scenes engraved upon
grocer's bill-heads, even in provincial towns, a series comparable for fantasy and imagination to the chinamen of Herold
upon Dresden porcelain. The painted papers vary much in their
set limits,[1] the blue ground being particularly rare. The boughs
of the flowering trees may be hung with Chinese lanterns and
with songbirds in cages. Chief flower is the paeony, which is the
rose of Chinese gardens, while among the birds may be recognised the golden and the silver pheasant, already, by that date,
domesticated for the aviary, but we would search in these

---

[1] Other examples are at Badminton, Cobham, Bowood and Nostell.

wallpapers, were there opportunity, for the Amherstian, which is the most magnificent in plumage of all the pheasants, living in aviaries as readily as the gold and silver, but not known in Europe till Lord Amherst's embassy of 1816. No experience could be more delightful than to waken in a bedroom hung with 'painted paper of Pekin'; unless it be to imagine ourselves, in pleasant company, drinking fragrant hyson or orange pekoe out of cups of porcelain, while the clock chimes, the mandarin nods his head from side to side, and the false nightingale jumps out of his gilded box to sing.

WOODHALL PARK   Woodhall Park, near Hertford, is the most important country house from the hand of Thomas Leverton that has come down to us, built for the 'Nabob', Sir Thomas Rumbold, Governor of Madras. Like Broadlands and Althorp, by Henry Holland, it is a white brick house. The entrance hall is one of the Etruscan rooms, with a ribbed or fluted ceiling to be known, immediately, as the work of Leverton, and white walls with garlands and painted medallions in chocolate, and red, and yellow. Behind this, a staircase of altogether exceptional dexterity and lightness rises in a spiral curve, with a balustrade somewhat like that of No. 1 Bedford Square in London (see p. 167), and fully equal to any of Adam's stair rails in elegance and finish. The walls of the stair have elaborate stucco panels, the fans of Leverton spread open under the spandrels of the dome, while we can attest his hand in the mouldings of the doorcases, in the bookcases of the library, and in the characteristic ornament of a 'Bossi' mantelpiece of inlaid, coloured marbles. But perhaps the most beautiful object at Woodhall is the carpet in the drawing-room. This will have been drawn by Leverton, and carried out at Moorfields or at Axminster. The ribbed or fluted centre, so dear to the architect, with the wreaths of grapes and vines upon a yellow ground, recall the carpets at Syon and at Saltram in Devon. This is as good an example as any of the Adam carpets of that English style which verges on the Russian-Bessarabian, and only proves the existence of another art that is lost, and unlikely in modern conditions ever to be born again.

BUCKINGHAMSHIRE

GAYHURST   At Gayhurst the tomb of Mr Speaker Wright and his son was long accepted as a masterpiece by Roubiliac, his first commission in England, but it is now thought to be the work of

Durham Cathedral and Castle from the north-west.

Tithe barn of the Black Monks at Abbotsbury, Dorset.

St Patrick's, Patrington, the 'Queen of Holderness'.

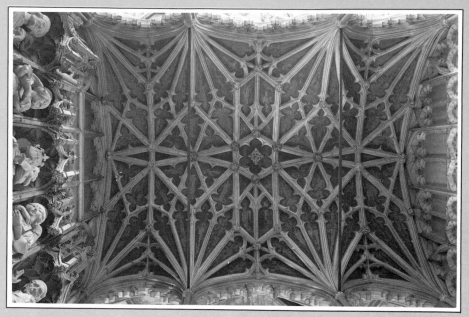

Above: Vaulted
ceiling of William
of Wykeham's
chantry chapel in
Winchester
Cathedral.

Right: Angel
ceiling at
All Saints,
Necton,
Norfolk.

Parish church of St Andrew at Mells, Somerset.

Left: Tiered
steeple of
St Bride's,
Fleet Street,
one of Wren's
City churches.

Below: Nicholas
Stone's effigy of
Dr John Donne
in his shroud,
in the chancel
of St Paul's
Cathedral.

Tomb of Alice Spencer, Countess of Derby, by Maximilian Colt, in Harefield church, Middlesex; beside it are a funeral helm and gauntlets and one of the Attic funerary vases of the Newdigate family.

Brass, in the French style, of Sir Robert de Setvans in armour complete with *ailettes*, or shoulder protectors, engraved with his heraldic device – the winnowing fan; at Chartham, Kent.

Thomas Carter. Indeed, it is entirely in the English style with the two full-length figures in splendid wigs, standing side by side under a canopy, framed by Corinthian pilasters and a broken pediment.

CLAYDON HOUSE   At Claydon we are again among the chinoiseries. But there is more to say, besides, of this house, which was decorated for Lord Verney. First, the stair with its treads inlaid with ebony, ivory, and holly, and its wrought iron balustrade, from top to bottom, perhaps of Italian workmanship, composed of wreaths and ears of corn that rattle together as you walk up the stair. The staircase and library at Claydon have stucco-work by Joseph Rose, long employed here. But there were wood carvers, as well, who made the magnificent overdoors to the north hall, Palladian in shape, but enriched with Rococo. However, the most remarkable feature of Claydon is the Chinese room. The doorcases have 'pagoda' overdoors and Chinese masks or faces at the sides; the chimneypiece is elaborate, with more masks of Chinamen; but most complicated of all is the tremendous alcove, with niches to hold china mandarins and pagodas, and probably, originally, a bed which, as one authority reminds us, may have been such as found a place in Bubb Dodington's 'Managarith' or Chinese bedroom at Eastbury, in Dorset. This bedroom at Claydon may be the most complete instance in England of chinoiserie.[1]

BEDFORDSHIRE

WOBURN ABBEY   With Chinese Chippendale, speaking for our own personal taste, we are not so much in sympathy, though we have not seen what must be the best of its kind, the Chinese Dairy at Woburn Abbey, all complete. This was the work of Henry Holland, who also built the sculpture gallery and the south wing of the Duke of Bedford's house, which had been redesigned by Flitcroft. SOUTHILL   Southill, for Mr Samuel Whitbread, is the more complete specimen of Holland, tasteful and discreet almost to extinction.

LUTON HOO   At Luton Hoo, we would wish to be able to admire once again the work of Robert Adam in the huge project he undertook for Lord Bute. It contained a circular hall or tribune,

---

[1] But there is a Chinese room, too, at Mawley Hall, in Shropshire; while no account of these lively fantasies should omit the room at Badminton, in Gloucestershire, with its Chinese bed by Chippendale (now in the Victoria and Albert Museum), its chinoiserie furniture, and imported Chinese wallpaper.

probably on the lines of that at Kedleston, and (we follow Mrs Delany): 'then into the Library. . . . It is, in effect, three or five rooms, one very large one well proportioned in the middle, each end divided off by pillars, in which recesses are chimneys: and a large square room at each end, which, when the doors are open make it appear one large room or gallery.' This library had 30,000 books, and was 150 feet in length; and Mrs Delany goes on to notice the beds, 'damask, and rich satin, green, blue and crimson; mine was white satin'. Dr Johnson visited Luton Hoo with Boswell, and this is his comment: 'The library is very splendid; the dignity of the rooms is very great; and the quantity of pictures is beyond expectation, beyond hope.' Luton Hoo has been altered out of recognition.

EAST ANGLIA

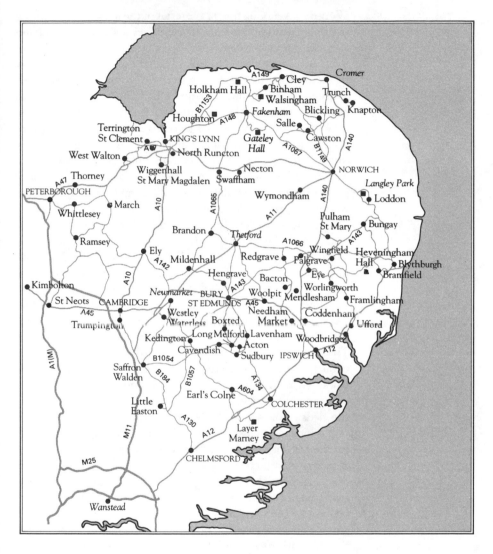

Cromer
Cley
Holkham Hall • Binham
Walsingham • Trunch
Fakenham • Blickling Knapton
Houghton A148 Salle
Terrington Gateley Cawston
St Clement KING'S LYNN Hall
West Walton • North Runcton
Wiggenhall • Necton NORWICH
Thorney St Mary Magdalen Swaffham Langley Park
PETERBOROUGH Wymondham Loddon
March
Whittlesey Pulham Bungay
Brandon St Mary
Ramsey Thetford Wingfield
Ely Redgrave Heveningham
Mildenhall Palgrave Hall Blythburgh
Hengrave Bacton Bramfield
Kimbolton Newmarket Woolpit Eye
St Neots BURY Mendlesham Worlingworth Framlingham
CAMBRIDGE ST EDMUNDS Coddenham
Westley Needham Ufford
Trumpington Waterless Boxted Market
Kedington Long Melford Lavenham Woodbridge
Cavendish Acton IPSWICH
Saffron Sudbury
Walden
Earl's Colne
Little
Easton COLCHESTER
Layer
Marney
CHELMSFORD

Wanstead

CAMBRIDGESHIRE AND HUNTINGDONSHIRE

ELY   We are back among the monasteries of the fens. Ely is at the far
end of these, if we think of them and their subordinate churches
as going from Ely towards the Wash and on either side of that
into Lincolnshire and Norfolk. The fens must be conceived of
in the days of the monks as alive with waterfowl of all sorts,
avocets, grebes, godwits, whimbrels, knots, dottrels, yelpers,
ruffs and reeves in their thousands, to but mention what are
now the rarest of them; the peasants had their huge flocks of
geese; but the paradise of the monks had also its ague-stricken
inhabitants, known into Victorian times as 'fen-slodgers' or
'yellow-bellies', when it would be true to say that quite a large
proportion of the population took laudanum to counteract the
wet of the climate, and were in a mild sense opium fiends.

Of all this district Ely was the capital, and does it not look
that still now seen perhaps from fifteen miles away across the
heath from near Newmarket? There is no more wonderful and
imposing building in England, varying, as it does, from the
castellan turrets and modulations of its exterior towers to the
fern-frost delicacies of its Lady Chapel, and to the miraculous
Octagon, an engineering feat without parallel in its day – still
less in ours when there is much work of engineers but little art.
The whole kingdom was searched for oaks of scantling or spread
enough to give the huge timbers necessary in its construction; a
whole grove was inspected, paid for and cut down, and the
roads and bridges into Ely widened and made strong enough for
the sleds or ox-wagons to bring them in.

It is indeed an advantage in a thousand to be approaching Ely
for the first, or fifth, or it could be the hundredth time. For this
is a sensation that does not stale. It can be seen from miles away;
from a distance that in my experience is only matched when the
twin steeples of Chartres rise from ten or fifteen miles in front of
you out of the cornlands of La Beauce; or when from a comparable distance over the olive groves you see the huge bulk of
the amphitheatre of El Djem. Or there is the Pyramid of
Cheops, to mention in the same breath as Ely, but with the
proviso that neither amphitheatre nor pyramid are works of
art. This, Ely is most emphatically, and at nearer view one
might almost add with a vengeance, for there is something
militant as of a soldier-minded Prince-Palatine about the castel-
lation of its west tower, and no less so the castellated turret to its

side.[1] It would be no surprise to see bowmen or archers on duty and at look-out on those towers. The nave of Ely in severe Norman style is in the same uncompromising mood till we arrive at the soaring Octagon, which is something unique in cathedral building. The petrified stalks of the vaulting, stalks stripped of their leaves, spread wide their symmetrical and open fans into the star vault of the lantern, which is in fact more like a passion-flower or clematis. The choir beyond this is of pointed architecture with, for lighter and later relief, the seething and prickling of the stone stalagmites of Bishop Alcock's chantry chapel in chamber-music Perpendicular. Bishop Alcock died in 1501, and his chantry chapel, begun thirteen years earlier, has lost any theatrical purpose or wish to impress with anything of solemnity or terror. The interior with its many canopied niches empty of statues, and therefore lifeless as a huge stable without horses, is too richly crowded and verges on the Manoelino of Portugal. Bishop Redman's tomb chapel with but room for a priest to stand at the altar, lies under three cusped arches with bird-cage panelling rising to the capitals of the clustered piers. A stone bird-cage, but suspended in air and centrifugally up-held, for it has no supporting columns. Beyond, to the left-hand side, the Lady Chapel, of earlier elaboration, is of rich sub-aqueous effect owing to the green lights in its chalky whiteness, and is the marvellous finish to a morning or an evening that opened in militant spirit and ends at this foretaste of the calm, empty churches of the nearby fens.

In preparation for visiting these we would recall the highway and bridge hermits of the Middle Ages, and the ferry hermits, also, who guided across rivers. These were especially useful in marshy districts and in the fens; and the Bishop of Ely in an indulgence of 1458 writes:

> Since our church is surrounded by waters and marshes and the relics of the Holy Virgins lying in it can only be visited over bridges and causeys, requiring daily repair, we commend to your charity William Grene, hermit, who, at our command with consent of the church of Ely, has undertaken the repair of the causeys and bridges of Stuntneys and Some

two villages now calling themselves Soham and Stuntney.

---

[1] Bishop van Mildert, last Prince-Palatine of Durham (d. 1836), is buried in the Cathedral. He continued to the end to wear his own version of a full bottomed, or judge's wig, much to the annoyance of Ernest Augustus, Duke of Cumberland and King of Hanover.

THORNEY   There was a proliferation of monasteries and their subject
churches in the fenlands, Thorney coming next for our
purpose, this like most of the others being of Benedictine
foundation. All that is left of Thorney is that fragment of it
which is now the parish church, but Thorney Island, as it then
was, having made its début into the religious life earlier still as
Ancarig, 'the island of the anchorite', became under Benedictine auspices the chosen paradise of mediaeval authors.
There are ecstatic accounts of it by William of Malmesbury,
writing in the thirteenth century, who came from Wiltshire at
the other side of England, from what would seem considerably
more of a rural paradise than the cold, wet, bleak fens. Thorney
Abbey was small in number of inmates, but rich out of all
proportion in the fruits of cultivation. He praises the orchards
and the improbable vineyards of the monks in his dog-Latin
which is so much easier to read than Esperanto.

WHITTLESEY   St Mary's, Whittlesey, was one of that group of churches
which were built by the abbots of Thorney and that, famous like
Whittlesey for their spires and whether or not due to the abbots
of the local monasteries, spread to the south of here across the
face of Rutland. Impressive as it is now, its effect must have
been much greater when it stood not above the fens only but
over its own Whittlesey Mere of more than fifteen hundred
acres of water, and above Whittlesey Wash. The tower is in four
storeys, entrance and west window, bell-chamber above that,
and then the exquisitely fanciful parapet and pinnacles or
obelisks in the midst of which springs up the spire, more than
one writer having drawn attention to 'the graceful manner in
which the spire is united to the tower'. I found this Perpendicular spire to be among the most beautiful of all; but how to
explain its grace and elegance, without pointing, not very far
away and in the same county, to the brass of Sir John de Creke
in the church at Westley Waterless? It will be seen from the
description below that no Japanese warrior in his laced lobster-
armour could be more elaborately garbed than Sir John de
Creke but, withal, he is waisted and of an excessive thinness, as
elegant indeed as the spire of Whittlesey rising above the fens
and meres not many miles away.

RAMSEY   Ramsey Abbey in Huntingdonshire, another of the great
Benedictine monasteries, with twenty-nine monks at the Suppression and with an income of £1,700, which puts it among
the ten richest monasteries in the kingdom, now enters the lists
of competition in church building, and many of the village

churches in this region, as rich in this respect as Norfolk and parts of Lincolnshire, but of less repute perhaps only because the villages are situated in this small and little known county, must be due to the Black Monks of Ramsey. But to which of the fenland abbeys was due the church of St Wendreda at March in MARCH Cambridgeshire with its 'angel' ceiling of the unique East Anglian kind, a double hammerbeam roof with angels with outspread wings, a hundred and twenty of them in all, eight pinions to a wing for every pair of them, in double tiers and along the runway of the ceiling, a roof that flutters and darkens with its rookery of golden wings, in its way as marvellous and poetic a work of art as any in mediaeval Europe? The rest of the church at March is entirely uninteresting. Why there should be this extraordinary concourse of angels at March is unexplained.

KIMBOLTON It was in the old house at Kimbolton, near Huntingdon, that Catherine of Aragon died, but it was rebuilt by Vanbrugh for the Earl, later Duke of Manchester. This nobleman had been Ambassador in Venice, Paris, and Vienna, and was something, therefore, of what the age called a virtuoso. We find Vanbrugh writing,

> I thought it was absolutely best to give it something of the Castle Air, though at the same time to make it Regular . . . so I hope Your Lordship will not be discouraged if any Italian you may Shew it to, should find fault that it is not Roman. . . . I am sure this will make a very noble and masculine show.

Later, in another letter, he writes, 'I shall be much deceived if People do not see a Manly Beauty in it . . .'. Kimbolton is, in fact, a four-square building, typical of the new manner of Vanbrugh which was to lead him in the end to Seaton Delaval. The phrase that intrigues is his invention of the 'Castle Air'.

ST NEOTS At St Neots we are back with the Perpendicular, in the tower of the church, adorned with elaborate corner pinnacles with a touch of Tudor Nonesuch on them. But the scale is small, looking down upon the streams bordered with willows and distant cottages thatched with reed. At St Neots, as in the Norfolk churches we shall visit shortly, the delight is in the slope and reduction of the stone outline of the buttresses; their set-offs, their drip moulds (to throw off the rain), all calculated with extreme precision and through their good sense and utility giving aesthetic beauty and satisfaction. But here it has not quite the expertise and taste of the Norfolk towers where every alteration of line has been long considered; while the roof-turrets are a little too flamboyant and could be flying the pennons of a tournament.

WESTLEY
WATERLESS

The church at Westley Waterless, the other side of Cambridge, contains the brass of Sir John de Creke, mentioned above. That pocket-Adonis of a knight, for there was never so slight a figure or so slim a waist, wears every garment proper to the knightly wardrobe; chaussés of banded ring-mail, a new species, consisting of rings of steel attached to strips of leather fastened, in turn, to another underlining; jambarts of plate; spurs of rouelle form; a hauberk; a haqueton padded and stuffed; vambraces of plate; demi-brassarts complete with coudières; roundels fashioned to resemble lion heads upon his arm joints; for helmet, a fluted bascinet of plate; the wambeys or gam-beson, stuffed with wool and padded with lines of needlework; and a special or particular garment, the so-called cyclax, laced at the sides, and cut very short in front. One authority on brasses thinks that he can detect yet another garment, to which he cannot give a name. Yet Sir John de Creke is excessively

TRUMPINGTON

attenuated and thin. Sir Roger de Trumpington in the church of that name near Cambridge, in entire ring-mail, not con-sisting, that is to say, of links of steel interlaced and tied with rivets, but of rings of steel sewn upon leather or quilted cloth, has his head resting upon his tilting-helm, at the apex of which may be seen the staple from which floated the scarf of his lady-love during the mock battle of the tournament. The shield of this paladin carries his appropriate armorial bearing of a pair of trumpets in pale; and the two trumpets appear again on his ailettes or shoulder plates, which stand up, rigid, behind his shoulders, very different in intention from the pair of ailettes garnished and fretted with pearls that were among the effects of Piers Gaveston, minion of Edward II.

CAMBRIDGE

In Cambridge itself, we first visit King's College Chapel, where the fan vault floats, one could almost say it waves or shivers, above high Perpendicular walls that are largely win-dow. The fans touch in the middle with what one could term a two years' growth of palm frond. And now a note of caution comes creeping in. One of the most learned and cautious critics of this architecture writes that 'the fan vault was cheap because it was standardised in its parts; all the ribs were of the same curvature; it was easy to build because rib-and-panel design was only apparent, and in most cases the whole work was cut from the solid block; it was consequently less 'alive' than other vaults and needed less buttressing'.[1] Not, as one would have thought, more, but less buttressing is what he states. And he warns one only to look out for supreme examples that were the work of great masters. Decidedly the ceiling of King's College Chapel is among the latter, although every one of its fans has had to be bound in by an extended rib that arches across the whole ceiling. And from another authority we learn the astonishing information, destructive of all accepted canons of admiration, that the great vault of King's College Chapel was to have been painted; and there are estimates for the painting and gilding of the twelve bays of the roof amounting to £320 in all, 'equal to between three and four thousand pounds of our money', but this was in 1911 before two World Wars. So the roof of King's College Chapel was to have been in gold and colours; and this may be as surprising to some tastes as that the sculptures of the Parthenon were once coloured. As, too, the sculptures on the porches of Chartres Cathedral. To which it can only be added that those who carved them will have been the best judges of such things. The fan vault of King's we can perhaps take on trust, but it is difficult to envisage the Elgin marbles or the porches of Chartres ablaze with gold and colours. But, then, again, many tastes would not approve the chryselephantine statues of the Ancients, though we should have learned by now to prefer the live flesh to the skeleton.

Pembroke Chapel, as we have stated earlier, was the first work of Christopher Wren, built on a commission from his uncle, the Bishop of Ely, who was later buried there, and who desired the chapel to be a thanksgiving for release from his eighteen years' imprisonment in the Tower of London. It is a correct and charming building, with its engaged Corinthian pilasters and the hexagon belfry with the dome above it, but we would not compare it with the chapel of Emmanuel, the first building Wren completed after his visit to France. A little removed from the other colleges, Emmanuel gives a shock of delight to the visitor from the moment he enters the court and sees, opposite to him, that delightful front with its four pilasters and columns, the swags of fruit between them, the broken pediment above, and the ingenious belfry. More than this, the chapel has on either hand, flat with its façade, a gallery of five round arches raised upon a cloister; and, as though we were in

[1] John H. Harvey, *op. cit.*, p. 129.

some Italian town, we remember that in the interior the altar-piece is by the Venetian, Amigoni.

To reach Wren's Library at Trinity, we pass through the great court with its canopied fountain standing in the centre,[1] that vision of what a Renaissance monastery cloister might have been in England. The library is one of the most loved of all Wren's buildings; as much, indeed, for its associations as for its actual beauties. For it is open to criticism. The first project was for a circular building with a dome, to which the access was to be by a double stairway, through a portico. Instead, it was decided to complete the second, or Nevile's Court of Trinity, by which means, too, the Library would have arches under it, and damp would not destroy the books. But the front towards the Court is by far the happiest. Its flight of eleven windows, with their columns, suggests the magnificence that waits within. Yet the floor has been sunk so low, to gain interior height, that it blocks one-third of the arcades below, and makes dull and meaningless what should have been, in contemporary language, the 'piazza' underneath, which is in fact but wasted space. The four statues on the roof line, upon the balustrade, are from the hand of Gabriel Cibber, the sculptor from Denmark. Unfortunately the water front of the Library is a disappointment. The lower floor is monotonous with its three tall doorways and the blank space above the windows, nor is this redeemed by the flat pilasters between the windows on the upper storey. Wren failed in his opportunity. He did not anticipate the possibilities of this Cambridge water architecture that was to make the slow journey by punt along the College Backs, by the soft lawns and weeping willow trees, into the only architectural experience of the kind that can compare to being rowed in a gondola down the Grand Canal. We enter the Library by a stair which has a splendid stucco ceiling, and find ourselves among the bookcases with their wreaths and cyphers carved in limewood by Grinling Gibbons, and with busts by Roubiliac upon the pedestals above. Here is a splendid, enriched wooden doorway. The Library of Trinity has, of course, books and relics of the highest interest, and it is ungenerous to say that, personally, we prefer the Library of Queen's, at Oxford, even though its architecture is not by Wren, and its carvings, which we prefer again, are more probably by Grinling Gibbons's pupils.

[1] This was perhaps designed by Ralph Symonds, who built some of the courts at St John's, Emmanuel and Sidney Sussex.

We return to King's for introduction to the work of James
Gibbs in Cambridge, for he made designs for three sides of a
court here, the fourth side being the chapel, and the three
blocks of buildings to stand separately, unlike the usual
arrangement in college buildings. Only one wing was built, the
fine, plain Fellows' block of King's, which is an epitome of good
commonsense, but no more than that, when we realise of what
Gibbs was capable. For he designed what is, after King's College
Chapel, the most beautiful of Cambridge buildings, the Senate
House. King's Parade, in actual fact so much more architecturally rewarding than the High at Oxford, even if the good
buildings be on one side only, has this delight which perpetually
renews itself each time we see it. As usual, the Senate House is
the curtailment of a larger plan, being one wing only of a
three-sided group of buildings, of which the present Library was
erected later, but not from Gibbs's plans. The functions of the
Senate House are comparable to those of the Sheldonian
Theatre at Oxford and it contains, therefore, a large hall for
the conferring of degrees. Gibbs, it appears, was not entirely
responsible for the design, which originated with the amateur
Sir James Burroughs, Master of Caius, for the Syndics made the
order that 'Mr James Gibbs do take with him to London Mr
Burroughs' plan . . . and make what improvement he shall
think necessary upon it.' In the result we have one of the
supreme elegancies of the eighteenth century, and a building
which, for Gibbs, is strangely feminine. The proportion of the
Senate House is an unending pleasure; the coupled pilasters at
the corners strike such a perfect balance with the engaged
columns of the centre. Both the depth of the cornice and
balustrade, and height of the pediment, achieve a mathematical, or, we would have it, a musical perfection. The comparison of the Senate House at Cambridge is not with Italian,
but with French architecture; with the Place Stanislas, at
Nancy, and with the twin buildings by Gabriel at the corners of
the Rue Royale, in Paris, facing the Place de la Concorde. But,
in the case both of Héré and of Gabriel, it is work of a
generation later than Gibbs. The Englishman (or Scot), as we
would expect, is more solid and less fashionable. There are
differences, too, inherent in the different stone. But façade-
making, that pastime or plaything of the eighteenth century,
here reaches to its climax. We should compare Vardy's front to
Spencer House, St James's. English architecture, on occasion,
as in this pair of instances, can surpass the French in elegance,

just as English furniture designed by Adam and carried out by Chippendale, a rare occurrence, can be of a quality unmatched even by the greatest of the French *ébénistes*.

NORFOLK

If we make north again towards the Wash, we can once more strike that line of churches, not in the fens but in the marshland, lying between Spalding and King's Lynn, but this time following it into Norfolk. We come then to Terrington St Clement, Tilney All Saints, Walpole St Peter, West Walton with a detached tower like an Eastern church, Walsoken, Wiggenhall St German, and Wiggenhall St Mary Magdalene with its beautiful carved benches of the early sixteenth century, until we reach King's Lynn.

KING'S LYNN   This is one of the most fascinating towns in England, and the mediaeval Guildhall is by no means its only attraction, for there are the delightful buildings by Henry Bell: the Custom House, reminiscent, it is true, of Hoorn and Alkmaar, for Lynn is so near to Holland, of Portland stone with a Doric and an Ionic order, a statue of Charles II, perhaps by Cibber, upon the front, and an open turret ending in an obelisk upon which a figure of Fame perched on one foot; the old Market House, unhappily pulled down, with a peristyle of sixteen Ionic columns and a 'neat octagonal room' above, with four niches on the outside and statues of the Virtues; a church at North Runcton, three miles from Lynn, with Ionic columns on high pedestals and a dome; and perhaps the house in Queen Street with its twisted Corinthian columns at the door. Bell, a competent engraver, as witness his own print of the Custom House, was a local architect of the type found in so many parts of Europe, unknown outside his native town, but forming for posterity the character of a particular place. The doorway to the house in Queen Street – or do we imagine this? – is not entirely like a doorway in any other town. It bears the date 1708, and we remind ourselves that it belongs to the generation of the Fleming, John Nost, who made use of twisted Corinthian columns in his tombs at Silton and at Durisdeer.[1] There can have been no personal contact between the Flemish sculptor and the King's Lynn architect, but such conceits were in the air, and, indeed, with

[1] Sir Hugh Wyndham at Silton, Dorset, and the Queensbury monument at Durisdeer, near Drumlanrig Castle in Scotland.

its empty quays and old brick houses, it resembles some Dutch harbour on the Zuyder Zee. But, also, for some peculiar reason King's Lynn is where the merry-go-rounds and roundabouts were made for fairs. Mermaids and winged lions were no strangers in its yards and warehouses. While near by, upon a Sunday morning, you may see the old ladies of Castle Rising Almshouse crossing the road to church, and wearing the high peaked witches' hats and red cloaks with a badge of a white horse which were prescribed for them by their founder, one of the Howards, in the reign of James I.

HOLKHAM HALL   Not far away are Houghton and Holkham with their incomparable treasures. Holkham is William Kent's biggest work, though we admit that its exterior is no more prepossessing than that of the proposed palace in Hyde Park for George II, of which the wooden model is still shown in the Dutch House at Kew. The ground floor of Holkham is treated with an ugly and mechanical rustication, a rustication without the Italian poetry or grandeur, while the white brick of which the house is built is inevitably depressing, and must ever be, even under the skies of Italy. The disposition of the windows is too bleak and formal, while the windows, again, are too small for their surrounding walls, so that the effect is blind and empty. There is a portico, but without light or shade, and dragged in like the 'fugal' portion of an overture or symphony. The fugue has been called, in such instances, 'the composer's friend', for the tendency is to fill up blanks with it. So it is with this portico; it is quite unnecessary, but a large house, like Holkham, had to have one. As a whole, the exterior of Holkham has a disconcerting Victorian air. It is dull and disappointing.

But the interior of Holkham is splendid from the start. The great hall, with its pillars raised upon a balustrade,[1] its glorious frieze and coffered ceiling, is of Roman grandeur, only matched by the great halls of Kedleston and Syon, which are the masterworks of Robert Adam. All of them, not least Holkham, rank among the monumental instances of the whole Renaissance in Europe. They are strictly Classical, not tainted with their age, and worthy of what we may imagine the Golden House of Nero to have been, where the best craftsmen of the Greek decadence were employed. There is nothing to criticise in the great hall at

[1] 'Its stately range of fluted columns enriched with purple and white variegated alabaster,' as remarks Robert Brettingham in the *Plans of Holkham Hall.* He was the nephew of Matthew Brettingham (see below). Most of the interior of Holkham was in fact executed after Kent's death, and the design of the hall altered.

Holkham. One can but admire, and admit that during his long years in Italy, Kent had learned his lesson. The other rooms at Holkham reveal him in masterly treatment of mantelpiece, doorway, and coffered ceiling. His doorcases are endless in their Classical variety, being perfect models of their sort, as are his chimneypieces and overmantels, one of which, with wonderful appropriateness, is frame to an antique mosaic.

HOUGHTON

But the imagination of Kent is most conspicuous in his furniture. He is the master of the eagle and the dolphin. If his overdoors and coffered ceilings are at their best in Holkham, his finest marble chimneypieces are at Houghton, where Colen Campbell was architect and Kent decorator. Both the stone hall and the dining-room have superb chimneypieces, framing bas-reliefs by Rysbrack, and it is difficult to choose between them for magnificence. The former has a pair of terms or caryatids carrying baskets of flowers upon their heads, a bold projecting cornice in three portions carrying a bust in the centre, and then the broad and splendid frame to the bas-relief, topped with a cornice and a broken pediment. The other is more simple, without human figures, but has a pair of fabulous creatures above, in the opening of the pediment, that are feeding from a bowl of grapes. The gilt furniture by Kent at Houghton must be among the wonders of English interior decoration. No Italian palace of the High Renaissance has such furniture. It is worthy of Mantua or Urbino; and it must always be a mystery as to why Kent's pre-eminent merit, or even genius, in this matter is not recognised.[1] It can only be because of the private uses of this furniture which, consequently, is never seen and never advertised. The only rival of Kent is Chippendale at his very finest, working under Adam, but that is superlative workmanship with marquetry of rare woods and mounts of ormolu. This is gilded furniture, settees and chairs and tables, superbly carved, but the material is unimportant, it is but carving and then gilding. This Kent furniture, however, could stand in the Vatican or in the Doge's Palace. It does not need a setting of its own time. It requires the golden age of the High Renaissance.

LANGLEY PARK

Matthew Brettingham, a Norwich architect who worked with Kent at Holkham Hall, designed Langley Park in the

[1] The saloon at Houghton has a set of twelve armchairs, four stools and two settees in mahogany, part gilt, and covered with cut velvet. They have shell aprons and female masks upon the knees. The Kent furniture at Houghton, all told, is among the greatest splendours of interior decoration in England, and it is unmatched in any other country in the world.

distant south-eastern corner of the county.[1] The house contains one of the loveliest works in stucco in the panel of Diana and Actaeon, so providing an instance of Rococo in a Palladian setting. The panel depicts Actaeon in Roman costume, in a warrior's kilt, with leather jerkin and short sleeves, bow in hand, having just this instant been changed into a stag, and averting his gaze from Diana and her nymphs as though miming the part of the Prince in *Le Lac des Cygnes*. The three naked young women are bathing in a brimming basin from which the water overflows. We can see their nether limbs perfectly, under the water, and they have even entangled the huntsman in their garments for a part of a scarf is round his chest and they are pulling him towards them in that gesture with which the Indian Rajahs have their waistbands wound, and unwound, by their attendants. This subject, by the Anglo-Dane, Charles Stanley, is the beginning of the stucco landscape. Another Norfolk
GATELEY HALL ceiling, at Gateley Hall – is it by the same master? – shows a whole pastoral scene, with trees and hills and windmills, flocks and herds, a church spire, farm buildings, and the squire in a cocked hat looking on.

WALSINGHAM   At Holkham and Houghton we were close to Walsingham, which was one of the chief destinations of the mediaeval pilgrims. One legend is as good as another, and in the Middle Ages the East Anglian countrymen thought the Milky Way in the heavens pointed to the shrine at Walsingham; while in Spain it led to Compostela and was called St James's Way. A path still traceable in places through the countryside is known as 'Walsingham Green Way', or the 'Palmers' Way', though, no doubt, of much older origin than the shrine. Everyone in the villages round knows by heart 'As I went to Walsingham', the pilgrims' song.[2] It is the land of warrens. One warren alone sends forty thousand rabbits in a year to the London of Dick Whittington. There is even a particular warren famous for its rabbits which have valuable silvery-grey fur. This is the district of the 'brecks', wide-open fields mixed with warren and sheep walk, the haunt of the great bustard. Here, too, are pits of the

[1] Brettingham was also responsible for Cumberland House, Pall Mall, and Norfolk House, St James's Square, both now pulled down. He had some share, too, in the original designs for Kedleston, and his son was one of the first architects to go to Greece, in company with 'Athenian' Stuart, the result of which journey was *The Antiquities of Athens* of Stuart and Revett, a work of much influence on the younger generation and a determining factor in the taste and style of the later eighteenth century.

[2] On which song sets of variations were composed by both William Byrd and John Bull, the virtuoso player of his day.

flint-knappers, which is a pre-historic industry. All of which is but prelude to finding nothing left at all of the shrine and Augustinian monastery which Erasmus visited and wrote of, and which Henry VIII attended as a pilgrim not so very many years before the Dissolution, walking barefoot from Barsham, a memorable sight in itself, in order to hang a chain of gold around the Virgin's neck.

BINHAM

At Binham Priory, which is near Walsingham, there is but the nave of the church still standing, which became the parish church and occupies, it is said, but one-sixth of the area of the original building. The aisles, the cloister, the guest house, are all in ruins. But there is forlorn and masculine splendour in what is left, for there is little or nothing at Binham Priory to interpose between ourselves and the early thirteenth century.

And now we may embark on one of the unique themes of this part of England, for the mediaeval carpenters made wooden ceilings as intricate and as specialised as shipbuilding, and indeed the process of installing the start of a double hammer-beam ceiling must have resembled, in reverse, the laying down of a ship's hull. The craft reached to extraordinary heights of execution and imagination and must have been in the hands of particular families and of 'mysteries' or guilds who guarded their secrets, and who only took on apprentices under stringent rules of secrecy. There could be arch-braced roof timbers, curved beams, that is to say, hewn from the wood; or they could be brought down and joined into a horizontal or hammer-beam projecting from the wall; or even, arch on arch and two projecting beams in support of them, which formed the double hammer-beam. The arched braces projected upwards from the wall-posts, and supported carved figures of angels with outspread wings. Such were the angel ceilings.

NECTON

They are the masterpieces of English carpentry. To start with a simple example, at Necton, where there are winged angels, and less obtrusively winged than some others, on every other or alternate beam, and statues below them standing on pedestals on the wall-posts. But this is one of the less elaborate of the angel ceilings. At Necton the angels – or are they saints, it is not quite the same thing! – though gilded, have their wings folded, beetle-wise, as though in wing-cases, and do not look capable of prolonged flight. They even have the look of winged priests in surplices, with wings only for ceremonial purposes and not for use.

Such roofs or ceilings are notoriously difficult to photograph, and must be more awkward still to draw. But, as is nearly always the case in this restricted field, a Victorian book more than a hundred years old comes to the rescue.[1] And demonstrably open timber roofs they are, in contrast to the flat roofs of Somerset, Devon, and the West Country! In the book in question there are careful coloured drawings of three of the roofs KNAPTON including that at Knapton,[2] where the prevailing tint is yellow, I would call it an almost laburnum-yellow. We do not know enough of the Brandon brothers to determine how subtle or unsubtle was their sense of colour; and of course the colouring will have deteriorated further during the hundred and forty years that have passed, and, also, there may have been, there almost certainly will have been repainting. But the interest lies in the fact that this work of the Brandon brothers chose to depict what are by no means the most interesting of their kind. Murray merely remarks of Knapton, 'there is a rich open roof of the Perpendicular period', albeit one of the most conscientious of modern authorities says of the church, 'It is worth going a long way to see the wonderful double hammer-beam roof here,'[3] a criticism that I can fully endorse for I have seen it, as, also, the open timber roof of Trunch near by.

SWAFFHAM At Swaffham, a market town back towards King's Lynn, the choir of winged angels are impressively angelic, and are in two rows or positions to take flight and flutter about the open roof; and, lastly, there are the famous pair of villages near Aylsham, SALLE, CAWSTON Salle and Cawston, a mile or two apart, but at the latter the romance is a little tarnished by the ridiculous aspect of the winged figures on the cornice of the roof which look like a hybrid of fish and cherub, though the life-size angels on the projecting beams look ready to take wing. Now, a species of shark that has a curious projecting dorsal fin used to be called an 'angel' by the Southwold fishermen, and it is tempting again to connect the 'mysteries' of these angel ceilings and of ship-building.

[1] *Open Timber Roofs of the Middle Ages*, by Raphael and J. Arthur Brandon, 1846. Cf. also *Murray's Handbook, Eastern Counties*, 1878 ed.; and *Collins Guide to English Parish Churches*, edited by John Betjeman, London, 1958. Asterisks are prodigal in this latter. Norfolk has 78 'starred' churches; Suffolk 77, and Lincolnshire no less than 130. A long life of leisured ease would be needed to see all 285 of these.

[2] The others are of Palgrave and Bacton in Suffolk (see below).

[3] 'With a total of 138 angels, all with spread-out wings and certainly not all genuine.' *North East Norfolk*, by Nikolaus Pevsner, Harmondsworth, 1962.

Beside the open timber roofs the other feature peculiar to East Anglia is the flushwork, or the facing of buildings with split or knapped flints and brick or freestone. It was a discovery of the Perpendicular style; and the county of Buckinghamshire apart, where it was used to much less purpose, it is found nowhere else. There is no trace of it in France or in the Netherlands, and nowhere but in England in the absence of building stone was it thought worth while to make use of the flint pits of the sea-shore. But flints are found inland, too, where the sea once was, and flint-knapping or the chipping of flint stones according to the line of cleavage is still, or was till very recently, the local BRANDON industry of Brandon. It was here that, over a hundred years ago, a sand mound was excavated, and a passage was found eighty feet deep, and in the side of it a pick-axe made of a flint stuck into a stag's antler. At Brandon flints must have been worked in this way for many centuries, perhaps for four or five thousand years, until during the Perpendicular heyday of East Anglia the industry greatly expanded in order to supply flints for building; for church towers, particularly for porches, and for the parapets that are a feature of churches like Lavenham or Long Melford in Suffolk, and which have elaborate schemes of ornament, and often long and ornate inscriptions worked into them.

In the hands of the Perpendicular craftsmen a quite extra-ordinary variety was given to the use of this seemingly un-promising material; not only in use of ornaments and patterns but even in alternations of colouring. As much use was made of flint, if with very different effect, as with the blue and white *azulejos* of Portugal, and the mental vision of East Anglian building is to a great extent composed of flushwork. The units are of course much smaller than with tile-work, and the results, correspondingly, if less pictorial, that much more subtle. It more resembles some form of exterior mosaic work with a restricted palette, but with shades of white, black, green, and even other colours; and someone used, like the writer, to see pieces of 'clinker' or ironstone upon the roads of Derbyshire in their startling hues of blue and jade-green could wish there had been an admixture of these into the darker flint stone when a coloured architecture might have been achieved of startling brilliance. Even so the effects are remarkable enough, and at least they are unique and to be seen nowhere else.

NORWICH The church of St Michael Coslany is an extreme instance of flushwork carried nearly to the point of the tattooing on an old-time Maori warrior. It is a strange sight standing there in the middle of Norwich. One writer comments that the best time to see its beautiful panelled flintwork is during the winter months. Then, the trees at the side of it are not in leaf and, also, the winter light works the best advantage from the trimmed flints. It is late in date, probably after 1500; offering, it is certain, a better prospect of what might have happened but for the coming of the Renaissance, than can be deduced from Flamboyant Gothic. It is an extraordinary feat to have produced this sobriety and dignity from building material which might seem to offer a good deal less promise than the broken china that gives gaiety and pantomime fantasy to the pagodas of Bangkok. The old authority is not to be contradicted who said that 'no better example can be pointed out of the advantage to be gained by the judicious use of local material.' A good deal of the flint surface of St Michael Coslany has been refaced, and the flushwork was completed about a hundred years ago, so that St Michael Coslany is now in pristine order, having been well repaired. Its high Perpendicular windows of varied tracery have no less beautiful blind panels of flushwork beside them, and the frieze of flintwork ties in, and binds as it were, and completes the building.

LODDON At Loddon there is a fine flushwork porch in two storeys, richly panelled with knapped rough flints producing, that is to say, a slightly obtruding surface.[1] It is not unreasonable to compare this porch and chamber over it to the very similar

CLEY porch at Cley, which I have seen in the unforgettable semi-darkness and mystery of a November evening. At Cley the upper storey windows are lancet-shaped and higher and more important, and there is the rich cresting of its battlements; but it lacks the flushwork panels of Loddon, which yet is but a façade of flint, and it has not the wonderful recesses and angles

PULHAM ST MARY of the porch at Cley. And there is Pulham St Mary: a two-storeyed porch with the importance of a separate building on its own, with rich 'Isabelline', as it would be called were it in Spain, cresting to its parapet; niches that once held statues either side of the door, and figures of eight angel musicians, with trumpets to their mouths or playing lutes and viols. Over this are as many carved shields, heraldic or religious emblems, and canopied niches over those for statues; while Mr Wearing

---

[1] An invaluable guide to these Norfolk churches are *Beautiful Norfolk Buildings*, Norwich, 1944; *More Beautiful Norfolk Buildings*, Norwich, 1947, and *Beautiful Norfolk Buildings*, Norwich, 1960. All three volumes are by Stanley J. Wearing and are illustrated with his pencil drawings.

draws attention to the 'black' flint panelling to the sides, buttresses and plinth of this fantastic porch which, were it not for its many local compeers, it would be difficult to believe is but a rustic village building.

WYMONDHAM   A few miles to the north-west is Wymondham Abbey, and I remember, at a time it was but a name to me, a late autumn afternoon when I saw its nave and two towers looming through the November mists. It looked at that moment like some great vessel washed ashore; turned-turtle, even, with the roof of its nave for keel and the pair of great engine-rooms or power-houses of uncertain purpose floating upside down in the tideless air of dusk. The great tower of Wymondham is in fact octagonal and, sinister thought, it will have been from one of the upper openings in this steeple that William Kett, a leader of the Rebellion of 1549, was hanged in chains. Had one entered the Abbey only a few years ago 'when services were only conducted under great difficulties owing to the intrusion of wind and rain through cracks and crevices in the fabric', the illusion of entering the hull of a wrecked vessel must have been stronger still. But the angels of the hammer-beam roof still look down on us, while the double storey of Norman arches that form the nave are of the stern, the quasi-military school of Ely. What can be said of it to bring it once more alive, not in its parochial sense? That Henry I conferred on it the right to all the wrecks along a stormy section of the Norfolk coast, and to two thousand eels a year from the parish of Elingey? And we come away from Wymondham looking back at its towers just as the rooks are wheeling in the winter mists.

SUFFOLK

At Woolpit, near Bury St Edmunds, begins the legend of the Green Children, who came up, a boy and a girl, out of the ancient trenches or 'Wlfpittes' at harvest time. The bodies of the Green Children of Woolpit were of a green colour. At first they could speak no English; but when they were able to do so, said that they belonged to the land of St Martin, an unknown country, where as they were watching their father's sheep they heard a loud noise, like the ringing of the bells of St Edmund's monastery. And then all at once they found themselves among the reapers in the harvest field at Woolpit. They stand hand-in-hand, the boy half a head taller than the girl, and wear short tunics of some unknown stuff, with belts or girdles round their waists, and well-worn sandals. The have come up into our world no differently from the French boy who went rabbiting with his dog during the War, saw his dog had disappeared into a hole in the ground, and found himself in the cavern at Lascaux with mammoths and wild horses painted on the walls.

'They were caught and taken to the village', so it is evident they tried to run away, running awkwardly, as would children who are not good at games, and the village children ran behind and in front, teasing and imitating them. So do rooks and starlings circle round any strange bird that comes among them, and drive it off.

But the children were caught and taken to a cottage, where 'for many months they would eat nothing but beans'. They gradually lost their green colour. The boy soon died. The girl survived and was married to a man of Lynn who courted her at the Michaelmas Fair, when she went to market carrying a green goose under her cloak. They had no children, and you may look in every churchyard in Lynn, and not find her tomb, or hear mention of her.[1]

BURY ST EDMUNDS

St Edmund's monastery at Bury was the chief religious centre of eastern England. Here was the shrine of St Edmund who was martyred by the Danes, and here were buried a sister of the Conqueror and a Queen of France, Mary Tudor, sister of Henry VIII. There were fifty to sixty monks here at the Suppression, and the still surviving splendour of the city's cathedral (formerly the church of St James) can only testify to what may have been even finer buildings at the East Anglian abbeys. The monastery had no fewer than four gatehouses; and a gate to its vineyard described as 'ad soladium infirmorum et amicorum',[2] words which infer a convivial property to the wine made from its grapes and must point, as is probable, either to special and tried varieties of vine, or to another climate from that which would only produce a thin and sour vinegar in our own day.

St Mary's, at Bury, can be the introduction to the angel ceilings of Suffolk. This is a wonderful specimen with winged

---

[1] The source of the legend of the Green Boy and Girl is William of Newburgh (Hist. Anglic., Lib. i. c. 27). The children declared that their country was a Christian land and had churches. There was no sun there only a faint twilight; but beyond a broad river there lay a land of light. The bell ringing, the river, and the green colour of the children all belong to the true old fairy mythology; cf. *Murray's Handbook to East Anglia*, 1875, pp. 175, 176.

[2] 'For the comfort of the sick and of friends'. The monks at Ely also had vineyards and made wine, which seems stranger and still more improbable than at Bury.

angel figures standing against alternate hammer-beams; winged angels but, again, it could be said, flightless, and described in Murray, unaccountably, and surely without reason, as 'constructed in France'. Woolpit – whence arose the Green Children – has a wonderful double hammer-beam roof which is no less of a marvel than that of Bury St Edmunds and must be among the masterworks of all carpentry. Then again, there is Needham Market, not half-way between Ipswich and Bury St Edmunds, where the open roof earns the highest encomiums of all; 'the climax of English roof construction': 'the culminating achievement of the English carpenter' and so on; but its details, and not only its details, owed a lot to the Victorian restorers. The effect is like the projection of an inverted ship's hull into the body or vessel of the church, and the woodwork hangs up there with as much or little of magic as the glass ship in a bottle. How does it keep there? How was it put up there? And yet it is heavy, and looks as though it might slip down the walls. Its mathematical certainty of construction delights the pundits, but it does not please as do Woolpit, Mildenhall, or others not even mentioned here.

WOOLPIT

NEEDHAM MARKET

MILDENHALL

Mildenhall, much further inland, and on the way to Ely, has a double hammer-beam which is an extraordinary feat of its sort. The master-carpenter must surely have had the skill to make careful preliminary drawings, and the planning of such a roof to cover nave and aisles was no less a feat of mathematical planning. There could be a dozen or more of the angel ceilings in Suffolk, both in market towns but often, too, in out of the way villages. Two only may be cited, which are illustrated among the coloured drawings in the Brandons' book mentioned earlier, at Palgrave and Bacton, in both of which the prevailing tint is shown as a vinous-red.

PALGRAVE
BACTON

The two great, nearby, flint and freestone Perpendicular churches of Long Melford and Lavenham, well known to hundreds or even thousands of persons here, are, it could be said, unknown outside this country, a fact which is not without its own degree of satisfaction in it. Perhaps it is the length of Long Melford church which impresses at a distance (one hundred and fifty feet)! And then, on nearer approach, the flushwork ornament along the plinth, above the tall three-light windows, and so many of them in a line – and higher up again, above the clerestory windows and along the battlements where the flushwork spells out the names of donors and benefactors in late Gothic lettering. The church at Long Melford is of course

LONG MELFORD

more beautiful than St Michael Coslany in Norwich, and it is difficult to take one's eyes off the intricacy of its flintwork where, incidentally, the expense was considered, and there is more flushwork ornament on the south side than on the other. LAVENHAM The church at Lavenham is no less extraordinary, and would call forth volumes of praise were it anywhere but in Suffolk. It is not so long as Melford, despite its flight of a dozen windows in the clerestory, but it has a flintwork tower of utmost magnificence, a veritable campanile of the sheepfolds, both churches being due to rich wool-merchants and the cloth trade. The CAVENDISH church at Cavendish, close by Long Melford, has a clerestory panelled in flushwork that must be of like provenance.

BOXTED In the church in a neighbouring village, Boxted, we can see the standing statue of a warrior in armour with a golden frog hanging from his right ear. It is Sir John Poley, a soldier under Elizabeth and James I, who also fought under Henri IV of France. He was made a Knight of the Danish Order of the Elephant, the oldest order of chivalry in Europe after the Garter, and his frog-earring is one of the emblems of that order, its import being, perhaps, that the elephant and the frog, respectively, were the biggest and the smallest quadrupeds ACTON known in nature. Also nearby, at Acton, is another knight, Sir Robert de Bures, who has the reputation of being the most perfect of the military brasses, and his figure is wearing the 'cuisseaux gamboisez', or padded and quilted trews, while at Long Melford itself there is a brass of a lady of the Clopton family who wears a butterfly headdress.[1] At Ketton, or Ked-KEDINGTON ington, in this same corner of Suffolk, we can look in at the tombs of the Barnardistons, at one time the most important family in the county, who are to be traced back to a time when surnames were not yet hereditary, and 'who flourished for twenty-seven generations in a direct line'. The church contains life-size statues of four knights and six ladies; one lady of the family, Grizel Barnardiston (1609) kneeling in a curious penthouse headdress and pleated farthingale that give a memorable and characteristic silhouette;[2] another wearing one of the completest of sculptured farthingales; Sir Nathaniel, at whose

[1] Another butterfly headdress, and no less beautiful necklace, appear upon the brass to Elizabeth Cheyne, at Blickling, Norfolk.

[2] The kneeling effigy of this young girl, more closely described, is notable for her hair mounted over a frame, with the back curls looped and knotted with ribbon, for her skirt which is ruched and gathered over her farthingale, and for the epaulettes of her sleeves that are prolonged in spikes falling almost to the ground, recalling the fluttering ribbons of certain birds of paradise.

death a precious book, *The Teares of Suffolk; Elegies on that renowned Knight,* was printed, looking out from a monument upon the wall, his wife beside him, and both leaning their heads upon one hand; a knight in a 'peascod-bellied' breastpiece; and Sir Thomas Barnardiston recumbent, while his two wives face one another. In all these monuments, and throughout the church, on pew and hatchment, is their beautiful crest of a heron or bittern standing in a bed of reeds.

BLYTHBURGH

EYE

MENDLESHAM

Throughout the county of Suffolk there must be examples beyond number of satisfying and appropriate flushwork mixed with brick or freestone; as at Blythburgh, on the sea-coast with a clerestory of eighteen windows divided by flint panels, and flushwork initialling along the parapet; and with the hundred-foot tower of Eye, all of flushwork, at the other side of Suffolk, near the Norfolk border. There are, too, the parapets on the towers of Woodbridge and Walberswick, and in particular the former of these two; the clerestory of Coddenham, with arched panels and initials, all in flushwork; and the porches of Halesworth, Blyford and Mendlesham.[1] Of these last, Mendlesham is the most elaborate, and it is in an upper chamber there that the most complete armoury of any church in England is preserved, of all dates from 1470 to 1610.

UFFORD

WOODBRIDGE

WORLINGWORTH

SUDBURY

There remain other and outstanding minor works of art, of which the chief may be the font cover at Ufford. This is eighteen feet high, all crockets and pinnacles, once coloured and gilded, and articulated so that its three tiers or storeys can slide into and over one another like the parts of a telescope. It is so fine a work of art that even the Cromwellian iconoclast and image-breaker Dowsing – neither the first, nor the last of his sort – writing of it in his diary, 'there is a glorious cover over the font, like a Pope's triple crown, a pelican on the top picking its breast, all gilt over with gold' – even Dowsing spared it and passed by. Another wooden font cover, at Woodbridge, has freestanding pinnacles at its sides, taller, as it were, two-light windows pierced into it, and a less exciting spiral finish; but the stone bowl of the font, to make up for this, has a pair of ladies with butterfly headdresses carved upon it. At Worlingworth is one more of the spired canopies, which is twenty feet high, taller even than the font at Ufford; while at Sudbury is yet another of them, 'one of the finest mediaeval font covers in the

[1] Illustrated in *The Use of Flint in Building, especially in the County of Suffolk,* by Frank T. Baggallay, in Vol. 1 of *Transactions New Series* of the RIBA for 1885. A peculiar technique for rendering flushwork is used in these drawings.

country', [1] 'very lofty, towering far above the piers of the nave arcade, and, from the traces which remain, once splendid with gold and vermilion'.

BRAMFIELD   Near Blythburgh, in the north-east of the county, where we have already seen the flushwork and where there is a fine carved and painted roof with a row of angels along the ridge, is the village of Bramfield, whose church contains one of the most notable works of Nicholas Stone, the altar tomb of Arthur and Elizabeth Coke. The lady, who died in childbirth, is shown with her husband kneeling in a niche above her, and in her arms, her babe in swaddling clothes. The head of this figure, the headdress, sleeves, and collar, are incomparably beautiful. She lies with her head upon two pillows of an exquisite rendering, while the laced coverlet that lies over her, once again, is incomparable in workmanship. The manipulation of the material is really extraordinary. Nowhere else are we so conscious of the pathos of death at the hands of an infant in arms. This is one of the great works of art of England. Indeed, for sheer technical mastery the Mrs Coke, at Bramfield, invites comparison with Bernini's famous *Ecstasy of St Theresa*. In itself it may even be considered as great a work of sculpture, but then we have to acknowledge the awkwardness and rigidity of its setting and its failure to flow into and form part of the architecture. But it even anticipates, in time, the St Theresa, for that was not completed until after Nicholas Stone was dead.

HEVENINGHAM   Two or three miles further, we come to Heveningham Hall,
HALL   which dates from the end of the following century, being undertaken after 1780, and is the most important example of James Wyatt's Classic style. It took the form of the decoration of an earlier house by Sir Robert Taylor, though the north front with its great columns raised upon rusticated arches in the style, it seems to us, of Chambers, was but just completed when Sir Gerard Vanneck, son of a Dutch merchant settled in London, called in Wyatt and 'Capability' Brown. The serpentine paths and winding waters and the great group of cedar trees are due to the landscape gardener, while the beautiful Orangery with its semicircular pillared portico, its niches for sculpture, and high windows is the work of Wyatt. Vanneck, later to become Lord Huntingfield, allowed Wyatt his opportunity in the interior, which is of unusual interest because it retains some of the furniture designed by him.

[1] Dr Nikolaus Pevsner, in *Suffolk*, Harmondsworth, 1951.

We enter by a magnificent hall, with no fewer than eight doors of mahogany, and scagliola pillars in imitation of yellow Siena marble. The walls are pale green, and the floor is of stone with inlays of red marble and black marble lines. Behind this hall lies the staircase, simpler and less grand than those of Heaton Hall near Manchester or Dodington in Gloucestershire, with a baluster painted blue and white and with lead enrichments like the Flaxman-Wedgwood cameos. Close to the foot of this staircase is an Etruscan room, the work, as at Heaton, of Biagio Rebecca, with pale green walls and white doors and stucco. Upon this background Rebecca painted his figure subjects in the approved Etruscan red of the vases, the women paler in hue than the Etruscan men. This is closer to the original than any others of the Etruscan rooms of Wyatt or Adam; but Wyatt had a more personal share in it than at Heaton, for he designed the furniture and the painted wooden candelabra. Out of this leads the painted saloon, entirely by Rebecca, a room with paired apses at the ends, and perhaps too much of Rebecca's delicate brushwork in green upon a biscuit ground. The decorations by Wyatt are completed by a dining-room and library, both in the same wing as the saloon and the Etruscan room. In the dining-room, Rebecca has submitted to control and Wyatt has taken most of the trouble to himself. The result is one of the enchantments of the late eighteenth century.

The double mahogany door into the dining-room may be the most sumptuous of all these English ornaments from the West Indies, inlaid and veneered, with strips at the edges that shine like ribbons of watered silk, and panels that are as rich as damask. But the doorway, in itself, is superb in composition, with its painted lunette by Rebecca, and its fan-shaped surround of stucco. The whole wall, indeed, is an architectural composition, with painted roundels in square frames on each side of the door, above oblong niches in which stand Wyatt's candelabra, delicate tripods with term legs, above which rise, like little rostral columns, serpent-coiled columns ending in a pineapple. The wall opposite, similar in composition, but with two lesser serving doors, and the space in the middle for a sideboard, has a mural candelabrum in the form of a stucco ornament, a bowl with ram's head corners, from which project ormolu candle branches. The fireplace wall has two hemicycle niches, while the mantelpiece has a painted panel and, over it, a great oval painting by Rebecca. The dado and deal sideboards of this dining-room have been specially designed by Wyatt, the tapering legs of the latter to match those of the mahogany chairs. A beautiful but simple frieze and delicate stucco ceiling complete the scheme of decoration. The library is a beautiful room, with pillars at each end of porphyry scagliola, a colour which is repeated in the mantelpiece, and as background for Rebecca's painted heads, in roundels, of the famous poets. The same colour occurs again on the prevailing white of the library, along the dado, and on the cornice and the ceiling. This latter has painted medallions or cameos by Rebecca in a graceful stucco setting, while the scheme of decoration includes a pair of tables for the display of drawings and engravings carried out in mahogany, with swags and garlands in satinwood.

There are other tombs still to visit in the north of the county. REDGRAVE At Redgrave, on the Norfolk border, is a most imposing monument to Lord Justice Holt, seated or enthroned, with amorini and much heraldry, among the details of which may be seen the heron or bittern of the Barnardistons, this huge architectural composition being signed by Thomas Green of Camberwell. And we are reminded of the bucolic or Arcadian BUNGAY butter-cross of Bungay nearby, an octagon of Tuscan pillars, domed, and with statue of Justice with her scales as a threat to WINGFIELD rustic crime![1] At Wingfield, John de la Pole, second Duke of Suffolk, and his wife, Elizabeth Plantagenet, lie buried, he, wearing the mantle of the Garter on his effigy, and she, the barbe or widow's plaited covering for the neck; while at FRAMLINGHAM Framlingham, a few miles inland from the flat Suffolk coast, there is the tomb in freestone of Henry Fitzroy, Duke of Richmond and Somerset, natural son of Henry VIII by Elizabeth Tallboys. It is a tall chest or sarcophagus with a curious frieze of sculptures, and concise and splendid shields-of-arms. But his is not the only body of a young man of great promise to lie buried here. The poet Earl of Surrey, familiar from his portrait at Hampton Court in trunk hose and cap and jacket of bright red velvet, lies, beheaded, in his tomb, having fallen victim to Henry VIII only a week before that despot's death. His three children, in red robes, and ruffs, and ermine collars, kneel on a step behind the statues of their father and their mother. His father, third Duke of Norfolk, who only narrowly escaped with his life, is portrayed with peculiar long beard and coroneted

[1] How many miles hence to its Arcadian sister, the butter-cross of Swaffham in Norfolk, another rotunda of Tuscan columns with lead dome above and figure of Ceres on top?

head upon another tomb, his wife by his side and a stag with great antlers lying at the foot. Nor is this all. Yet another tomb, with coats-of-arms and antlered stags, commemorates the two wives of the Duke of Norfolk who succeeded him. These tombs at Framlingham are instinct of Henry VIII as much as the halls and passages of Hampton Court. What stories Surrey or his spade-bearded father would have to tell us of the gigantic King, of his bluff voice, his failing strength, who had once been the strongest and handsomest man in England, and of his six, and more, encounters with the monstrous regiment of women.

HENGRAVE   At Hengrave, back now near Bury St Edmunds, Thomas Darcy, in a wall-monument under an elaborate architectural canopy, kneels in the baggy trunk-hose of his day, his obsolete tilting-helm at his knee, and hung from his shoulder, a tabard or shield with his armorial bearings. Near the church is the red brick Tudor Hengrave Hall, with architecture that marks the transition from Gothic to Renaissance. The entrance gateway has a triple bay window, the corbelling below terminating in a shield-of-arms that is supported by a pair of amorini dressed in Roman armour. They are in fact perfectly Italian, while the window above them is Perpendicular Gothic, and the turrets to either side carry those domed caps which are so curious a feature of the Henry VII Chapel at Westminster, and that look as though the pennons of the tournament should flutter from them.

IPSWICH   Bishop Sparrowe's House at Ipswich was built in the late fifteenth century, though the armorial bearings of Charles II on the front betray the date of the decoration. It is a captivating house and we must describe it, noting on the way, that the vault of the Sparrowe family in St Lawrence's church in the town bears the inscription 'Nidus Passerum' or sparrows' nest.[1] This type of house is peculiar to Suffolk and to Essex. It is quite different from anything that we have seen, being built of grey wood and yellow plaster. The ground floor has wooden balusters, richly carved, with brackets above them that support the projecting upper floor. This has four oriel windows, and another on the side, with as many gables corresponding; but the entire two fronts of this first floor have been treated to a fantastic decoration. There are pilasters between the windows

---

[1] In another of the twelve ancient parish churches in Ipswich, St Mary Tower, is a brass to a notary-public, that is to say a scribe or conveyancer, where are to be seen his ink-horn and his pen-case, and upon his left shoulder, his curious cap or turban, worn with a hood and a long scarf that tucked into the girdle, or trailed upon the ground.

and heavy swags between them; the lower part or embrasure of the oriels and the space between the pilasters being full of figures and devices. Those in front of the oriels represent the four quarters of the world; while the oriels themselves are most delicate in conception, being set with small panes of glass with a central arched panel framed in carving, the whole effect being that of a carved and embossed casket, contrived of the materials of a nest or bower, but owing much also to the proximity of the sea. It is not uninfluenced by the shipbuilders, and its images are mariners' or merchants' images. There is nothing comparable across the North Sea, in the Netherlands. It is indigenous, but breathes the adventures and romance of ocean.

The country in Suffolk is wooded, with gentle hills and corn-fields, the very landscape of Gainsborough's early painting of Squire Andrews and his wife, by consent of many lovers of pictures, the most beautiful painting ever done by an Englishman. Gainsborough himself was born within a mile or two of this landscape which we see. The scene is Auberies, near Sudbury, which was his birthplace, and the date must be 1750, as near as may be.

It is August, or September: the corn is cut and Mr and Mrs Andrews are at the edge of it, in a green field. He has come out with his gun to look for a hare, or perhaps the partridges are already in the stubble. They are at the foot of a great, old tree. His gun, with an immensely long barrel, is under his arm and he wears white stockings, dark breeches and a coat of primrose buff. He has a three-cornered hat with laced edges. His other arm is on the elbow of the bench, while a retriever looks up at him, waiting for the sport to begin. What is wonderful in his figure is the loose, flapping lapels of his coat, the wrinkles of his sleeves and waistcoat, his gloves creasing at his wrist, and the twisted bags of powder and shot that dangle from his pocket.

His wife sits stiffly beside him on a hard iron bench, or garden seat, which gives the period by its curves. Her expression is demure and vaguely disapproving and she is very young, probably not yet twenty. Her hands lie straight in front of her, upon her lap. She has the long, thin bodice and the wide panniered or hooped skirt that was the fashion. Out of this, her two feet rest one upon another on the grass. The billowing extent of this skirt or pannier is so charged with the light blue, that is its colour, that the sensation of it is indescribable in words. It would be wrong to say that this blue is charged with electricity; but it has the colour of blue spray on one day in ten years in the Baltic or Northern Seas. It is no blue of the Mediterranean. Perhaps it is the blue of a freshwater lake, where the ripples have slight blue crests and the light runs through the bulrushes out to the swan white calm. There they ride, and arch their necks and look into the depths; and blue light breaks back from them into the reeds. This is that blue, in synthesis, billowing upon the panniers and down their crumpled sides.

The landscape is harvest and high summer. Yellow green grass spurts or fleeces from their feet into the harvest edge. The corn is cut and tied into stooks, leaving the bare stubble and its wounded stalks cut to the quick. All the cornsheaves are bound as prisoners: not a cornstalk stands. There are oak trees at the far edge of this, and then the harvest becomes pasture, through a white barred gate. There is a field of sheep, their fleeces flashing white in the distance, more fields and wooded slopes, not tall enough for hills. On the left, there are high elms for owl and ringdove, and through the boughs a church tower, near enough to hear the bells. The sky has great chariots and bastions of cloud, so there is wind and a far-off lowing of the herds.

The landscape of England has never been painted as in this picture. And so close is its identity that it would be pleasant to walk in the fields, in September, and recognise the scene. This painting has a fourfold or quadruple point. It is the primrose buff shooting coat, the blue pannier, the yellow green grass and the golden straw of the cornstooks. On two occasions the writer of these pages has had the good fortune to come upon this painting suffused, of a sudden, with the afternoon sun shining in from the west, and from low down in the heavens, for it was April. This made of it such an intermingling of buff and straw, or yellow, and light green and blue that the impression of it is unforgettable. It becomes light blue and greenish golden yellow in the memory. The colour of her dress remains, and the grass and cornfield; and then his coat comes back with its miraculous untidiness and its appurtenances for shooting, the press of the iron bench upon the knoll of grass, the tied and bearded cornstooks, the white gate, the far-off pastures and the elms.

No King in Christendom hath such a subject as Oxford. He came in with the Conqueror, Earl of Guynes; shortly after the Conquest made great chamberlain, above five hundred years ago by Henry I, the Conqueror's son, brother to Rufus . . . no other Kingdom can produce such a peer in one and the self-same name and person. . . . I have laboured to make a covenant with myself that affection may not press upon judgement; for I suppose there is no man that hath any apprehension of gentry or nobleness but his affection stands to the continuance of so noble a name and home and would take hold of a twig or twine-thread to uphold it. And yet Time hath his revolutions; there must be a period and an end to all temporal things, *finis rerum*, an end of names and dignities and whatsoever is terrene; and why not of de Vere? – for where is Bohun? Where is Mowbray? Where is Mortimer? Nay, what is more, and most of all, where is Plantagenet? They are entombed in the urns and sepulchres of mortality.

Such were the noble words of Chief Justice Crewe giving judgement in 1625, after the death of the eighteenth Earl of Oxford, in favour of the male line of the de Veres, a family whose name, in itself a synonym for the nobility of high descent, together with their crest of the blue boar or verres and their badge of the mullet or white star of five points, and their armorial quarterings and ensigns, is to be found emblazoned, far and wide, throughout the old halls and churches of East Anglia.

This aspect, as of the bones of the proud and gentle long crumbled into dust, composes, we might say, one half of the poetry of the sepulchre or tomb. The other half of it is concerned, necessarily, with the mortality of more humble beings. With this in mind, let us contemplate the tomb of de Vere, ninth Earl of Oxford, Marquis of Dublin, and Duke of EARL'S COLNE Ireland, at Earl's Colne in Essex, with his second wife Lancerana Serjeaulx, the joiner's daughter, wearing the piked-horn or high headdress introduced by Anne of Bohemia, Queen of Richard II, to whom she had been maid-of-honour, a headdress which Horace Walpole says is 'exactly like the description of Mount Parnassus, with two tops'. This pair of mutilated effigies, from the different spheres of birth of their originals, amount to both sorts of poetry entombed together in the one grave.[1]

LITTLE EASTON

Not far away, at Little Easton is Charles Stanley's monument to Lord Maynard. Stanley was among the most exquisite craftsmen in the great age of taste, whose beautiful Rococo stucco ceilings at Easton Neston, in Northamptonshire, and Langley Park, in Norfolk, we have already admired. His Maynard monument is entirely of that style, exhibiting the theatrical device of a dark pyramid against which the white marble effigy stands out in full relief. Lord Maynard, in semi-Roman dress, leans upon a marble urn and round him are busts and medallions of his family. Completely Rococo is the device of the higher medallion pinned like a medal to the tapering face of the pyramid. It is interesting to think that this rare master was invited to Denmark where he spent fifteen years (1746-61) as sculptor to Frederick V. Ceilings, mantelpieces, monuments, perhaps garden statues, in the old castles and court chapels of Denmark must exist by him.

SAFFRON WALDEN

And remembering the house of Bishop Sparrowe in Ipswich, in Suffolk, let us visit the little pargetted Sun Inn at Saffron Walden, which is not less imaginative.[2] But Saffron Walden lies inland. It is further from the sea. The house in question has two overhanging gables and was the work, probably, of a village plasterer. One whole panel has the figures of two giants who are holding up the sun. The other is an all-over decoration of birds and flowers. It is decoration and not, like the other house, neat construction. There must at one time have been a quantity of the pargetted houses in Suffolk and Essex, and no work on architecture must fail to take account of them, for they form so musical a dialect of our vernacular. The Sun Inn at Saffron Walden is as simple as the design on a smock or on a warming pan. The smocks, we do not digress, were worn in different colours, white or bleached in some counties, deep blue, black worked with white, or olive green in Cambridge, Essex, and some parts of Suffolk. In imagination we would have an entire street of such houses. They are pleasures that are akin to needlework, to the birds and flowers and figures on a counterpane, and we would look at them on a sunny morning when the country folk are come in to market in their colours.

[1] The monument has now been moved to St Stephen's Chapel at Bures, in Suffolk.

[2] The house, on the corner of Church Street, still stands, though it is no longer called the Sun Inn.

COLCHESTER   At Colchester, all that is left of the abbey is the Perpendicular flushwork gateway, with its flint-panelled and pinnacled turrets, a beautiful exercise in the local style; but nearby
LAYER MARNEY   is Layer Marney Tower, a wholly typical example of red brick
Tudor architecture, because it is plain but lavish, yet not
enriched with too much heraldry and gilding. This is a tall
building. The double towers to either side of the doorway are
eight storeys high, and they are in a hybrid style, for the
panelling, so to speak, of the mullioned windows is Perpendicular Gothic, while the design of the parapets, with their
dolphins leaping over semi-circular panels, is taken direct from
the French Renaissance of François I. The material, here, is
the typical thin, red brick much in use in East Anglia because of
the scarcity of stone, but also under the influence of the brick
houses of Bruges and Ghent, not far away, and even profiting, it
may be, from the red bricks of the local Roman villas.

WANSTEAD   As we near London, the destruction increases. Wanstead,
built for Sir Richard Child, is another of the great houses that
have gone. It had nineteen rooms upon the ground floor, with a
vista through them; a ballroom with olive and gold wainscot;
painted and stucco ceilings; and 'a parlour finely adorn'd with
China paper, the figures of men and women, birds and flowers,
the liveliest I ever saw come from that country'. But Wanstead
was pulled down in 1822. It was the most complete work of
Colen Campbell. Only in the parish church can we see one of
the previous generation of Childs in the monument by John
Nost, an architectural frontispiece reaching from floor to
ceiling signed and dated 1699. Sir Josiah Child, periwigged, in
Roman costume, stands on a plinth between pillars, below a
canopy. Above him on the cornice, figures of fame blow their
trumpets, and a semi-recumbent effigy in marble lies at his feet.

OLD LONDON

London has the most true-sounding name for a city that has ever been invented. It contains in it the rumbling of a million wheels, of a million wheels rolling into the town across the bridges. It is the very sound of traffic; and the hubbub and the roar seem, in the sound of it, to be moving in a fog. It is like a pall to cover and deaden the confusion, and we know by instinct that the great and vast body of it can never be seen in its entirety, but only, as it were, wheel by wheel, street by street. That is the old London, the London described in identical terms of horror by such different minds as Dostoevsky and Verlaine. It is the gas-lit London. This is London, burning in its lights; but lit, now, by the light of summer. A morning when metal is too hot to touch, when the pavement is too hot to tread. All the contemporary world lies open to us; the streets are thronged, and there is not even enough wind in the still air to shake the flags upon the skyline. For it is June, in the streets of shops.

As far as the eyes can see there are shop fronts, bow windows, every enticement that painted lettering and a pane of glass can offer.[1] There is more to buy than in the bazaars of Damascus or Grand Cairo; under the arcades of the Palais Royal; or in the toyshops of old Nuremberg. So let us start from Charing Cross and walk along the Strand. In the distance hangs the white dome of St Paul's. Straight in front is Gibbs's steeple of St Mary-le-Strand, a little masterpiece of elegance and good manners, paying tribute in its pagoda or pepper castor form to this mart for foreign lands, and recalling in every detail works of the silversmiths in the reigns of Charles II or Queen Anne. Behind it must be the other church of St Clement Danes; and were we to climb upon a roof, or mount that very tower, we would see seventy or a hundred white steeples, all of Portland stone, curving away in the distance, past St Paul's to Greenwich, as in Canaletto's painting, where as a foreigner again he

---

[1] This view along the Strand is taken from the drawing by George Scharf, who was born near Munich in 1788, and died in London in 1860. He studied in Antwerp and Paris, and accompanied the Allied armies in their final campaigns against Napoleon, being occupied chiefly in painting portraits in miniature of the British officers. He arrived in London in 1816. His private hobby seems to have consisted in making watercolour drawings of old London, with particular regard for beadles, night watchmen, and other vanishsing figures of the past, and a special enthusiasm for old shop fronts and for the little details of costume and street architecture which would appeal to someone of foreign origin as being characteristic of his adopted capital. An enormous mass of these small drawings, amounting to several hundreds in number, were deposited by his heirs, a year or two after he had died, at the British Museum, and are to be studied in the Print Room.

seized upon this feature of old London. They are London's minarets, in form and variety not less capricious than that name
suggests. Works of an earlier age; for the Strand, as we see it
this fine morning of a hundred and sixty years ago, is nearly
contemporary with him. With few exceptions, the shops and
houses date from not later than the beginning of the century.
They must be modern enough to suit the requirements of busi-
ness and trade. Many of them are gilded and painted to look
new. But, for ourselves, they have the newness of any mediaeval town, of any place intangible because of physical im-
possibility, be it Antioch or Ephesus, Byzantium or ancient
Rome, made a living reality, and known and touched by us.

We pass by the shop of an ivory and hard wood turner and
carver. He advertises chessmen, and billiard, pool, and baga-
telle balls supplied; his sign, which we should find again upon
his billhead, the figure of an elephant standing in a forest
clearing, with a pair of ivory tusks, lying like crossed swords, at
his feet. Next door, a grocer or fancy warehouseman has in his
window: English, French and Spanish chocolates; Westmore-
land and Westphalian hams; Parmesan, Gruyère and Chapzugar cheeses; Dutch beef for grating; Russian and Reindeer
tongues; Vermicelli and Cagliari pastes for soups. A curious
mingling of past and present; for, among so much else that is
familiar, what are Spanish chocolates, Chapzugar cheeses,
Dutch beef for grating? After this comes an ordinary or eating
house. The slate reads: 'giblet soup, roast ribs of beef, Cheddar
or red Leicester cheese, cheap oysters, Colchester or Whit-
stable, Cornish or Dutch Zeeland, jellied or smoked eels'.
Inside, there are high wooden pews, and top hats everywhere,
as in an Eton class room. For we begin, now, to take notice of
the crowd. Figures in black and drab and bottle green, with
nankeen breeches, dressed with that contradiction which turns
the townsmen of one decade into countrymen of the next.
Outside a chemist's window it would be impossible not to
linger. We read announcements of Sim's only genuine white
and musk brown Windsor soap; mottled and Naples soaps;
Rowland's Macassar oil, in an older packing; notices, respect-
fully worded, addressed to the nobility, gentry, and the clergy,
calling attention to the advantages of certain preparations,
composed, as it were, in a particular language, the jargon of
elocutionist or dancing master. Authentic Eau de Cologne,
guaranteed against imposture and pleading, vociferously, its
address: 'Gegenüber dem Julichs Platz', with fulmination and

threat of action against all other persons who called themselves Farina, took up the centre of one window. It is, plainly, the wrappings and labels that are the fascination.

In another window, Hannay and Dietrichsen's Fragrant essence of Rondeletia, for the toilet or handkerchief, prepared expressly for the use of the Royal Family.[1] We read:

> The lovers of elegant perfumes are solicited to call and try this article on their Handkerchief, for which purpose a Bottle is always open free, to which Handkerchief, so perfumed, the combined fragrance of the choicest conservatory must yield precedence.... Perfumers, whose appearance of respectability would induce a belief that they would not sell a counterfeit article, are even guilty of this.

And we come to Hannay & Co.'s Oriental Oil.

> A pure limpid white vegetable substance. . . . The great care is proverbial, that is paid to the cultivation of the luxuriant tresses of the fair Captives of the Harem, and Art is there well known to succeed in outrivalling even the far-famed beauties of Circassia. The Oriental Oil, as prepared by Messrs. Hannay & Co. has been employed for the purpose during the period of three centuries.

Close to it, is Gowland's Lotion: 'Distinguished as a safe and congenial appendage of the toilet during a period of nearly eighty years. A copy of that popular work, "The Theory of Beauty", is enclosed with every bottle.' And there is, also, Shaw's Mindora Oil, known, too, from 1750. By its side, goods and an advertisement of Brewster's:

> Haircutter and Manufacturer of Ornamental Hair to the Royal Family. Makes Ladies' Headdresses, Gentlemen's Perruques, Scalps, etc., of the finest natural curl. Hair distinguished from all others for their lightness, durability, and exactness in fitting. W. B. most scrupulously excludes all common hair from his house, and being the greatest buyer of that of the first quality, he can always ensure such a supply as cannot be had in any other house. Brewster's Almond and Honey Soap, combining the emollient and balsamic proper-

---

[1] According to *The Art of Perfumery*, by G. W. Septimus Piesse, London, 1855, essence of Rondeletia was composed of cloves, lavender, musk, and vanilla. He suggests that its inventor took the name of this perfume from the Rondeletia, the Chyn-len of the Chinese, or from the R. Odorata of the West Indies, which has a sweet odour.

ties of the honey with the finest Almond Oil soap. Sold in squares, at a shilling each. The only house in London where Chardan Houbigant's Pâte d'Amande au Miel can be had as imported.

And, in a corner, next to Rowland's Kalydor, Rowland's Essence of Tyre, for changing red and grey whiskers to black or brown. We pass on, and come to the Maison de Deuil: 'Mourning Furnisher by appointment to the King, H.R.H. the Duchess of Gloucester, H.R.H. the Duchess of Kent, H.R.H. the Duchess of Cambridge, and the Grand Duchess of Mecklenburgh Strelitz.' 'Mr. Pugh,' we read,

> Takes pleasure in introducing to his numerous patrons and the public his highly approved materials for Family Mourning, the Royal Bombazin Cloth, and Amphomoion or Widow's silk, to be had only at his house. Widow's Mourning in a hitherbefore unknown variety. Mourning costume, Pelisses, Paletots, Polish Mantles and Cloaks, in velvet, satin, glacé, gros royal, moiré, and other silks, in every variety.

And, close to this, the next window has a label, 'Mock Turtle always ready'.

This prospect of the Strand, seen not in detail but in all its length, is a wonderful and characteristic vision. We would like the enlargement of it upon the curtain or backcloth of a theatre. So many dramas could be played in front of it; Dan Leno or Little Tich equally with Shakespeare or Ben Jonson. For many reasons. Because anything, so exactly dated, is true to all time, and for the vast human history of this thoroughfare and parallel to old Thames. It is east to west of London, and includes it all. But, looked upon without regard to this, simply for its appearance to the eyes, with no thought for its purpose or its meaning, the shops and houses are in simile the bows or stern galleys of many ships tied side by side; an endless collection of bow windows looking upon the sea, ghosts, therefore, of seaside terraces and parades; temples of Aesculapius, with magic waters of the alchemist in great glass jars and cruchons in the windows; altars of the green turtle, where it was brought alive and slain; counters loaded with the golden saps of sugarcanes; the white sugarloaf, in sign and emblem, in reminder of gaiters and pipeclay and the moustachio'd grenadiers; Tegg's printshop and the colourists at work; a tea and coffee warehouse, terminus of the green tea hills; the seedsman with a window of bright seed packets; the painted carnation and the picotee; a baker's shop with, at back, the dusty clowns or scullions of the oven; mercers and haberdashers who had slaves of the needle working for them in the slums; elegant establishments where there was not heard the weeping of the children; the clock-shop and its traps for time; the funeral furnisher; sugar cakes for weddings and baptisms; the tallow chandler; the shop of the East Indiaman, with clothes to take out to India and Madeira and curries for the traveller returned; on and on, until we get to Ludgate Hill and, climbing that, see the spire of St Martin's, Ludgate, giving measure and proportion to the dome of St Paul's. We are in Fleet Street, in Grub Street; and it is before the stamping of the presses. No one's ruin is called out on the hoardings. And we come back along the Strand of shops and warehouses.

The curious part of this perambulation, if we would have the experience with our own eyes and senses and not surrender into another time, has the effect, precisely, of poverty among so many riches. We may go where we will, and look into the windows, but we have no money in our pockets. We are as the children who gnaw a crust of bread and pass along the gutter. Our translation from this time into that other could be effected no more simply than by making a purchase and having it handed, wrapped, or in a parcel, across the counter. There would be a touch of hands, a communion or sacrament, and such contact, perfunctory and superficial, would be all we needed. We long, even, for a thing so trivial as the folding of the paper and the knotting of the string. To watch the packet being sealed, and the sealing-wax held into the flame. To ask the shopkeeper for a simple direction and be told how many doors away, up or down the Strand. And, stepping down into the street, to have living persons brush against us, hear their voices, and stand still for a moment, at a corner, to listen to the hurdygurdy.

No! we cannot buy: we are penniless and wandering. We can look into the shop-windows: but we dare not enter. Another street musician is standing in the gutter. A little Savoyard, with an old barrel organ strapped round him, of which he grinds and grinds the handle: a dwarf, or an ugly child, with nothing of the child about him: with a mouth that only gnaws or snarls: never his mother's darling, but kicked into the world to bring back halfpennies with a hired organ. He wears a little peaked hat, the hat of a Calabrian brigand, of Masaniello, and boots and trousers that are too big for him. This child has known the secrets of his parents since the day that he was born. There has been no privacy for him. He has the cleverness of a little mongrel cur, to pick up crusts and dodge the traffic. We wonder to what dark den he creeps to sleep. As for the hurdygurdy, it is played by a pigtailed sailor with a wooden stump. His trousers, bell-bottomed, are of white canvas, and he has a wide brimmed hat; he is swarthy and bearded, and cannot read or write. His heavy build is that of a picador, who rides out to the bull upon a starving nag and is lifted, horse and all, and thrown back against the barrier. Here there is no bullring; but there is much of the bull about this burly hurdygurdy man. Such are the persons with whom our lot would be thrown were we to stay here until the gaslit dark. There are so many beggars and ragged children, with frayed ends to their trousers like a torn and ragged cuff. Who has ever seen a beggar in a top hat? We shall know, presently, that he may not be the strangest of his brethren. For, in an age when all men were top-hatted, there is nothing peculiar in this. It is not his top hat; what is frightful is the condition of it, as though it had been found floating, face downwards, in the river Styx after being worn at many funerals in fog and rain. The women beggars are, perhaps, more fearful still; but, if the finery of one generation becomes the garb of old landladies and charwomen in the next, in example of which were to be noticed, less than fifty years ago, the black mantles and bonnets of the 1860s worn in the back streets of great cities, it may be imagined how the beggar women wore the rags and tatters of the age of coal. We hear cracked voices singing, and watch the slow walk that we know so well, looking up from the gutter into the windows of the houses and listening for the falling of a copper coin.

The shopkeepers, meanwhile, would be in their back parlours drinking sherry. It is the arts of the shipbuilder and the fairground that have raised them to comfort. Or we see in those arts, still living, as to one of them, their descent or perversion into special purposes. And we pass, at that moment, by a toyshop. It is their world in little, not in literal copy, but for the flight and fantasy of their imaginations. The faces of the dolls have an especial horror and repulsion; and there are musical boxes with dancing or moving figures that are part of them. One, in particular, has a little dining-table set with little dishes, with little figures sitting in their chairs round the table, their heads being formed like mice – or could they be real mice? – who move their hands and roll their beady eyes to music. They make a clatter, too, and lift their knives and forks. They are dressed in shawls and bonnets; or wear tailcoats. One, indeed, is a soldier; and, another, a mouse notary. What can their bodies be underneath their clothes? An ordinary doll's body, wired and articulated in order to improve it from a mere image into an automaton that moves. For not only do they raise their knives and forks but they turn from side to side as though dancing in their chairs, becoming more staccato as the music finishes, and the mouse notary is left looking up, with his knife and fork held high into the air. Their heads are, certainly, the heads of mice, treated by the taxidermist and given back their beady eyes, then sewed on to the doll's body, a little mouse homunculus, a little mouseheaded man or woman, with mouse hair brushed and treated and mouse whiskers glued on, one by one. Somebody will buy this and, years later, it will be found in the lumber room, where the hands that played with it will scarce dare to touch it. The dolls' heads made of china are repellent, too; never the right size, but with the horror of nanisation, the midget freakishness, even in proportion to their build. They have the cretinous, the goitrous stare, dolts of the mountains, from Aosta or Courmayeur. There are, also, of course, painted hoops and painted carts: toy soldiers: glass ships in bottles: windmills: model shops, even a toyshop. It is the land of red cheeks: marionettes in wood: wax dolls and wooden dolls: bells and hearts and cradles.

LONDON

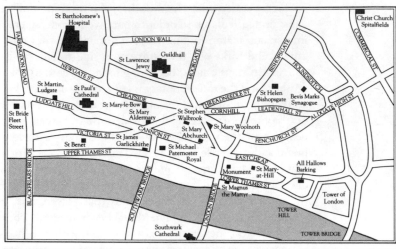

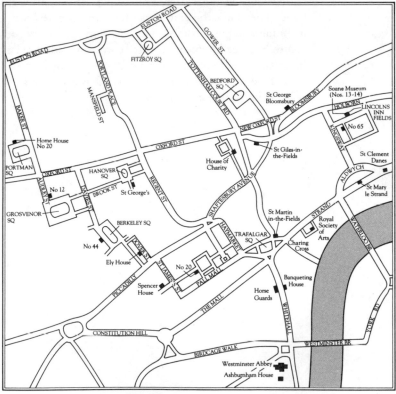

Westminster Abbey, whose church already by 1300 in the words of Dom David Knowles 'was probably the most lavishly appointed and gorgeously decorated in England', is more Plantagenet than Benedictine in provenance and origin, both as to its fabric and more still for the works of art it contained. For it was the place of coronation and royal attendance and the fane which certain of the kings and Henry III in particular took into their especial care and protection. Westminster Abbey, as we see it today, has little of the monks left in it and much of the lay person, royal or commoner. Tombs of kings and queens, great nobles, generals, admirals, men of politics, writers, even poets, have only given all the additional weight of tomb and tablet to this direction.

The bronze gilt figures of Henry III and of Eleanor of Castile (wife of Edward I) are both by William Torel, goldsmith of London. Though they may not be portraits, for the art was only advancing towards that stage, it is difficult indeed to imagine any more kingly conception than that of Henry III, or a figure at the same time more touchingly feminine or more aristocratic in type and mien than that of Eleanor of Castile, the foreign princess to whom the Eleanor Crosses, masterpieces of the lightest and most graceful period in Gothic art, were raised by the love of her husband, wherever her corpse had rested on its way to burial. These two figures are still to be seen in unparalleled splendour, with their gilding, done from the melting-down of Flemish golden florins of Bruges and Ghent, as bright and untrammelled as when new. Wholly admirable are such details as the King's shoes, with their heraldic diapering of golden leopards, set in lozenges; while the Queen's tomb has above it the wonderful iron grate by Thomas of Leighton with its patterns of vine and corn motifs, ending in trefoiled spikes, which may have been used as prickets for wax candles.

No less impressive, but different, is the effigy of William de Valence, half-brother to Henry III. His mailed figure is in oak covered with thin plates of copper, and there is much enamel in Limoges champlevé upon his cushion, his surcoat, and his shield that is charged with the arms of Valence with diapered field. A vision, not of a king or ruler, but of a knight or warrior of royal blood. But it is Edward III who takes our breath away. His tomb is by John Orchard, 'latoner'. Some authorities describe it as 'an idealised type of a venerable king', but though his crown is lost, as, also, the original pillow beneath his head, though he has lost the sceptres that he was holding in each hand, we are unwilling to believe that his high-nosed features, his long hair and flowing beard, his stiff coat or tunic, like a prophet's nightgown, can be anything else than the portraiture of a great king, dead or living. Below the tomb are little bronze figures, probably portraits, of the Black Prince and four other of the king's children. The effigy of the Black Prince in Canterbury Cathedral, a mailed figure as romantic as the name implies, may be by the same hand. As to the figures upon the tombs of Richard II and Anne of Bohemia, these are at last portraits, unmistakably and to be recognised as such, the work of Nicholas Broker and Godfrey Prest, coppersmiths, while the tombs, themselves, were the work of Stephen Lote and of Henry Yevele, the King's master-mason, the greatest, it may be, of English mediaeval architects. Nevertheless, they do not compare altogether favourably, as works of art, with those of their predecessors just mentioned. They are a little coarse and clumsy in their likenesses. More beautiful than the portrayed features of Richard II are the King's badges, the white hart, the sunburst, and the broom-pod of the Plantagenets, punched into the gilt metal of his robes, and the powdering of the mantles of both King and Queen with their initial letters of A and R.

The tomb of Edmund Crouchback, Earl of Lancaster, brother of Edward I, is of stone and was once entirely gilded and with 'the hollows and recesses coloured bright red and green in transparent lacquer colours'. Aveline, his wife, and Aymer de Valence, near by, were no less brilliant. At a later date the effigy of Henry V, hero of Agincourt, who died at only thirty-five years old, was of oak plated with silver gilt, and the head, which must have been a portrait, was of solid silver, but these massy riches fell victim to the Reformation. It lay in the King's chantry chapel, of which there were a great number in the Abbey, although it could be said that the number of royal tombs alone made the erection of individual chantry chapels somewhat of a difficulty. The chantry of Henry V is of curious construction for it is in the form of a bridge across the ambulatory, and in a cathedral in Spain might well have been intended not for a tomb-chamber but for a *camarín*, or a room in which to keep jewels and dresses for the images of the Virgin. The exterior of this bridge-chantry, which has octagonal stair-turrets at either end, has many statuettes in niches. It has indeed an extraordinary number of small carved figures standing under two-tier canopies, the mullions of which carry over them heraldic figures of chained swans which were the badge of the de Bohuns, his mother's family. Under this row of figures, and a frieze of more chained swans and other heraldic animals, are angels in pairs holding heraldic shields with the lions of England and lilies of France, while in the middle of them is a group portraying the act of coronation with two mitred bishops placing a crown on the King's head. This is on the south side of the chapel; and on its other wall amid similar figures is a central group representing the act of homage.

The chapel of Henry VII with its tomb by Torrigiani is the chantry chapel *in excelsis*, but this is also the supreme example of fan vaulting, being both the most extreme and by far the most beautiful of these conceptions. It is here in the middle of London, in the midst of the Thames fogs, within sound of the tugs, and in the face of the parrot-house of Parliament, that there is this unique and special fan vault the transcendental beauty of which puts it on a par, however much the purists may cast up their eyes at the comparison, with such architectural gems in their different kinds as the Sainte-Chapelle, the Cappella Palatina, the pilgrimage church of Die Wies, or the Shaikh Lotfollah mosque on the Maidan at Isfahan.

What, then, is the effect of coming into Henry VII's Chapel at Westminster and looking up at the ceiling for the first time? As an impression it is indubitably beyond precedent and very extraordinary. The ceiling has been described, not as a fan vault but a transcendental parody or set of transcendental variations on a fan vault. A musical analogy is not unreasonable. I think the sensation given is that if you listened you would hear these hanging pendants ringing. In the unlikely event of our being left alone for the night in the chapel one would expect to hear some sort of noise from them. 'Musical stones' were a feature in ceremonies and processions in past Imperial China. They were struck with wooden or stone hammers and gave out a note. There could even be a stone orchestra. And if the uncouth and awkward stones of the lake-bed, why not the highly worked and articulated stone stalactites above us? One would anticipate high notes and scales as on a seraphic glockenspiel. Some sound or other must emerge and come down from that colourless, yet coloratura ceiling. The stone ribs with their fringed edges arching across the whole vault would seem even to hold and bind in the ringing.

But musical anticipations apart, entry into the chapel provides a very strange sensation which, too, seems capable of change or alteration within itself, even as you look up at it.

Coming in part, perhaps, from the play or change in the stalactites as they move and take up new positions, as you walk below them, within their hierarchy. Those circular fans or funnels, or that inflorescence but perhaps of marine not terrestrial flowering, is whirring, spinning, while perfectly and visibly motionless and still. Particularly if you can look up at it from a little to the right or left, and at an angle, the ceiling seems unprecedented and extraordinary. It is then that you get the sea-cavern, polyp-hiding, madrepore-growing effect of it, and could almost expect to see little brightly coloured fish swimming in and out between the pale stalactites and hanging lanterns. Being not natural, however, but artificial, and, at that, the height of artifice, the effect of the fan vault ceiling is Oriental. Had our Indian dominion come a little earlier, and coaeval with that of Portugal, one could think it the work of imported craftsmen from some Dravidian or other temple.

To describe its structure in words is far from easy. The 'fans' are in fact not fans at all; nor are they palm-fronds, nor funnels, nor umbrellas. Here, for about the first time, and the last (the dates are given as 1503-12, well into Henry VIII's reign) the stone shapes are complete circles, in their turn held out there, balanced, as it were, kept spinning, each by a fan or hemicycle on the wall, that touches the edge of it and gives it motion. We have the illusion that the pattern of the circles is not in their stillness but in their spinning. The bay or far end of the chapel over its three windows has no fewer than four of the stone tops or gyroscopes filling the whole compartment of the roof over the apse, loaded, otherwise, with little traceries and ornaments for a surround to the smaller or central gyroscope or parachute, it now resembles, ending in a dependent boss shaped like a lantern. But the stone stalactites or parachutes, choosing the term carefully, are suspended, held up in their descent from below, or from the side, at least, by a buttress coming out from the wall and passing into them, gripping them, midway in their stone folds. The purpose is that of the pedestal sometimes to be seen in an equestrian statue coming up out of the ground and supporting the horse by the middle of its belly. All along the chapel roof there are those stone struts or supports coming up out of the wall, providing in themselves a part of the scheme of ornament, but offering their aid to hold the stalactites or parachutes in place, to keep them up and prevent them coming down. There are in all three compartments of the ceiling twelve of the larger stalactites or parachutes, and four of the ones in the centre of the ceiling; each, and all of them with its dependent boss or lantern.

It is the planning and working out, and the paper, or, rather parchment stage of the designing, and resultant effect that makes the wonder of this fan vault ceiling. And it is this complexity or inflorescence that calls to memory such an Oriental marvel as the Shaikh Lotfollah mosque of Isfahan. It is of so extraordinary and exotic a nature that it calls for far-fetched compliments and comparisons. Were it in the East it would count among the wonders of the Orient; and it is strange indeed to find it only a stone's throw from the Thames. A peculiar and striking feature of it is its pallor. It has no colour but that of its stone which may have paled with age.

The English monument or effigy, in whatever form, is now at the moment when Pietro Torrigiani came from Florence at the invitation of Henry VIII to make the tombs at Westminster. The King's employment of Holbein and of Torrigiani compares, as has often been noted, but is true, with the patronage of Titian by Charles V, and of Leonardo and Benvenuto Cellini by François I. Particularly, the works of Holbein were to have much following in England. Torrigiani, a superb craftsman, is less important in this respect. It is even arguable that he adapted his style while over here to suit the English taste. Margaret Beaufort, Countess of Richmond and Derby, mother of Henry VII, through whom the Tudors drew their succession to the throne of England, was the first commission that he executed.[1] It may have been designed by William Bolton, Prior of St Bartholomew's, and by a Flemish painter, but it was cast in bronze gilt by Torrigiani, the recent cleaning having shown that her headdress was not gilt but painted white and that her face and hands were flesh pink. The double tomb of Henry VII and Elizabeth of York, his wife, is altogether more magnificent, and it is of Torrigiani's own design. But, even so, Humfrey Walker, founder, and Nicholas Ewen, coppersmith and gilder, were the chief workmen. Of more interest, certainly, than the tombs, splendid though they be, is the surrounding screen or grate of copper gilt designed by Lawrence Imber, with crowned initials and heraldic details.

Among later monuments in the Abbey every style of sculp-

[1] This is situated in the south aisle of Henry VII's Chapel, as is the tomb of Mary Queen of Scots, for which the sculptor Cornelius Cure was paid immense sums. Tombs in the north aisle include those of Queen Elizabeth and of the little daughters of James I, one lying in her hooded bed, the other reclining on her tomb, works by Maximilian Colt, a Huguenot from Arras.

ture is represented, from the painted Jacobean tomb and beyond the marble frontispiece to the 'monstrous' allegory, and it may be only the comparative dullness of many of them, and the dust of ages, that blind us to the freaks of morbid imagination that are in our midst. The examples are innumerable. It is only possible to point in admiration to a few of them, for in number they are beyond counting.[1]

THE MONUMENT But we should go down to the City if we wish to see the Baroque at play in England, for here we may admire the work of Caius Gabriel Cibber in his relief on the pedestal of the Fire Monument, a work that Mrs Esdaile describes perfectly with the remark that 'it recalls the illusionist reliefs of the age of the Flavian Emperors'. The chief actor is Charles II, periwigged, baton in hand, and in the costume of a Roman Emperor. Cibber was a Dane, or rather a Schleswiger, born in Flensburg, who studied in Rome and was well acquainted, therefore, with Bernini's sculptures. This relief is, all things considered, probably his best work, making one think of the contemporary Trinity Column in the Graben at Vienna, with the more coincidence because the Kaiser Leopold I, who appears among its sculptures, bore so strong a family resemblance, Bourbon-Habsburg-Medici, to our Charles II. Cibber's most famous works were his figures of melancholy and raving madness, which were placed upon the gate piers of Bedlam and were moved, later, to the Guildhall:

> *Close to those walls where Folley holds her throne*
> *And laughs to think Monroe would take her down,*
> *Where o'er the gates, by his fam'd father's hand*
> *Great Cibber's brazen, brainless brothers stand.*

These are Pope's immortal lines from the first book of *The Dunciad*. The models for the statues were two of the patients of the hospital, one of whom is said to have been a servant of Oliver Cromwell. They are lying, naked, with shaven heads, upon mattresses of rushes, and are an appalling reminder of Bedlam's horrors. The Monument itself is by Wren, but unlike

---

[1] Let us mention the tomb of Sir Francis Vere, in all probability by Maximilian Colt; the altar tomb by Nicholas Stone of Sir G. Villiers and his wife, the Countess of Buckingham; the monument to Dr Busby, the famous headmaster, by Francis Bird; the medallion of Congreve, in a great wig, by Francis Bird, with open playbooks and masks of comedy below him; the Shakespeare and Dryden monuments by Scheemakers; Sir Henry Cheere's monument to Captain de Sausmarez; and the Argyll and Nightingale monuments, great set pieces created and executed by Roubiliac.

him, for it is as foreign to London as the *guglie* of Naples. Originally he designed a Doric column with sprigs or tongues of flame burgeoning out of the shaft to hide the narrow stairway windows; but the sketch was rejected, and in the present scheme, as executed, a great statue was to stand upon the column, in place of the fiery urn which Wren did not design. The Monument, with its plinth half-sunk into the ground, stands in one of the most characteristic backwaters of the City, until recently so undisturbed that we would look round, unconsciously, for the lodging-house where Mr Pecksniff and his daughters stayed, as described by the City lover, Dickens.

ST PAUL'S CATHEDRAL We have only a step or two to go, in any direction, and there stands St Paul's. We should be glad, one and all of us, that this structure comes down to us from the Age of Reason. Were it Old St Paul's, it would be but another Westminster, while the Classical portico added to the west front by Inigo Jones so closely resembled the portico of All Saints Church, Northampton, that we may dismiss it with few regrets, preferring, indeed, the statue of Charles II in Roman armour and a periwig, at Northampton, to the pillars and statues that could only have spoiled the mediaeval fabric of Old St Paul's.

Wren had already been consulted upon the rebuilding, and had drawn up designs, when the Fire of London demolished the old Cathedral and made it necessary to begin again from the beginning. Several separate plans were prepared, over many years, besides that executed, of which the principal ones are known as the 'Greek Cross' design (with its variant, the 'great model', which was Wren's own favourite), and the 'warrant' design, because it was accepted by Royal warrant. The schemes are most curiously different. In addition, there is an earlier plan, dating from before the Fire, when Wren, comparatively, was inexperienced in architecture, and culminating in a dome consisting of an inner and outer shell, and the outer dome to be sheathed in lead with a lantern at the top and above that an open-work pineapple, sixty-eight feet in height. What is known as the 'great model' design was approached by a portico'd vestibule, with a pair of domes, a lesser and a greater, one behind the other. Wren had set his heart upon this, and is said to have wept when he was told of its rejection. This would, in fact, have been an aisleless building, without chapels, and it was, in all probability, because of the novelty of this plan that it was refused. But the later 'warrant' design is more peculiar than original, for it provides for a most extraordinary dome, that alters its mind, half way, starts to be a dome again, and then ends in a pagoda or steeple in six tiers or stages that diminish, like the steeple of St Bride's, in Fleet Street.

Old St Paul's had fallen in the Great Fire with dramatic suddenness. In the words of Evelyn, 'the Stones of St Paul's flew like Grenades.' The clearing away of the fragments was a Herculean labour, made dangerous by the collapse of great portions of the ruins. At least one of the great piers was blown up by Wren with gunpowder; while in another place he improvised a battering ram. No less than forty-seven thousand waggonloads of rubbish were removed, during which time the architect stood on a platform in the middle of the ruins like a general with his staff around him looking at his plans. The foundation stone was laid at last, in 1675, and the new St Paul's was opened for worship at the thanksgiving for the Peace of Ryswick, in 1694. The last stone of the cupola was laid in 1710.

There can be no hesitation in the opinion that St Paul's is the most magnificent domed building of the Renaissance. By comparison, Brunelleschi's dome at Florence is coarse and clumsy. Michelangelo's dome of St Peter's is more gigantic. It dominates the entire air of Rome. All lovers of architecture must sigh for that moment, gone for ever, when the *vetturino*, reining in his horses, cried 'Ecce Roma' and there, fifteen miles away, hung the dome of St Peter's. But the Vatican lies beside St Peter's. Our eyes are dazzled by the splashing fountains, by Bernini's colonnade, and by his splendid stair that mounts into the palace of the priest-king, past his parti-coloured halberdiers. St Paul's is very different. It stands over the City of London and its merchandise. It presides over this meeting of the four ends of the earth. The fugue of its architecture is more correct and classical. There is more imagination in this colder architecture. The twin campanili of St Paul's are fantastically elaborate in invention. The porch or frontispiece is rich and magnificent in its light and shadow. The north and south doors advance their pillars in a hemicycle. We may walk all round St Paul's and look at it from every angle, and its fugal structure is for ever moving. We may look up at the drum or peristyle, at the circle of pillars that stand below the dome, thinking with astonishment of the mathematical miracle of its construction, for the dome is supported on a cone of brick within. We may cast our eyes up to the beauty and delicacy of its white stone lantern. All this, we are thinking, is the work of one man, and he lived to see it finished.

The interior of St Paul's is Protestant, instantly, and from the entrance. It has Corinthian and Composite pilasters, and our eyes follow the stone vaulting to the gilt balcony, far up, and so into the enormous dome. We will not state that the interior of the dome is aesthetically beautiful, but it is overwhelming as a work of engineering and construction, and probably this is all that a Renaissance dome can be. The decorative work at St Paul's is magnificent in quality, and due to four great craftsmen. Sir James Thornhill painted, originally, the eight monochrome panels in the spandrels, but only his sketches have been preserved; Francis Bird, a sculptor who had worked in Rome, carved the Conversion of St Paul over the great pediment; Grinling Gibbons worked on the choirstalls, though much of the carved woodwork is by other hands; and Jean Tijou made the wrought iron railings.

In the chancel stands Nicholas Stone's effigy of Dr John Donne in his shroud, of which Isaac Walton tells us, in his *Life of Donne*:

> Several charcoal fires being first made in his large study, he brought with him into that place his winding-sheet in his hand, and having put off all his clothes, had this sheet put upon him, and so tied with knots at his head and feet, and his hands so placed as dead bodies are usually fitted to be shrouded and put into their coffin or grave.

Upon a wooden model of an urn he stood 'with his lean, pale, and death-like face', while his picture was drawn by a painter upon a board. Another beautiful instance of Stone's work is the wall memorial in the crypt to Sir Simon Baskerville, a wooden scroll, we would describe it as, though carried out in stone; and there, too, are the memorials of the family of Sir Christopher Wren. In the monument to Jane, daughter of the great architect, Francis Bird has portrayed her as St Cecilia, while another memorial, to a daughter-in-law, could hardly be improved upon for grace and liveliness, but its cupids, death's heads, hourglasses, are conspicuously Italian. Of actual Italian workmanship is the Cornish porphyry sarcophagus which now holds the body of Lord Nelson, for it formed part of a tomb begun by the Florentine sculptor Benedetto da Rovezzano for Cardinal Wolsey. This was seized by Henry VIII and the work continued for his own use. It was set up in St George's, Windsor, but never completed, and in the end was broken up and sold by Cromwell, all that remains being the four huge bronze candlesticks by Benedetto, now in the church of St Bavon, Ghent, and Nelson's sarcophagus in the crypt below St Paul's. The rest has gone.

But this vast building has other wonders. There are vaulted chambers or vestries for the Deans, the Minor Canons, and the Lord Mayor; while the foot of the Geometrical Staircase, by the Dean's door, is a most beautiful and satisfying composition, led up to by the curving stone wall of the balustrade till it becomes a stone niche, framed in carving, with a really splendid rail above it by Jean Tijou, after which the handrail of the stair goes up again. This little work of detail has the swing and balance that characterise the greatest masters of the Baroque, and it is completely satisfying. Finally, there is the library with its limewood bookcases in an upper chamber. St Paul's is the most entire and unanimous of the great buildings.

LONDON CHURCHES

During all the years of its construction Wren was engaged upon his London churches. In all, fifty-four churches were designed by him. The variety of the steeples alone is perfectly extraordinary, and if we add to them the later churches built by Hawksmoor and by Gibbs we can understand how the London steeples of white Portland stone are so conspicuous a feature in the painting of London from the garden of Richmond House, by Canaletto. They formed nothing less than the architectural character of old London, and in the painting are as numerous as minarets in Cairo or in Istanbul. The steeples that were actually of Wren's design can, of course, be classified under different forms. Many persons will have realised for themselves the exceeding cleverness of the spire of St Martin's, Ludgate, to give contrast to the great mass of St Paul's, beyond. The belfries of St Bride's, Fleet Street, and St Mary-le-Bow are famous. The imagery, so to speak, of these belfries is that, appropriately, of the shedding of the sound of bells; from the diminishing tiers of St Bride's, Fleet Street, like a pagoda, that in themselves suggest a peal of bells, to the type that is like a sugar castor that should be turned upside down and shaken and would then sprinkle forth the sound. There is, too, the stricter campanile type of bell turret, that, for instance, of St James Garlickhithe, or of St Michael Paternoster Royal.[1] And there are as well Wren's 'Gothick' steeples.

[1] The spires of these nearly adjacent churches, both in the shadow of St Paul's, are of a different suggestion. They convey, in their shape, the sound-symbolism that they should turn round and *grind*. Not, then, a shedding or sprinkling of the bells, but a turning, turning, as of a musical box or merry-go-round.

The most famous, and rightly, of his City interiors is St
Stephen Walbrook, with its panelled dome on sixteen pillars,
eight of which support the arches. But another domed interior,
St Mary Abchurch, is scarcely less remarkable; while it is
necessary to mention St Antholin, Budge Row, a church demolished long ago, because of the peculiar octagonal arrangement of its pillars, like a Roman or Byzantine baptistery. What
a contrast to St Benet, Upper Thames Street, in red brick, and
like a Quaker or Moravian meeting house. St Lawrence Jewry,
another contrast, could have been a church in Italy or Spain,
with its picture by Spagnoletto and the stuccos and painted
ceiling by Isaac Fuller in the vestry. This showed the apotheosis
of St Lawrence. An angel played the gridiron as though it were
a harp. We could have been in Naples or Valencia;[1] till we
remember this is the church to which the newly elected Lord
Mayor of London and the Sheriffs used to come, in all the pomp
of crystal coaches, coachmen in three-cornered hats, and the
huge fur hat of the City sword-bearer, costumes and ceremony,
indeed, that make the Lord Mayor of London into a figure not
very different from the Doge of Venice, did he but survive into
our day. The Wren churches had, of course, much other ad-
ventitious aid from carvings, and even fonts, a few by Grinling
Gibbons, or attributed to him, and from such characteristic and
delightful details as the carved Lion and Unicorn of the Royal
arms at St Mildred, Bread Street (another church which was
destroyed), or the wrought iron swordrests at St Mary-at-Hill.[2]
The Spanish-Portuguese synagogue in Bevis Marks, said to be
copied from the synagogue of the Sephardic Jews in Amster-

[1] St Lawrence Jewry, hopelessly gutted in the blitz, has since been restored as
far as is possible, but all the interior decoration perished.

[2] These swordrests were intended for the sword of the Lord Mayor when he
visited the church in state. Authorities differ as to whether each Lord Mayor
came once in state to his own church, where he was a parishioner, during his
year of office, or whether until the middle of the last century it was customary for
the Lord Mayor to attend in state one or other of the City churches every
Sunday, which, if true, compares with the state visits of the Doge of Venice to
the different parish churches of Venice. Earlier wooden swordrests remain in St
Helen, Bishopsgate, St Mary Aldermary, Southwark Cathedral (from St
Olave's, Tooley Street), and two in City Company Halls. The earliest, dated,
iron swordrest (1708) is at St Magnus the Martyr. The most splendid examples
were at All Hallows Barking, where at least one still survives, while St Mary-at-
Hill, near the Tower, has no fewer than six, one of them the gift of Alderman
Beckford, father of the 'Caliph Vathek'. Cf. *The Old Churches of London*, by
Gerald Cobb, London, 1941, and an article in *Archaeologia*, LIV, p. 41, by E. H.
Freshfield, in which that writer enumerates, as existing in his time (1891), a
total of sixty-three swordrests in the City churches, fifty-eight of which were of
wrought iron. York, Norwich and Bristol are other cities where fine swordrests
are to be found in many of the churches.

dam, is a plain but beautiful interior under Wren influence, and should be seen also by all who are interested in the City churches.

Hawksmoor and Gibbs both profited from the passing of Queen Anne's Act for the building of fifty new churches. The most considerable works of Hawksmoor are his London churches, and it is very evident, in these, that he was no mere imitator of Wren. St Mary Woolnoth must be a familiar sight to a public of many tens of thousands who have never heard of Hawksmoor. This curious church, in style, could be a fragment of Blenheim built again in Lombard Street, and the twelve Corinthian columns of the interior are in keeping, though so complete is the hand of degradation that if we follow down the street we may find it difficult to determine where the architecture of Queen Anne comes to an end and the Metropolitan Railway begins. The steeple of St Anne, Limehouse, is again in the style of Blenheim, but with 'Gothick' finials, and an interior that is more interesting than St Mary Woolnoth. The hand of Hawksmoor appears, too, in St Alphege, Greenwich, but not in the tower, which is by James of Greenwich.[1] This church of Portland stone stands at the corner, before we come to the Hospital, and is a first intimation of the architectural and marine glories that lie beyond. St George-in-the-East is a church by Hawksmoor that is unknown to me. Christ Church, Spitalfields, is the finest of his London churches. The exterior is a work of the utmost originality, though a result of intellectual processes and not of inspiration. Its steeple and portico have been considered, and considered again, from every angle. No sculpture or ornament is employed. The whole effect comes from its abstract plans and masses. The interior is no less deliberate with its projecting lateral arcades of Corinthian pillars.

Hawksmoor did not repeat himself. Those persons, and they would be the majority, who could not identify Queen's and All Souls Colleges in Oxford, on visual evidence, as works of the same architect, would hesitate to connect together Christ Church, Spitalfields, and St George's, Bloomsbury. But to those who haunt the Reading Room and love the part of London that lies round Shaftesbury Avenue, two of the endearing monuments are the white steeples of St George's, Bloomsbury, and St Giles-in-the-Fields. The stepped pyramid of St

[1] John James also built the familiar St George's, Hanover Square.

George's is one of the curiosities of London, but it attracts no more attention than do the living curiosities who come to and fro, every day, from the Museum. A statue of George II sails aloft, through sun or fog, on top of what purports to be a model of the Mausoleum of Halicarnassus, one of the ancient Seven Wonders of the World. The top of that was adorned with a chariot drawn by four horses, a sculptural animation that probably inspired Hawksmoor to the Lion and Unicorn that played at the base of his pyramid. A thousand pities that they were taken down! The Unicorn sat upright at one corner of the pyramid, with its long tail curled up behind it. Probably the white Portland stone hinted that this heraldic animal was as much the white horse of Hanover as the British Unicorn. The Lion, more like a huge mastiff, was climbing, head first, down the pyramid at the other corner, lashing its great tail for some two or three steps towards the summit. Between the front paws of both Lion and Unicorn stood, and still stands alone, the Royal crown.

The most beautiful London steeples of all, in our own opinion, are by James Gibbs, a Scotsman, born near Aberdeen in 1682, as remote a provenance as could be imagined for so typical a product of the European eighteenth century. Instead of studying in Paris, Gibbs went to Rome where he 'conversed with the best masters'. On his return to England, he met and made friends with Wren, and before long was appointed one of the surveyors for Queen Anne's fifty churches. This was his opportunity, and we shall see that it took the form of a skilful blending of the Italian with the style of Wren. To the extent that we could almost say of Gibbs's churches, that it was as if Wren was young again and had been to Italy.

St Mary-le-Strand is the first of Gibbs's London churches. How many tens of millions of men and women have passed it by; more than ever floated under the arch of the Rialto! But, indeed, its situation in the flow of traffic of the Strand, broken again by St Clement Danes behind it, is as unique as any building on the Grand Canal. What echoes of old London we hear in Pope's lines from *The Dunciad*:

> *Where the tall Maypole once o'erlooked the Strand*
> *But now (so Anne and Piety ordain)*
> *A church collects the saints of Drury Lane.*

Gibbs writes, himself, that 'this church being situated in a very publick place, the Commissioners ... spared no cost to beautify it . . .'. And he continues, 'it consists of two orders . . . the wall of the lower being solid, to keep out noises from the street.' Gibbs had, in the first place, designed a small campanile or turret, and no steeple. In front of the church there was to be a column, two hundred and fifty feet high, with a statue of Queen Anne. But Queen Anne died, and Gibbs built the steeple. In his *Book of Architecture* he writes: 'Steeples are indeed of a Gothic extraction, but they have their beauties when their parts are well disposed, and when the plans of the several degrees and orders of which they are composed gradually diminish and pass from one form to another without confusion, and when every part has the appearance of a proper bearing.' This aim he certainly accomplished in the steeple of St Mary-le-Strand. The interior of the church is too cramped and narrow to give him scope. Perhaps only the brothers Egid Quirin and Cosmas Damian Asam of Bavaria could have made the most of it. But the exterior is a lesson in good manners to the passing crowd.

A year or two after St Mary-le-Strand was finished, Gibbs completed Wren's church of St Clement Danes by adding the steeple. So both island churches in the Strand had Gibbs's steeples. They delight by contrast; that of St Mary-le-Strand being of the flat sort, like a canister, or the top tiers of a cabinet; and that of St Clement Danes, square, with cut off angles, and then octagonal, like an Oriental pagoda, in symbol of the fragrant teas, the golden sugars and the spices come up old Thames, by sail, and unloading at the City warehouses round St Paul's, and beyond, to Wapping.

Gibbs's next project was St Martin-in-the-Fields, a splendid masterpiece in the midst of London, and aesthetically the most successful of all London churches. If we look at this dispassionately, we may not feel certain there is a finer building in all Rome or Venice. His first two designs were for a circular church; and we may wish that this had been realised, remembering his Radcliffe Camera. But the plans were too expensive. The present building was an alternative design. Its portico can be admired endlessly, and not found wanting, together with the manner in which Gibbs has combined portico and steeple in one unit or member. The steeple is of the sprinkler or sugar castor sort, ingeniously designed in a series of diminishing octagons, till it forms an obelisk pierced with openings, and points away. No other single London building, save St Paul's, is so worthy of its situation. It is true, however, that the interior of this church is not particularly interesting, though it contains the first stucco or 'fretwork' of Artari and Bagutti.

But the history of London steeples does not end with Gibbs. A favourite specimen is that of St Giles-in-the-Fields, in the waste land between New Oxford Street and Charing Cross Road. This church, one of the last examples of the style of Wren, is by Flitcroft, the architect of Woburn Abbey and the huge and ugly Wentworth Woodhouse. The tower has a de-lightful first storey, above the entablature, like a room in an arch put up to get the view, then an octagonal belfry with open windows, and a closed spire of stone. 'Light, airy, and genteel' describes it perfectly, and indeed nothing could be more elegant than that octagon, rising over Bloomsbury. St Leonard's, Shoreditch, by the Elder Dance, must be our last example, a steeple modelled, obviously, upon St Mary-le-Bow, but in fact surpassing that, for its Classic elements are more defined and clearer. The actual belfry is yet another octagon, with balconies and curving buttresses below it.

GREENWICH The London steeples of white Portland stone lead on to Greenwich, down the Thames. Here we find a masterpiece of Inigo Jones and the grandest of Wren's secular buildings. Queen Elizabeth was born at Greenwich Palace, and it is a site as splendid as anything that Venice offers, looking between the pair of columns towards San Giorgio Maggiore, over the lifting gondolas. The visitor to the Queen's House, built by Jones for Henrietta Maria, Charles I's Queen, must feel his spirits lifted by the health-giving, the therapeutic proportions of the in-terior, as at the wonderful Villa Maser, which is the greatest work of Palladio upon the Venetian terra firma. The river front of King Charles's block of Greenwich Hospital is also in the manner of Jones, and could be called the 'masculine and un-affected brother' of the Banqueting House at Whitehall. But, in actual fact, King Charles's block was begun by John Webb as part of a palace for Charles II.

The Royal Hospital of Greenwich was a project of Queen Mary II, and the conditions imposed upon Wren were that he should not interfere with the Queen's House, built for her grandmother, or with the existing block. He decided, there-fore, to leave a clear vista from the Queen's House down to the river, and to co-ordinate the scheme of Inigo Jones by an extension of the palace. To this end he designed the colonnade of coupled Doric columns facing each other across the open vista, and down at their corners, by the river, he placed his pair of domes. One dome is above the Chapel, and the other above the entrance to the Painted Hall. In order to effect this, Wren completed the one building begun by Webb and added another in exact facsimile. He is working, therefore, at Greenwich, in the Palladian manner not in the Classical Baroque in which he built St Paul's. Greenwich Hospital is, in fact, a double building in two separate wings that complete each other, and compose the whole, with the pair of domes at their nearest point, and the Queen's House seen far back, and in between.

The purposes for which Greenwich Hospital was intended confine its interior magnificence to the Painted Hall. But this cannot be mentioned otherwise than as the only frescoed room in England that can compare with the painted walls and ceilings of Italy. It is from the brush of Thornhill, who worked for nineteen years upon it, and it is his masterwork. His scheme of fresco covers the Lower and the Upper Hall, and as it progressed it became a dedication to or apotheosis of, respectively, William and Mary, Queen Anne, on the two ceilings, and George I and the Hanoverian dynasty upon the west wall of the Upper Hall. We will quote some passages from the contemporary description by Sir Richard Steele:

> In the centre is a large oval frame supported by eight gigantic figures of slaves . . . the King tramples tyranny under with his feet, which is expressed by a French personage with his leaden crown fallen off: cardinal's cap, triple crowned mitres, etc., tumbling down. Over the Royal canopy is Apollo in his golden chariot, attended by the Horae, the morning dews falling upon him. . . . In the centre of the gallery going into the Upper Hall is seen, as though on the stocks, the taffrail of the Blenheim man-of-war, with her galleries and portholes open. . . . In the centre of the opposite gallery is the stern of a beautiful galley, filled with Spanish trophies; underneath is the Humber, the Severn, with the Avon falling into her; and other rivers. In the North end of the gallery is the famous Tycho Brahe, a noble Danish knight; near him is Copernicus, with his Pythagorean system in his hand, and an old mathematician. In the South end are portraits of Mr Flamsteed, the first Astronomer Royal, and his disciple, Mr Thomas Weston. In Mr Flamsteed's hand is a scroll of paper, on which is drawn the great eclipse of the sun which happened in April 1715; near him is an old man with a

pendulum, counting the seconds of time as Mr Flamsteed makes his observations of the descent of the moon on the Severn, which, at certain times, forms a roll of the tides, very dangerous to shipping, called the Eagre. This is also expressed by rivers falling, through the moon's influence, into the Severn. The great rivers at each end of the Hall have their product of fish issuing out of their vases, etc., etc.

In other places we see the four quarters of the world: a wall painting in gold and sepia, to imitate a bas-relief, of the landing of William III at Torbay; in another place, the disembarkation of George I and his family at Greenwich; and, in one background, the dome of St Paul's. Particularly appropriate are the paintings of the men-of-war. We admire the panels in chiaroscuro. What is it all about? Copernicus, Archimedes, Tycho Brahe, and Mr Flamsteed? The Four Elements, Earth, Air, Fire and Water, represented by Cybele, Juno, Jupiter and Neptune, who are accompanied by their lesser deities, namely, the Fauni, Iris, Vulcan and Amphitrite, with their proper attributes? Fame descending, riding on the winds, sounding the praises of the royal founders? We could see portraits of Frederick, Prince of Wales, the Queen of Prussia, the Duke of Cumberland and his five sisters, the Electress Sophia; and besides, the Lord Mayor of London, with the Arms, Sword, and Cap of Maintenance, supported by Thame and Isis, with other rivers offering up their treasures. What does it mean? We can but admire, and point to the Art of Fresco.

ST BARTHOLOMEW'S HOSPITAL

Thornhill's Painted Hall at Greenwich was the inspiration for the only monumental paintings by his son-in-law, William Hogarth, *The Pool of Bethesda* and *The Good Samaritan*, upon the staircase of St Bartholomew's Hospital in the City. Did we not know these to be by Hogarth, we would ascribe them to a Neapolitan, to Francesco di Mura, 'Franceschiello', the pupil of Solimena. The wall paintings have elaborate scrollwork or framing at the sides, and the whole conception is Rococo, not the grouping of the figures only, and their sentiment, but the hemicycle of arches or ruins that forms the background of *The Pool of Bethesda*, and is so theatrical that it may remind us of Bakst's scenes for *The Sleeping Beauty*. These works are peculiar and unique in Hogarth. Never again did he attempt the Grand Style. Did he have the advice, in this instance, of his friend George Lambert, the scene painter of Covent Garden, of whose talents we cannot speak, for such works, of necessity, have perished long ago? This is, at least, possible.[1]

Returning from Greenwich, if we like to imagine ourselves upon the river, we see again in their multitude the steeples of white Portland stone, and in their midst the dome of St Paul's. Let us not be led, though, into an exaggeration of that whiteness! We have contemporary evidence to prove that the stone of St Paul's was black with soot long before the last stone of the cupola was laid. The quality of Portland stone, however, is its depth of light and shade. As we come nearer to the dome of St Paul's it is the more astounding, from every angle, that one man, and one man only, lived to see it finished. This is he who, according to Sarah, Duchess of Marlborough, 'suffered himself to be drawn up in a basket, two or three times a year, at no little danger'. We may begin to think of St Paul's as marine architecture, being come from Greenwich. That superb dome has the perfection of the rarest seashell. Of the most spectacular, or the most ordinary, of the seashells. For the cockleshell is as beautiful. The nautilus is as ingenious. But the most elaborate of the molluscs in their porcelain houses are not more wonderful. Wren has rivalled with Nature in his architecture. More than this could not be said of the greatest architect of the human race.

Although London was not rebuilt by Wren, his influence, if not his actual hand, appears in the brick buildings of the Temple; in the rubbed brick doors, models of quiet beauty, in King's Bench Walk; and in a lovely composition, more Dutch than usual, with the wooden doorway of St Paul's Deanery, with its double steps and railings. The Halls of the City Companies, which are so unique a feature of the City, do not seem in any instance to be directly due to Wren, though certainly, in ignorance, we would look here for him. The brick architecture of his school came after him; or was the vernacular of his own time, studied and spoken by him, and left to his successors, who, in this branch, inclined to be builders more than architects. To see the hand of Wren himself in this vein we should go CHELSEA to Chelsea Hospital, upon which we may quote the remark of HOSPITAL Carlyle, who loved not architecture and had no understanding of aesthetic matters. 'I had passed it almost daily for many years without thinking much about it, and one day I began to reflect

[1] It has been conjectured that Lambert may even have painted the landscape backgrounds to Hogarth's two paintings. Though no scene paintings have survived, many other of Lambert's paintings and drawings are known.

that it had always been a pleasure to me to see it, and I looked at it more attentively and saw that it was quiet and dignified and the work of a *gentleman*.' Outside the Hospital is a statue of Charles II by Grinling Gibbons, who, we must remind ourselves, was sculptor as well as woodcarver. This is a pair to his statue of James II outside the National Gallery, and they are fascinating alike because of their classical costume and their Stuart physiognomy.

WHITEHALL   The great London palace of these kings and their forebears was Whitehall, of which the Banqueting House, the masterpiece of Inigo Jones, alone survives. For a year or two after his return from Italy, Jones had little opportunity for the new architecture he had learned. It is, however, the symptom of what is coming that the following sentences should be found written in his sketch book, under date, January 20th, 1614 (1615):

> In all designing of ornament one must first design the ground plan as it is for use, and then adorn and compose it with decorum according to its use. . . . For as outwardly every wise man carries himself gravely in public places, yet inwardly has imagination and fire which sometimes flies out unrestrained, just as Nature sometimes flies out to delight or amuse us, to move us to laughter, contemplation, or even horror; so in architecture the outward ornament is to be solid, proportionable according to rule, masculine and unaffected.

The Banqueting House at Whitehall, the living proof of those principles, is the most beautiful building in London; there is, indeed, nothing whatever that can compare with it except St Paul's, and it is worthy in every respect of the hand of the great Italians, Sansovino, Vignola, Palladio. Yet how few have the curiosity to know its history! How many of the public know that its painted ceiling is by Rubens? The exterior of the Banqueting House is a work of art that can bear comparison with the Library of Sansovino at Venice. From one of the upper windows Charles I stepped out to execution on the scaffold. But the most interesting fact about this building is its early date. It was finished in 1622, during the reign of James I. The architect, who at his first effort broke with the mediaeval style, was close on fifty years of age, but he was to continue in his maturity for three decades more. The Banqueting House was the result of many years' study in Italy, and much reflection on Italian buildings. Only thus can the mystery be explained.

But this building is but a fragment of a giant plan for the new palace of Whitehall, for which several projects exist, by Jones, his nephew John Webb,[1] and, later, by Christopher Wren; but none was executed. Of the buildings which now occupy the site, we mention only William Kent's Horse Guards. Its front is imposing, but it possesses a kind of aristocratic aloofness and self-effacement, at the far end of the parade ground, that compels us to take if for granted, and pass by. Is it not as English as the officials who used to dress for dinner, every night, in the far provinces of the Sudan? And we may add that were the Horse Guards a building in Paris or Vienna we should be reminded, perpetually, to admire it. Here the rustication is more alive and bold; the cupola is set perfectly upon the main body; the Palladian windows on the first floor are in proper proportion to their space of wall: the side pavilions project just far enough and are of the right solidity, in themselves, with their three windows side by side. It is one of the last buildings by Kent, and was left unfinished at his death. Vardy completed it. How well the white Portland stone matches, unintentionally, with the black chargers, the steel helmets and breastplates, white breeches, and scarlet or blue tunics of the Life Guards or the Horse Guards blue! How well it goes with the long-skirted yellow and gold surcoats and black Montero caps, with the kettledrums and silver trumpets of their mounted band! But this is fortuitous and not intentional, being due to the perfect manners of that Palladian façade. For the Horse Guards could, as well, be a country house in a great park with the hounds meeting at the door.

LONDON HOUSES My mother used to tell me that her father, who had beautiful horses and carriages and lived in a big old house in Berkeley Square, drove out to dinner in his coach with a coachman on the box, and a pair of footmen standing at the back holding long staffs, all of them in livery and wearing three-cornered hats and wigs of spun glass. And this latter detail I never quite believed until this week when reading a book of memoirs,[2] where the author remembered in the seventies and eighties seeing carriages waiting in Charles Street, round the corner from Berkeley Square, with coachman and footmen wearing

---

[1] The degree of their relationship is uncertain. Webb married Anne Jones, probably the niece of Inigo Jones, in which case Inigo Jones would be his wife's uncle.

[2] *Romantic London*, by Ralph Nevill, London, 1928, p. 19.

wigs of spun glass, and on occasion a coach standing at the door with postilions in blue silk jackets and white beaver hats.

Of the great houses of London, few have survived into the present age, but there is enough to allow us some idea of the works of the chief English architects in the metropolis. Ashburnham House, in Westminster, where the staircase is deserving of no less a title than that of masterpiece, has been connected with the names of both Inigo Jones and Webb. It would be a late work of Jones, done, like Wilton at the end of the Civil Wars, or during the Commonwealth, an unlikely flowering, especially when we remember that Inigo Jones was nearly eighty years old, and died in 1653. This staircase is too good, though, to be by Webb alone. The panelling and fluted columns of the walls are beyond praise, and so is the oval dome above, a wonderful decorative invention and of masterly ingenuity. It would be no exaggeration, remembering the staircases in Italian palaces, to say that this, within its modest dimensions, is as fine as any.

The only staircase to compare with it, for its enlargement of a small space into magnificence, is the interior of No. 44 Berkeley Square, by William Kent for Lady Isabella Finch, an affair of genius that in any other city but London would be famous. The Venetian stair, and the drawing-room on the first floor with its coved ceiling, are in fact as splendid as the interior of any Roman or Venetian palace. How these have been contrived within the small area of a London house remains something of a miracle, and it is the more absorbing because unsuspected from the outside.[1]

Kent also made many alterations at Kensington Palace, but here we would see first the work of Wren, surviving in two of his masterworks in little, a garden alcove and the Orangery.[2] The garden alcove, in its coupled columns and the niche and swags between them, and in the high panelling of its interior shaped like a hemicycle, was not without influence upon the garden architecture of William Kent. But the Orangery, built for Queen Anne, and in which she often dined or drank her tea, in Defoe's words 'was pleased to make the Green House, which is very beautiful, her Summer Supper House', is complete and perfect as a work of art. An Orangery was a new opportunity, as we may see in the Orangery at Versailles, or at Herrenhausen,

[1] This house has also two rooms in white and gold by Henry Holland.

[2] These are variously attributed to Wren, Vanbrugh or Hawksmoor, but it is the style of Wren, in the interior of the Orangery, in particular.

the Hanoverian palace, where today there are more than fifty huge orange trees in their tubs that are three hundred years old. But here the architect has made it into something as grand, in the classical sense, as an interior by Palladio. No praise could be too high of its fluted pilasters, its carved cornice, the doors and round arched doorways, and their niches. We can only say of the Orangery, one of the last of Wren's works, if it is indeed his, that in its way and for its special purpose, it is as beautiful as the Banqueting House of Inigo Jones at Whitehall.

In the presence chamber in Kensington Palace we observe Kent as a decorator in the vein we have already seen at Rousham in Oxfordshire, imitating the grotesques of Raphael's Loggie at the Vatican, while the walls of the King's staircase reveal him as not far inferior to the Italians. They are divided by painted pillars and a balcony into compartments, with a crowd of persons looking on; male courtiers, negro pages, women holding little spaniels, or fans. A young page stands, in trickery, on the near side of the balcony, and we should remark that there is a Beefeater, or Yeoman of the Guard, in every panel. Their originals were, of course, on guard above the stair, but Kent had a particular liking for the Yeomen of the Guard.[1] Certain paintings of masquerades which could be by a Venetian, have been attributed to William Kent, because in each there is a Yeoman of the Guard among the masquers; while we must recall, too, the guard room at Hampton Court which has a mantelpiece with carved Beefeaters for supporters, though this is probably designed by Vanbrugh rather than Kent.

BRANDENBURGH HOUSE

The spirit of the Italian theatre may have been evident too in Roger Morris's Brandenburgh House at Hammersmith, for Mr Wyndham, long ago destroyed, with a gallery of gilding and frescoes, a pair of columns of Sicilian jasper and columns for the doorcase of lapis lazuli; for the Florentine Servandoni, theatrical artist and organiser of fêtes and fireworks, who designed Saint-Sulpice in Paris, had a hand in this.

HOUSES OF ISAAC WARE

The chief work of Isaac Ware was at Chesterfield House, where the Rococo interiors in the French taste were due to him, of which we find the great Lord Chesterfield writing that it is to be 'finie a la Françoise avec force sculptures et dorures'. It had, in fact, some very gilded rooms. Here, too, till a few years ago,

---

[1] This predilection is also found, in curious form, in two oil paintings at Hampton Court, of *Henry V's First Meeting with Princess Katharine of France* and *The Marriage of Henry V*, subjects which, however weak in handling, point forward to Bonington and Delacroix, and initiate a new kind of painting.

Nicholas Hawksmoor's Mausoleum at Castle Howard.

Diana and her court; part of the coloured plaster frieze by Abraham Smith in the great chamber at Hardwick Hall.

Kirby Hall, Northamptonshire; part of the north façade of the courtyard,
built by Nicholas Stone.

Sir John Vanbrugh's bridge over the lake at Blenheim Palace.

Colonnade of the Palladian bridge at Wilton House, designed by the ninth
Earl of Pembroke and Roger Morris.

Above left:
Rococo stucco-
work, attributed
to Charles
Stanley, at
Honington Hall,
Warwickshire.

Above right:
Corner of the
ceiling of the red
drawing-room at
Syon House,
designed by
Robert Adam
and with panels
painted by
Angelica
Kauffmann.

Below: Sphinx
supporting a
gilt side table
at Houghton,
Norfolk; designed
by William Kent
for Sir Robert
Walpole.

Characteristic plaster fans of James Wyatt in the hall at Heveningham Hall, Suffolk.

Ashdown House, in the Vale of the White Horse.

could be seen the stair with marble steps and wrought iron balustrade from Canons, Edgware, a stairway that had known the tread of the great Handel.[1] Ware was the complete Cockney, his best work being done in London,[2] and his bust by Roubiliac shows a thin, pinched face, a character which we can corroborate from the *Life of Nollekens*, by J. T. Smith, where we read that the father of Nollekens told him the following story:

A thin, sickly little boy, a chimney sweeper, was amusing himself one morning by drawing with a piece of chalk the street front of Whitehall upon the basement stones of the building itself, carrying his delineations as high as his little arms could possibly reach . . . it happened that his operations caught the eye of a gentleman of considerable taste and fortune as he was riding by. He checked the carriage, and after a few minutes' observation, called to the boy to come to him; who, upon asked as to where he lived, burst into tears, and begged of the gentleman not to tell his master, assuring him that he would wipe it all off. . . . His benefactor then went to his master in Charles Court, in the Strand, who gave him a good character, but declared he was of little use to him, on account of his being so bodily weak. He said he was fully aware of the boy's fondness for chalking, and showed his visitor what a state his walls were in from the young artist having drawn the portico of St Martin's church in various places. . . . The gentleman purchased the remainder of the boy's time, gave him an excellent education, then sent him to Italy; and upon his return, employed him, and introduced him to his friends as an architect.

This story was told, too, by Isaac Ware to Roubiliac, when he was sitting for his bust, and we may fancy we see the same physiognomy in the engraving from that.

Upon the London houses of Isaac Ware there could be much argument and controversy. Engravings of a number of them are given in his *Body of Architecture*; in Hanover Square, Bloomsbury Square, Berkeley Square, Burlington Gardens, Dover Street, Bruton Street, Albemarle Street, and South Audley

[1] Chesterfield House was demolished in 1937.

[2] He was employed, too, at Houghton and published some engravings of it, while his adherence to the Palladian movement is proved in a book of designs by Inigo Jones, and in his translation of Palladio. He refaced Chicksands Priory, in Bedfordshire, for the Osborn family, together with Wrotham Park, nearby, in Hertfordshire, for Admiral Byng, who was related to them, a house with typical portico and wings, but it has been much damaged in a fire.

Street. But we have arrived at the age of the ordinary inconspicuous London exterior; and, also, the street numbers have been altered in the course of time. The problem explains itself if we take a pair of London houses. The 'House of Charity', at the corner of Soho Square and Greek Street, is a plain brick house, disarmingly simple and undemonstrative from outside, but containing a Rococo staircase and a room on the first floor that would be exuberant even in Naples or Palermo. The stucco, indeed, is probably Italian, but the architect may have been Flitcroft, or Isaac Ware. If it be the latter, then who designed the extreme Palladian room at the back of No. 12 North Audley Street, a house still smaller and more unpretentious from without? Was it Flitcroft, or Isaac Ware, or another?[1] For the same architect cannot have been responsible for both.

THE HOUSE OF CHARITY

12 NORTH AUDLEY STREET

SPENCER HOUSE

Vardy, who completed the Horse Guards when Kent died, will be remembered by Spencer House, St James's, even though the façade towards the park be by Colonel Grey, the amateur and dilettante. The 'painted' drawing-room here is to the design of 'Athenian' Stuart, and it provides a pretty setting for the joint brushes of Angelica Kauffmann and her husband, Zucchi, and a far echo of Florence, or even Fontainebleau. These are Italian arabesques; there is nothing Grecian about them. They are modelled on the painted decorations of the Renaissance, and are amateur beside the work of Adam or of Wyatt. By contrast, the decoration of Ely House, Dover Street, by Sir Robert Taylor is most elegant. The house has a plain stone front with a bishop's mitre on it, but the interior is light, delicate and graceful, and a long way from the Palladians; indeed, it is upon distinctly Adam lines.

ELY HOUSE

ADAM HOUSES

The dawn of Adam brought with it a brightening of the parts, till, indeed, no interiors have glittered with more brilliance of detail. But the works of Adam must be selected, and reselected, until we reach his best. We may not find it possible to admire Adam as architect of an exterior. Neither the south front of Kedleston, nor that of Stowe, has movement, nor any quality but that, like a triumphal arch, of standing still. But Adam is master of a flight of rooms, of the first, second, and

---

[1] Mr Laurence Turner, in *Decorative Plasterwork in Great Britain*, London, 1927, p. 209, suggests the name of Robert Harris as architect of No. 12 North Audley Street, and compares it to the stucco-work at Compton Place, Eastbourne. This little London house is said to have been built by George II for his mistress, Lady Suffolk. The Palladian room at the back, with its multiplicity of cornices and mouldings, according to Mr Laurence Turner's theory, is by the architect of Marble Hill, Twickenham, associated with the same lady.

third drawing-rooms, that communicate through high door-cases of mahogany and gold. Master, too, of the English dining-room, for it is to be observed that the French, who prefer female company, ate their meals anywhere, and joined the ladies. Not so the English. They sat for long hours over their port. Adam, therefore, was master of the sideboard and the wine-cooler; but his true genius lay in the frieze and ceiling.

20 ST JAMES'S
SQUARE

In London, No. 20 St James's Square, built for the Welsh magnate, Sir Watkin Williams Wynn, shows, for once more, the great architect in Robert Adam. The exterior is so correct and modest, with a lovely leaded fanlight over the door, that no one could suspect the courtyard at the back, or the architecture that hides within. We must mention the stair balusters of cast iron, and a pair of drawing-rooms, the second of them with an apsed end and a barrel ceiling, lately restored in bright colours from the original drawings; while the appointments of this Adam house were complete down to the sedan chair and the inkstand, the fire irons, silver dishes, and an escutcheon and knocker, 'in brass water gilt', for the outer door.

HOME HOUSE

No. 20 Portman Square, now the Courtauld Institute, reveals Adam in another and more fanciful magnificence, the date being 1776, a year when the elegance of feminine fashion for the whole of the eighteenth century reached to its height. Marie Antoinette had just become Queen of France and her towering headdresses had become the rage. This short period in history is immediately to be known and recognised in these details, and perhaps the most typical English relic or echo is to be found in the group of silhouettes by Thorond that date from just these years. It influenced Fuseli, too, in his mood of Beardsley, and the extremes of this fashion of hairdressing, dating from the time when he was a young man, haunted and obsessed him all his long life. It is curious, but not surprising, that No. 20 Portman Square was built for a woman, the Countess of Home. A drawing, by Adam, gives us the precise detail of the doorway and cast iron railing. It is a plain London façade of brick, with five windows, offering no clue to its interior wonders.

These can begin at the staircase, with a fine balustrade, rising, and then branching right and left, in a circular well which is elaborately painted. The back parlour or dining-room, downstairs, is a fine Adam room, but the music-room on the first floor, and the drawing-room behind it, are most wonderful in their elegance and minute detail. Drawings for this pair of rooms show the mirrors and girandoles that were designed for them. A little round ante-room and an Etruscan bedroom complete the first floor. But the music-room is particularly remarkable by reason of its wonderful ceiling, as complex and fine drawn as a spider's web upon a frosty morning, and because of the richness and intricacy of the apses for the side doors, the beautiful frieze, and the fan-like ornaments of the upper walls, from which the eyes go to the rayed circles of the ceiling, that is among the most elaborate works of Robert Adam in this class. It is difficult to arrive at any explanation of the extraordinary richness of this interior in Portman Square. The legend that Adam was in love with Lady Home is no more than a myth, for she was a middle-aged widow and died as soon after the completion of the house as 1784. The true reason would seem to be rivalry with James Wyatt, who was himself working on a group of houses only a few yards down the square. Wyatt was the most dangerous of Adam's competitors, and under that stimulus he surpassed himself.

DERBY HOUSE But this is not entirely true. Old Derby House in Grosvenor Square, dating from a year or two earlier, was in the same vein of fantastic elegance. This was the finest and most sumptuous of all Adam's London houses, 'clinquant, like all the harlequinades of Adam, which never let the eye repose a moment', as Walpole phrases it, but his old-maidish criticism in no way diminishes our longing to wander through the rooms. Our guide has to be Horace Walpole. The only other evidence comes from Adam's drawings, or the engravings in his works, for the house was long ago destroyed. Adam had been called in by Lord Derby to redecorate this house in Grosvenor Square about the time of the marriage of his son, Lord Stanley, with the beautiful Lady Betty Hamilton, daughter of the still more famous beauty, Elizabeth Gunning. We have Walpole's account of the ball given a year before the wedding, in one of his letters written to the Countess of Upper Ossory:

> The festival was very expensive, for it is the fashion now to make romances rather than balls. In the hall was a band of French horns and clarionets in laced uniforms and feathers. The dome of the staircase was beautifully illuminated with coloured glass lanthorns; in the ante-room was a bevy of vestals in white habits, making tea. . . . In six rooms below were magnificent suppers.

Adam's engravings of the second and third drawing-rooms

upstairs give us some of the brilliance of the scene. The rooms are empty; but we find ceilings like those at Home House; a wonderful mirror with caryatids, and sprightly figured arabesques for the overdoors, together with coloured ceilings, in lilac, pink, bright blue, and green and yellow. These harlequin coats and the spangled mirrors, were then bright and new. One or two of Adam's drawings for the ceilings are dated only a month before the wedding day. That is to say, on this night of the party, the house was not finished. Lord Stanley had 'burst open the side of the wall to build an orchestra, with a pendant mirror to reflect the dancers, à la Guisnes: and the musicians were in scarlet robes, like the candle-snuffers who represent the senates of Venice at Drury Lane.'

KENWOOD

Like Derby House, Roxburghe House, Cumberland House and Northumberland House are all demolished, only to be known from the great folios of the architect's drawings now in the Soane Museum in Lincoln's Inn Fields. But one other example of Adam at his best is the library at Kenwood, a room which has structural resemblance to the dining-room at Syon in Middlesex, for it has the same half-domed apses at each end, with screens of columns in front of them, only this feature is on a bigger scale at Kenwood, and the ceiling is in colours, not in white and gold. This ceiling is, indeed, one of the 'harlequinades' of Adam, and, as he describes it in his own words, in his *Works*: 'the grounds of the *pannels* and *freeses* are coloured with light tints of pink and green, so as to take off the glare of the white, so common in every ceiling till of late.' The stucco decoration of the half-domes in the apses and of the entablatures above the screens of columns in white and gold is richer and more elaborate than at Syon, the motif being a band of lions placed, heraldically, face to face, between Classical urns and antlered deer's heads. We must notice, too, the beautiful ornamentation of the bookcases along the walls, with their columns and the arched recesses that are above them.

THE ADELPHI

But we must turn from Adam's private palaces to his street architecture, an excursion shorn of most of its pleasures since the Adelphi, wilfully, and of cupidity, was pulled down. Adelphi Terrace, and its streets adjoining, formed a building project into which all four Adam brothers entered. A great mass of vaults and arches had to be raised upon the river bank to support the terrace; the project and the building operations were entered upon too hastily, and the brothers Adam, the ἀδελφοι, were involved in litigation and financial worry from which even the recourse of a State Lottery barely rescued them. Adam, himself, and David Garrick, were residents of the Terrace and occupied two of the more elaborately finished of the houses. Many others contained fine ceilings and mantelpieces; there were beautiful doorways, fanlights, balconies, and torch-snuffers; The Society of Arts, in John Street, had, or still has, its large paintings by James Barry, in one of which Dr Burney appears as a sea nymph; and, perhaps, it is possible to admire, and regret, the Adelphi, while remembering the words of Horace Walpole: 'What are the Adelphi Buildings? Warehouses laced down the seams, like a soldier's trull in a regimental old coat.'

STREET ARCHITECTURE OF THE ADAMS   Mansfield Street and Portland Place are instances of Adam houses built for sale, being, for that reason, in a different category from the Adelphi buildings. Mansfield Street has, still, at least one extremely beautiful fanlight and a fine pillared doorway with a little balcony above it. The interiors have good stucco-work, especially upon the staircases. In general, the detail is better than in Portland Place, which is later in date and, on the strength of an obituary notice, the work of James, and not of Robert Adam. The pairs of centre houses on each side, in yellow stucco, are imposing; there is one beautiful Adam doorway and fanlight, and the chance visitor waiting to see the dentist or the doctor may find a plain, but simple mantelpiece, a ceiling, or an Adam door. Two blocks of Fitzroy Square are by the brothers Adam, though built after the death of Robert Adam, with fronts of Portland stone, good, but heavy, pavilions at the ends, and in fact, in the architect's Edinburgh, or final, manner, for the houses much resemble those in Charlotte Square and St Andrew Square in the Scottish capital.

BRITISH COFFEE HOUSE   And, as postscript, there is the British Coffee House in Cockspur Street, long since pulled down, which was a favourite resort for young Scots in London. This was a miniature masterpiece by Adam, and there is an engraving of it in his *Works*. It had a shop front with pillared entrances on each side, and salons above flanked with urns in niches to suggest coffee roasting. It was 'surely an adaptation of the Porta Aurea', and Sir John Soane so much admired it that he had drawings of it made for his lectures at the Academy.

The picture is complete, but not the portrait of Robert Adam at work, for which we have recourse to Mrs Montagu in her letter to the Duchess of Portland, under date July 20th, 1779, at a time when she was decorating Portman House and indulging herself in the luxury of pitting together the rival talents of Robert Adam and James Wyatt.

Mr Adam came at the head of a regiment of artificers, an hour after the time he had promised. The bricklayer talked about the alterations to be made in a wall, the stonemason was as eloquent about the coping of the said wall; the carpenter thought the internal fitting-up of the house not less important; then came the painter, who is painting my ceiling in various colours, according to the present fashion.

BEDFORD SQUARE   There is little left in London of either Wyatt or Holland for the public to appreciate, but there remains one considerable artist, Thomas Leverton, unduly forgotten or ignored, but who, for many tastes, will rank only after Wyatt, according to whether we like the epoch in all its fanciful delicacy of gilt and stucco, or declining into the last period before the fall. Leverton, moreover, is of particular interest for his London houses. He can show us, in a single London square, all the resources of the Classic style. Leverton may be the last of our architects of the golden age, and the gilding has come down to an acorn, or the sharp leaf of a laurel. The fan, the grape, the tulip, and the hop vine, are his ornaments. His stairs are models for grace and lightness. Born within a year or two of Wyatt and Holland, in 1743, he lived till 1824, but practised little, if at all, after the last decade of the century; either because he fell out of sympathy, or because he had made his fortune and could leave fifty thousand pounds to friends and relations and twelve thousand pounds in charity. His houses in Bedford Square were built about 1775, a lovely moment in our architecture, and with the appropriate volume of *The Survey of London* (St Giles-in-the-Fields, vol. II) as guide, we may go round the square from house to house, beginning at No. 1.[1]

This has an oval dome, in the front hall, that is Leverton, not Wyatt, nor Adam. The design is fluted or umbrella ribbed, with an alternating ornament of formal scrolls and antique lamps. We shall find that Leverton, in stucco, is master of the fan. The staircase is contrived with masterly ingenuity out of the small front hall. In a back room, on the ground floor, there is an oval plaque above the mantelpiece, beautifully garlanded with ears

---

[1] It is not known how far Leverton was involved in the design of the exteriors of Bedford Square, nor in all the interiors, but those of nos. 1 and 13 seem certain to be by him.

of corn and hop vines, on a ground of blue, while the mantel-piece, itself, is carved with tripods and festoons of hops and ivy. The ceiling of the room above this has his characteristic fans in the corners, arabesques and moulded sphinxes, and painted medallions, perhaps by Zucchi, the frieze consisting of female figures holding garlands, and between fans. No. 6 has a fine staircase lantern; No. 9 beautiful wall plaques, one of which, in particular, has an exquisite garland round it. No. 10, on the first floor, has a ceiling with paintings by Angelica Kauffmann, or by Zucchi. We cannot pass by No. 11, at the corner, and not admire its admirable, plain exterior. The architect lived in No. 13; but there is a better ceiling next door. No. 15 has a rusticated Palladian door and a lovely fanlight; No. 25 a ceiling by Angelica Kauffmann and the fans of Leverton in the four corners. At No. 30 a ceiling, on the first floor, is exceptional with its outer panels of tripods and garlands, its centre fluting with sprays of hops, and the cameo paintings that surround it. At Nos. 32 and 40 there are exquisite stucco ceilings; another, at No. 44; and we come to the double houses, Nos. 46 and 47, that have façades of stucco. No. 47 has one of the best of the ceilings, with fans and urns and sphinxes; No. 50 a superb fanlight in the hall. We could continue round the corner, and admire the fanlights in Gower Street, at Nos. 68 and 84; or, were there time, we could walk to 65 Lincoln's Inn Fields for another of Leverton's ceilings, with the fans in the corners, his typical running, formal scrolls of foliage, his moulded sphinxes and antique lamps, and the almost finicking detail of his garlands tied with ribbons.

THE SOUTH-EAST

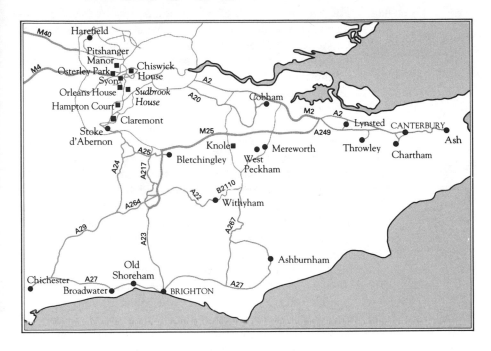

HAREFIELD The church at Harefield, which is a perfect treasure-house of monuments of all ages, has in its superabundance the tomb of the Countess of Derby by Maximilian Colt, which is a glorious hearse – a tester or four-poster stowed away, wedged in, rather, on the right side of the altar. Four pillars of touchstone, a domed canopy to represent damask that comes out again in the form of carved curtains that are knotted round the pillars. Comfortably within this bedstead, but with her feet emerging from it, lies the effigy of the lady, with long, flowing golden hair, below her waist, dressed in an immense farthingale, but no ruff, with the figures of three young girls, her daughters, kneeling below her, and the most delightful movable, or detached, heraldic objects, wherever opportunity offers. This is a monument that many persons would go a long way to see, were it better known. The painted and gilded river barges that Colt carved for the royal family have perished centuries ago, but his *Book of Monuments*, 1619, is preserved in the College of Heralds, a book made in accordance with an order of the Heralds and containing six or eight coloured drawings of the monuments under construction in one year, where one can admire the black testers or catafalques, red pillars simulating veined marbles, lying or kneeling effigies, and many coats-of-arms. Among the other sights of Harefield are the pillar tablet to a bishop of Gloucester, with mitre and coat-of-arms propped upon a pair of Bibles, cupids' heads and satyr masks, very Italian, this; and a wonderful, big wall tablet by William Stanton to one of the Newdigates with twisted columns; both specimens, moreover, being masterly in their clear lettering upon a bulbous or concave surface, a conceit dear to the Baroque imagination. The three great Attic funeral vases to the Ladies Newdigate are smaller works that are touching in sentiment and exquisite in detail, while on the outside wall of this church so full of monuments is a tablet to old Mossendew, gamekeeper by calling, and a lovely name.

CANONS The legendary Canons, near Edgware, was built for the Duke of Chandos largely by James Gibbs, but nothing but a few scattered fragments survives. The house was pulled down and sold. Its only relics were the marble steps and wrought iron rail that were moved to Chesterfield House, and now are elsewhere; the fine brick portico, moved to Hendon Hall, nearby; and the two lodges, it may be, in Cavendish Square, that headed the avenue leading down to Edgware, or so it is said, and we would believe it true.[1] Canons had every embellishment the age could offer, precious marbles, woodcarvings by Grinling Gibbons, stucco or 'fretwork' by Bagutti, painted walls and ceilings by Bellucci and Laguerre, perhaps some of the better work of Sir James Thornhill, a private Swiss Guard of eight retired sergeants from Marlborough's wars, a string band – and Handel at the organ.

CHISWICK HOUSE   On a quite different scale is the villa at Chiswick built by Lord Burlington, also a patron of Handel and, more to our purpose, the founder of the Palladian party. Under the direction of this aristocrat a band of architects swept the country and carried opinion with them. Colen Campbell denounces the 'affected and licentious works of Bernini and Fontana', together with 'the wildly Extravagant Designs of Borromini, who has endeavoured to debauch mankind with his odd and chimerical beauties'. Instead, the new model was to be 'the chaste cities of the North, Verona and Vicenza'. Chiswick was to be an adaptation of the Palladian villa, but without the vineyards or the Euganean hills. It was based upon a design which was nothing less than the warhorse of the Palladians, being a variation or adaptation of Palladio's Villa Capra, or Rotonda, at Vicenza. Colen Campbell had already given his version at Mereworth Castle, to which we shall come presently; and it may be added that, so popular was this problem, there were, in all, four specimens in England, another at Foot's Cray in Kent, lately burned down, and Nuthall Temple in Nottinghamshire, now demolished, but which was far more Rococo in decoration. This latter is, however, of much later date (1757). The domed octagonal hall, at Nuthall Temple, had a beautiful wrought iron balcony above, and on the walls, festoons of flowers and trophies framing medallions from Aesop's *Fables*. Chiswick is much more solemn, and contains one of the first copies from a Roman ceiling. Our criticism of Chiswick, as of Mereworth, is that the inconvenience and disregard for comfort laid at Vanbrugh's door apply with more truth to these Palladian villas. The *villeggiatura* of a Venetian noble in the sixteenth century, of one of Titian's senators, tempering magnificence with frugality by retiring for a few weeks in summer to a 'Roman'

[1] The pulpit from the chapel at Canons, traditionally ascribed to Gibbons, is now in Fawley church, Buckinghamshire, while its ceiling painting by Bellucci is in the church at Great Witley, Worcestershire.

villa on the mainland, was not adaptable to an England that had little summer and no vines. And the villa at Chiswick is heavy and the ceilings are too low. Yet it is fine in detail, or even splendid, if of low proportion.

ORLEANS HOUSE   Orleans House, up the Thames at Twickenham, was rebuilt for the Scottish politician, James Johnston, by James of Greenwich, who about the same time (1710) rebuilt Twickenham church. But, in 1720, the Octagon was added by James Gibbs, and this is clearly among his master works. It was built for the entertainment of Caroline of Ansbach, then Princess of Wales, and was approached by a corridor, like an orangery, used for a music-room. The Octagon, externally, is built of yellow stock brick, with pilasters of rubbed vermilion brick, and dressings of Portland stone. It has tall Palladian windows with rusticated blocks, and *œils-de-bœuf* above. The dome is internal only, with lunettes and busts. There is a splendid chimneypiece with mirror over it, and a pediment with reclining figures, perhaps by Rysbrack, and a magnificent picture-frame above. The two doorways support modelled *putti*, and medallions of George and Caroline. This Baroque masterpiece in little was rescued from destruction by the Hon. Mrs Ionides in 1927, when Orleans House was pulled down. It is tempting to think that Queen Caroline may have come here by water to enjoy the cherry gardens and the vine terraces, on board her son's barge. This State Barge, which was in use till 1849, is now in the National Maritime Museum. It was designed by William Kent for Frederick, Prince of Wales, in 1732, and 'The Queene came in the barge the first day it was upon ye water to Sommerset House'. Originally there were to have been twelve rowers, but eventually it was made for twenty-two oarsmen, eleven a side. The drawings for the decorations of the barge were carried out with meticulous accuracy. There is a sketch, too, for a waterman's costume and helmet, while in another drawing, a waterman can be seen standing on deck oar in hand, in an attitude reminiscent of the Procession of Boats at Eton on the Fourth of June.

SUDBROOK HOUSE   Across the Thames from Orleans House, at Petersham, is another work of James Gibbs, Sudbrook House, which has one of his best interiors. The cube room has five doors with architectural door-cases, coupled Corinthian pilasters, and a vaulted ceiling with *œil-de-bœuf* windows in the empty spaces. The detail is bold and noble, and there are splendid stucco trophies. Sudbrook Park, which is Crown property and part of Richmond

Park, is said to have been given by George I to the Duke of Argyll. His arms are above the fireplace, and he was the early patron of James Gibbs.

Neither Gibbs's nor Kent's work would have met with the approval of Sir John Soane. 'It is impossible,' Soane solemnly told his pupils, 'for me to impress too much upon your minds that modillions, mutules, dentils, and tryglyphs cannot be admitted into the interior of any edifice with even a shadow of propriety.' Soane, quarrelling with both his sons, because the elder of them would not make 'Restorations' of the 'Ruins' at Ealing during his spare time at Cambridge, an offence which he carried a stage further by 'becoming engaged' as a result of an excursion 'to one of those watering places where young ladies are to be found who are in haste to be married', dedicated his Memoirs, despairingly, to his grandson: 'To you, my dear child, I dedicate these "Memoirs" trusting that my success will be to you a stimulus and my mortifications serve you as beacons.'[1] None of the family, of course, became architects. Mr Bolton recognises Mr Pecksniff in Sir John Soane; and it could, indeed, be Soane, and not Pecksniff, whom Dickens makes address his new pupil as follows:

PITSHANGER MANOR

There are a cartload of loose bricks, and a score or two of old flower pots in the back yard. If you could pile them up, my dear Martin, into any form which would remind me on my return, say, of St Peter's at Rome, or the Mosque of St Sophia at Constantinople, it would be at once improving to you and agreeable to my feelings.

The 'Ruins' were in the grounds of Pitshanger Manor, and Soane continues, mournfully:

They were sources of amusement to the numerous persons visiting this place, particularly on the three days of the Ealing Fair. . . . On those days it was the custom for our friends to visit us by a general invitation, and it was not unusual to entertain two hundred persons to a *déjeuner à la fourchette*; many of whom, after contemplating the ruins and drawings, communicated their sentiments on the subject, which created a constant source of intellectual enjoyment. . . .

But 'the character of the place has been destroyed and the

---

[1] We are indebted for these quotations to the extraordinarily entertaining little guide to Pitshanger Manor, by Mr Arthur T. Bolton, late Curator of the Soane Museum in Lincoln's Inn Fields. Only rarely can so much information and amusement have been combined in a sevenpenny guide.

former Gothic scenes and intellectual banquets of Pitshanger are no more'. Pitshanger Manor, which was the country villa of Soane, is now the Ealing Public Library. It was built by George Dance the younger but largely rebuilt by Soane and exhibits the architect in a fantastic mood of elegance, as though wishing to compete with Adam. The entrance front recalls Adam's garden front at Kedleston, while the dining-room has arched windows, with arched alcoves opposite; an apse at one end with doors on either side and a ceiling of triangles and rectangles. On the first floor, one of the rooms has a ceiling of astonishing delicacy, a sort of combination of the Classical and Rococo, like Adam at his lightest, with octagonal panels backed alternately with fan-like ornaments, and in the middle of the octagon a round shape like the nimbus of a waterlily, with a spread of arabesque and acanthus round it. This is one of the most delicate of all designs in stucco, and proves of what he was capable when he so wished it.

SYON HOUSE

Adam's own invention and imagination is shown nearby, at Syon House. But let us first recall that the house is built into the cloister of a house of nuns founded by Henry V in the year of Agincourt. This was the only abbey in England of Brigittines, an order of Swedish origin, and a foundation immensely favoured by the Kings and Queens of England. Its income of £1,750 was the largest of any nunnery in England, and at the Suppression no fewer than fifty-one nuns, four lay-sisters, twelve monks, and five lay-brothers were given pensions.[1] We read of the Lenten store for their *refectorium* in the year 1481-2, which includes salt fysshe, stokfyssh (dried cod like the Portuguese *bacalhau*), white heryng, rede heryng, muddefissh, lyng, aburden, Scarburgh fysshe, salt samon, salt elys, a barrel of honey, and figs – with, later in the same year, a kilderkin of good ale, 15 lb of almonds and 39 Essex cheeses. In Lent also they ate dried fruits, particularly almonds, raisins and figs, these latter being made often into little pies like mince pies called rischewes, or russheaulx, the same word, in fact, as rissoles. That curious word (and confection) of Anglo-Norman invention – it means less than nothing in French – blancmange also makes its appearance. Syon had a famous library and a tradition of learning. The nuns, too, came of aristocratic families, Strick-

[1] The last abbess Agness Jordayn had the huge pension of £200 per annum, and her sepulchral brass is not far away in the church of Denham. But most of the nuns of Syon went abroad, first to Belgium, then to Lisbon, where they stayed nearly two hundred years, and are now (since 1861) at South Brent, Devon, our only living link with the nunneries of pre-Reformation England.

land, Scrope, Nevill, Bourchier, Tresham, and it is only for a relief from the tragedy of its fate and extirpation, with the execution of the chief of its priest-monks for refusing to take the oath of supremacy to Henry VIII, that with these nuns in mind, at dinner, young and old, we read of the table of signs drawn up for their convenience. These were to enable them to obtain what they wanted without breaking the rule of silence. Such practice was apparently nothing unusual but obtained in many convents. One who wanted fish would 'wagge her hande displaied sidelynges in manere of a fissh taill', and wanting milk would 'draw her left little fynger in maner of mylking'. For mustard the sign was to 'hold her nose in the uppere part of her righte fiste and rubbe it', and for salt to 'philippe with her right thombe and her forefynger overe the left thombe'. There were over a hundred signs in all in this dumb crambo, and great must have been its humorous openings, both purposeful and accidental. Impossible, indeed, to end this paragraph without quoting from the mediaeval cookery book which tells how to cook herrings:

The white herring by the bak a brode ye splat him sure,
Both roe and bones voyded, then may your lord endure to
eat merily with mustard,

adding, it may be, stewed eels and rice, hog's sowse, rissoles in their early and unfamiliar form, and for envoi quaking blancmange; and so to bed, and lights out, with no more talking until 2 a.m. and the cold night stair!

At Syon, in Adam's own words, the 'idea was to me a favourite one, the subject great, the expense unlimited'; and we would add that this house, the plain exterior of which is so dull and unprepossessing, is among the greatest works of art in England. The gateway with its little colonnades and porter's lodges is almost too elegant: 'all lace and embroidery, and as croquant as his frames for tables' (this is Horace Walpole speaking), and the white entrance hall we find uninteresting, but, perhaps, on purpose, for the ante-room leading out of it is as superb as any Roman interior in the palace of the Caesars. Its decoration consists of twelve columns, and as many pilasters, of verde antique, dredged, appropriately, from the bed of the Tiber, and ransomed by Sir Hugh Smithson, first Duke of Northumberland of the new creation, for a thousand pounds apiece. These verde antique columns have gilded Ionic capitals and neckings, and bases of white marble with gilt enrichments.

The entablature above the columns has a honeysuckle frieze in gold on blue, which brings out the yellows, reds and blues of the scagliola floor. Another feature of this ante-room is the two gilded, military trophies upon the walls, like paintings by Chirico, but played in serious. In admiring this Roman vision of a room we must remember what Mr Bolton points out, in his great work on Adam,[1] that the ante-room was never a living-room but a waiting room for servants out of livery, the hall being occupied by servants in livery in attendance. Walpole, inevitably, gives us further information: 'they (the Northumberlands) live by the etiquette of the old peerage, have Swiss porters, and the Countess has her pipers,'[2] and also, we could add, their fool or jester in his cap and bells, until 1798.

The dining-room, in white and gold, has an apse at either end, with pillars in front of it, and a good Adam ceiling, not too light or filigraine, in white and gold. This is the ordinary Adam; but the red drawing-room, next door, is a rich and beautiful masterpiece in another manner. The walls are hung with plum red silk, woven in Spitalfields, on which the pattern of flowers and garlands makes an effect of silver. The coved ceiling, flat in the centre, and divided into octagons and little diamonds, is painted by Angelica Kauffmann, like so many little cameos in gilt and coffered surrounds; and the pink and yellow carpet designed by Adam, woven and signed 'T. Moore', is exactly appropriate to the walls and ceiling. There are gilt console tables with ram's head masks and fretted legs, and there is a mantelpiece of ormolu and white marble, as fine, but different, in workmanship as the steel grates of Kedleston. Mr Bolton compares this 'to an overdress of brass lace thrown upon the white marble form', and there are magnificent doorways of mahogany with gilded panels, and pilasters and entablatures of gold on cream, in the Italian Renaissance manner, not unworthy of the doors in the Ducal Palace at Urbino.

The gallery leading from this is Adam's adaptation of the great gallery of Elizabethan or Jacobean houses, with bookcases along its length, low ceiling richly wrought, and arabesque panels in stucco upon the walls, entirely, here again, in the manner of the Renaissance. Few, indeed, are the critics, brought blindfolded into this long gallery of Syon, who would know it for the work of Robert Adam. At each end of the gallery

[1] A. T. Bolton, *Robert and James Adam*, London, 1922.

[2] The Northumbrian, not the Highland, bagpipe.

there is a little room contrived in the thickness of the turret: one of these little boudoirs or closets being circular, with a domed roof and columns, and with shelves for china; while the other is square, with Chinese paper on the walls, and held a collection of drawings and miniatures. From the centre of the dome, in the round closet or boudoir, there hangs a gilded bird cage of beautiful design.

Adam's full fantasy is apparent, too, in a project for a bridge over the canal at Syon, of which there is an engraving in his *Works*. This is a bridge of three arches, with a balustrade and lamps, and caryatids at every bridge pier who are holding up a long stone garland in their hands. We should also visit Isle-

ISLEWORTH

worth church, beyond the park gates, to admire Francis Bird's Hogarthian or Handelian mural monument to Sir Orlando Gee, a superb presentment of a man in a periwig, and framed in an architectural composition of pillars that have twisted bases.

OSTERLEY

After Syon it is natural to move to Osterley, near by, than which nothing could be more different. At Osterley we find ourselves, for once, admiring an exterior by Adam, or, at least, it is his portico or 'propylaeum', a screen in front of the court-yard and leading to the entrance. But the interior of Osterley is nothing comparable to Syon in fantasy or imagination. We may admire the State bed by Adam, but not want to sleep in it, and be impressed by the suitability of his furniture in the room made for the Boucher tapestries, but, in our own time, we cannot be taken by the novelty of his Etruscan room, which was, in its day, an entirely new departure. Far preferable, to our taste, is the Etruscan room at Heveningham in Suffolk, designed by Wyatt and carried through by Biagio Rebecca. But the happy invention of Adam is proved at Osterley in a Doric Orangery and a semicircular conservatory with high, round arched Venetian windows and coupled columns in between them.

HAMPTON COURT

Hampton Court is beyond argument the most historic and delightful of domestic buildings in the whole of England. Cardinal Wolsey's palace had been enlarged by Henry VIII, but it must have become dilapidated when William and Mary decided to rebuild it. Several schemes were drawn up by Wren, and only the death of Queen Mary prevented the pulling down of the greater portion of the Tudor palace. The great Tudor gallery with its bay in the centre was demolished. On the other hand, the new palace was not finished when King William died, and it was completed by Queen Anne, and by George I and II.

William Kent was employed here by the last of these monarchs, after whose death the palace has remained empty. Even so, in its two portions, the Tudor and the rooms by Wren, we may gather the sensation, respectively of reading Shakespeare and then discovering the refinements and elegancies of Pope's *Rape of the Lock.*

The building material of Wren's portion is a thin, mulberry brick, of exceptional quality, with coigns and ornaments in Portland stone. We first come upon the hand of Wren in the colonnade of the second or Clock Court, a stone colonnade of coupled columns with a balustrade of urns and trophies, in fact, a guard room in which it is impossible not to post, in imagination, the grenadiers of King William's reign, in their white gaiters, pipeclay, scarlet coats, and half sugarloaf hats, with powdered pigtails. A pair of sentries are on guard and, almost, we can hear their companions talking. How English is this Classical architecture compared with Bernini's Scala Regia at the Vatican, where the Swiss Guard are on duty! The doorway leads directly to the King's Staircase, designed by Wren, with walls and ceiling all painted in one huge composition by Antonio Verrio, and a wrought iron balustrade from designs by Jean Tijou.

But we continue into the Fountain Court, where we observe a certain monotony in the sameness of the windows, round three sides. This court is the nearest equivalent to an Engish cloister, and recalls Eton, or an Oxford college. The fourth side is lower in elevation, so as to allow more light, and being but a corridor, its two floors are given more fanciful treatment, as though it were an enclosed, or red brick version of the colonnade. This gallery connects the King's and Queen's apartments; and the set of portraits of the ladies of Charles II's court by Lely known as the 'Windsor Beauties', hang upon the walls. The interior of Wren's palace is divided in fact into two separate ranges of state apartments for the King and Queen, the King's Side and the Queen's Side, facing different aspects of the gardens, and each with its guard room, presence chamber, audience chamber, and state bedroom.

But we have climbed the King's Staircase, among the gods and goddesses of Verrio, and passing through the King's Guard Room, where the Yeomen of the Guard used to be on duty, traverse his state apartments, and find them uninteresting till we come to his State Bedroom and Dressing-room, both with ceilings by Verrio. On our way the 'Hampton Court Beauties' by Kneller do not distract our attention like Lely's beauties of an earlier reign. Passing into the Queen's apartments we shall find two more painted rooms; the Queen's Bedroom by Sir James Thornhill, painted for George I; and the Queen's Drawing-room by Verrio, with painted ceiling and walls like huge tapestries, Prince George of Denmark on the one, as Lord High Admiral of England pointing to the Fleet, while, opposite, Cupid is drawn by sea horses in a water chariot and the English Fleet rides at anchor in the distance. The Cartoon Gallery is the finest room by Wren, built for the cartoons of Raphael; and in the Queen's Guard Room there is a mantelpiece where the supporters are a pair of Beefeaters or Yeomen of the Guard. The sculptor has been most apt in this instance, for the Yeomen of the Guard in their Tudor uniforms must have been very appropriate to Hampton Court, and perhaps we should note that George II, the last King to live here, took them with him as his bodyguard to the field of Dettingen in 1743, the last occasion on which the monarch has appeared in person on the battlefield.

There is an influence in the interior of Hampton Court that we have not met before. It is that of Daniel Marot, a French Huguenot craftsman who worked for William III in Holland, and was brought by him to England. Marot drew designs for almost everything that could be imagined, but his influence appears, particularly, in the shelved mantelpieces for the display of china. Marot, as we state, a Frenchman, had become Dutch in deference to his patron, as can be seen in his decorations at the château of Voorst, in Holland; while Wren, as we may see in his delightfully detailed drawings from the All Souls collection, contrives to give a frieze and cornice, to a doorway or a mantelpiece, much of the Dutch manner. This, with the help of Grinling Gibbons, for Grinling Gibbons worked here, as did Gabriel Cibber, but the chief works of the latter were the stone vases for the gardens.

This brings us to the two garden fronts of Hampton Court. Both fronts have a centrepiece of Portland stone. The east façade, facing the Great Fountain Garden, shows 'The Triumph of Hercules over Envy', in the pediment, by Gabriel Cibber. For ourselves we admire, in particular, the two enriched windows of the south façade, above the Orangery, lovely compositions and identical, with a bold stone surround to the lower window and a carved mask as keystone, above which our pair of windows have a conventional ornament like a wreath or spray at their base, and then, above the window, there is a pediment heaped with flowers on which a pair of amorini are treading while they hold up an escutcheon, this being the work, again, of Gabriel Cibber. The wrought iron gates of Tijou, twelve in number, stand down by the river like an ornamented screen to remind us of such felicities as the river barge in *The Rape of the Lock*; or, indeed, of a band playing upon a barge as in the case of Handel's *Water Music*. This ironwork is the absolute embodiment of its age. It is as personal as the tread of the courtiers, the cut of their clothes, or the accent of their voices.

CLAREMONT Claremont, near Esher on the Surrey side of the Thames, was built by Vanbrugh for the Duke of Newcastle, but this is another of his houses that has been destroyed. It consisted of a recessed central body and two huge, solid wings, each with four towers, all in Vanbrugh's round arched, round windowed manner, and from the engraving quite plain and without ornament. It contained at least one splendid room, but Claremont was perhaps more famous for its gardens and pavilions, some of the latter in plain Classic, and others in this round arched mediaeval manner.

STOKE D'ABERNON Three or four miles away, at Stoke d'Abernon, is one of the earliest examples of a military monumental brass, dating from 1277. Sir John d'Abernon lies in a complete suit of interlaced chain-mail, the mere engraving of each link of which, in the words of one authority, must have cost many weeks of patient labour. He wears pryck spurs upon his heels, and a guige or shoulder belt, ornamented with roses and with fylfots, which in fact are swastikas, supporting his shield. And, for contrast, we

BLETCHINGLEY go to Bletchingley, where we are halted by the most splendid of all the architectural frontispieces in England. All things considered, the Clayton memorial is the finest monument of the Baroque in England. It is by the previously unknown sculptor, Richard Crutcher, who was Master of the Masons' Company in 1713. Apparently not even the dates of his birth or death are yet known. Sir Robert Clayton, who was Lord Mayor of London, is standing in his robes, a scroll, probably denoting his generous gifts to St Thomas's Hospital, in his left hand. At his side stands his wife, a most perfect presentment of the dress worn by a lady in the reign of Queen Anne. Between them, at their feet, lies their only child, one of the most beautiful little children in the whole art of sculpture, and instinct in every fold of its lace dress, in every curl of its hair, of the age of Queen Anne. But the pathos of the monument is that this same child had died no less than forty years before, and Mrs Esdaile has traced this baby to an effigy upon the floor of the vestry at Ickenham, Middlesex, where some other sculptor, name unknown, has carved it as dead, eyes closed, and wrapped up in the clothes in which it will be buried. The background of the monument is an immense inscription in curving lines, as upon a parchment or whole sheepskin, with cherub heads above it, and the whole gathered up into a knot or fold. But the architectural composition in which the statues are framed is really and truly magnificent, and one of the splendours of the age. It has two pairs of Corinthian pillars, one advanced and one retired, flanked by flat pilasters to the outside, so that each face of the monument has one project-ing and two retiring cornices, and above, a splendid broken pediment of the richest moulding. The effect of this is that the Lord Mayor and his lady, with the inscription at the back exposed to uninterrupted view between them, have each a position or corner to themselves in the angle of the pillars, much as though they were standing close to the footlights in the old architectural tradition of the theatre, near to the painted scene. The balance of the monument is completed by a weeping cupid at each corner, or we could call them foundling cupids or poor children, foster-brothers to the sleeping babe that lies between. The ascension or balance of the 'piece' is made perfect by this device, so that the eyes range from the outside cupids to the niche of pillars, to the statues, the playing cornices, and completing finish of the coat-of-arms at top. In its Corinthian manner that is, yet, not Roman at all, and still less Italian, but only English and of Queen Anne's reign, the Clayton monu-ment is one of the most entirely satisfying works of art in the whole kingdom. Not mentally great, or portending more than what it says, but a delight to the eye, musically perfect, that is to say, harmonious in detail and proportion, and a wonderful example of stage sense or of the art of presentation. On the merits of this one monument alone it is strange, indeed, that so little should be known of its mason and sculptor, Richard Crutcher.

KENT

CANTERBURY The way is now open over the chalk hills to Canterbury, only rather more than a half day's ride or walk by copses thick with primroses. Hop-fields are already in being and oasthouses in embryo, and the quincunxes play among the hop-poles as we go slowly past. It is one of the holy places of England of which in folk memory there are for campanili the pale blue spires of 'Canterbury Bells'. But the sound of bells was louder then than now. The cathedral which rose out of the ashes of the former building and which is, in fact, the third church to stand on the same site, is not by personal taste the most exciting or beautiful of English cathedrals. Perhaps because being so typical of them it represents the average or ordinary, remembering always when thinking more of individual persons, that the pattern or archetype can become extreme and exceptional in virtue of that very quality. So Canterbury is the English cathedral *in excelsis* with its Bell Harry Tower rising above the cricket fields of Kent, actual or hypothetical; and with Canterbury cricket week in mind, as close to and as much a part of them as the Moorish Giralda of Seville Cathedral which moves its shadow across the bullring during the bullfights of the Feria. Peculiar to Canterbury is its double set of transepts. The great central tower of Canterbury was added by Prior Goldstone in 1495, a late work comparable to the Perpendicular tower of Fountains in Yorkshire, the work there of Abbot Huby, and, like that, one of the glorious church towers of this, our native style or vernacular. The nave, too, of Canterbury is Perpendicular, finished under Prior Chillenden (1391-1405), though without fantasy in the form of fan vaulting or other fanciful excesses. A note of severity, with unfortunate after-effects in mid-Victorian times all the way from Manchester and Liverpool to Sydney and Bombay, is struck by the choir of Canterbury begun by the Frenchman, William of Sens, in 1175 and built of Caen stone shipped from Normandy. But he fell from a scaffolding and left Canterbury only three years later and his plans were completed by William the Englishman who succeeded him as architect.

Flights of steps lead up from the choir to the Trinity Chapel, also the work of William the Englishman, and here stood the shrine of Thomas à Becket, murdered in the cathedral in 1170. The jewels, the vestments, the reliquaries and other works of art accruing to Canterbury owing to his martyrdom are all gone, treasures that accumulated for three centuries after his burial here in 1220, until Erasmus, visiting the shrine in 1512, could write of it that 'gold was the meanest thing to be seen'. We are left with Becket's Crown, the circular chapel or Corona beyond the choir at the far end of the cathedral, which contained a fragment of his skull and still holds the 'Chair of St Augustine' or Archbishop's Chair. And on the east side of the Trinity

Chapel we have the tomb of the Black Prince, with his heraldic surcoat, gauntlets, shield, and helmet hanging above in romantic panoply; and things as unique to this country and as English of definition as the fan vaults in the ceiling of the Angel Steeple, Bell Harry Tower under its other name, a geometrically exact unfolding or opening of no fewer than eight fan-shapes of stone all fitting into the square, as intricate a work as any of Moorish or Mudéjar craftsmen, and a contraption which appears to fold in on itself at any moment with a shutting and a snapping of stone slats.

Several churches in the villages around Canterbury contain ASH   fine monumental brasses. At Ash, the memorial to an unknown lady offers the most extreme instance of the horned headdress of CHARTHAM   the Middle Ages, while at Chartham the brass of Sir Robert de Setvans, bare-headed, has a peculiar fascination by reason of the pair of fans upon his shield and the 'seven fans' displayed upon his person; but, and here comes the poetic touch, they are in fact fans of wickerwork for winnowing corn. What has been judged the 'finest collection of brasses in the country', at COBHAM   Cobham, includes one to Sir John de Cobham, a knight in full armour who is carrying a model of the church he built; in the same church is the painted 'altar' tomb of Lord Cobham and his wife, that compares in execution with the Howard tombs at Framlingham in Suffolk.

THROWLEY   Of slightly later date, from the end of Queen Elizabeth's reign, is the tomb at Throwley, on which two pairs of figures, man and wife, kneel facing one another, hands joined in prayer, one of the young women in ruff and farthingale (Margaret Lady Legh, at Fulham church, excepted) being the prettiest figure of a woman in all our early Renaissance sculpture. In two villages in this same neighbourhood there are tombs by Epiphanius Evesham. This exquisite craftsman and delineator of children is another of the discoveries or rehabilitations of Mrs Esdaile, a master who was all but forgotten until she recognised his signature from a single sentence in Walpole, and it emerges that he was born in Herefordshire and was, in view of his chosen profession, surprisingly, of gentle blood. His BOUGHTON-   elaborate alabaster monument to Sir Thomas Hawkins, dating UNDER-BLEAN   from 1618, is in Boughton-under-Blean;[1] while the Teynham LYNSTED   monument of 1632 is at Lynsted. And we conclude at West WEST PECKHAM   Peckham, where is another work that could be by Richard

[1] One of the four Kentish villages named Boughton; the others are Boughton Aluph, Boughton Malherbe and Boughton Monchelsea.

Crutcher, whose Clayton monument we admired at Bletchingley. This, without architecture, and but a simple canopy of
looped-up curtains, shows Leonard Bartholomew and his wife,
leaning, back to back, he in the clothes and periwig that he
wore in life.

MEREWORTH   In the next village we are back with the Palladians in the
person of Colen Campbell, who was the architect of Mereworth. Campbell, in fact, was first in the Palladian field, while
Kent was still studying in Italy, or painting halls and staircases
in England. Walpole – it is inevitable to quote from him –
writes of the wooded park of Mereworth, 'broke, like an Albano
landscape, with an octagonal temple and a triumphal arch'.
This is the earliest of the English copies of the Palladian villa,
but it should be remembered that whereas Lord Burlington only
intended Chiswick, outside London, not as a residence but to
house his works of art, Mereworth was to be a country house, a
full day's journey from the capital. By some curious alchemy it is
entirely appropriate to the Kentish scene, as much adapted as
Castle Howard to its Yorkshire vale, and eloquent of the same
great age of architecture. The exigencies of the plan, a round
domed building set into a square, have cramped the subsidiary
rooms into the corners; but how delightful is Bagutti's plasterwork in the hall, and how splendid are the porticoes! Upon a
summer day, from June to August, you may look right through
Mereworth, in at one portico and out through the pillars of the
other, while the smaller rooms in the angles seem contrived for
shade and cool. Unfortunately, we do not see the building as it
was designed for Lord Westmorland, when it was moated and
set in the water, when the grotto rooms were perfect, and the
stables and lesser buildings were laid out to plan. There is also a
mid-eighteenth-century parish church at Mereworth, a delicate
and graceful design with, as Mrs Esdaile notes, its 'lovely,
Wren-like spire, and amazing fan-like portico'.

KNOLE   Knole, nearby, is one of the most famous of the great English
houses, but it is an old and lovely range of building, more than it
is fine architecture. There is in fact not much of architecture
about it, compared with Spain, or Italy, or later England. It has
some of the best plasterwork, on ceiling and mantelpiece, in the
whole kingdom. But it is unrivalled in its furniture and
contents. Brocaded and cut-velvet beds of James I; costume
portraits of that curious age by Mytens and Van Somer; wonderful silk or velvet chairs in quantity; and silver furniture of the
reign of Charles II. But not great architecture.

SUSSEX

CHICHESTER The red brick 'vernacular' style of Christopher Wren is to be seen in two houses at Chichester which could have been designed by the great architect himself.[1] The pleasures of such red brick buildings come from the warm glow and neatness of the brick, in contrast with the white joints of mortar. We may be reminded of pictures by Van der Heyden, who painted brick architecture so meticulously that we may count the bricks, yet he never tires or fidgets, and is among the little masters even when his subject is a cobbled street. But the two little houses at Chichester are incomparable. One, in West Street, has pineapple gate piers – the pineapple, we may remind ourselves, had just come to England. There is a delightful painting by Henry Danckerts of Mr Rose, the Royal gardener, on his knee, presenting the first pineapple ever grown in England to Charles II. It is one of the best likenesses of Charles II, wearing the suit of brown that he affected, very tall and swarthy, much like a Habsburg or Medici, with two of his black and white King Charles Spaniels or Cavaliers frolicking at his feet – the other house has a pair of dodos, they can be nothing else, upon its gate posts; while both houses are of that red brick building that is one of the delights of England.

And, in the neighbourhood of Chichester, we should pause BROADWATER at the headstones in Portland stone at Broadwater, Sompting, OLD SHOREHAM or the altar tombs at Old Shoreham, with their honeysuckle ornament, cupids' heads, and festoons of flowers. Among the more elaborate monuments in Sussex, is the Sackville tomb at WITHYHAM Withyham by Cibber, with a mother and father kneeling beside their dying son, the kneeling mother resembling a lady from a ASHBURNHAM Terburg or Metsu painting. And at Ashburnham is a characteristic work of John Bushnell: William Ashburnham kneels, stretching out his hands towards his dying wife, and the same device is used as in the same artist's statue to Lord Mordaunt in Fulham church of four pedestals, like lamp burners, supporting globes and helms and coronets, while the statues stand up on black marble slabs. Bushnell remains in his few works an extreme exponent of the Baroque in England, but a sculptor more curious than successful, and never graceful, in his monuments.

[1] Wren House and Dodo House (also known as Pallant or Swan House) have been attributed to Wren, but there is no evidence that they are by him.

WESSEX

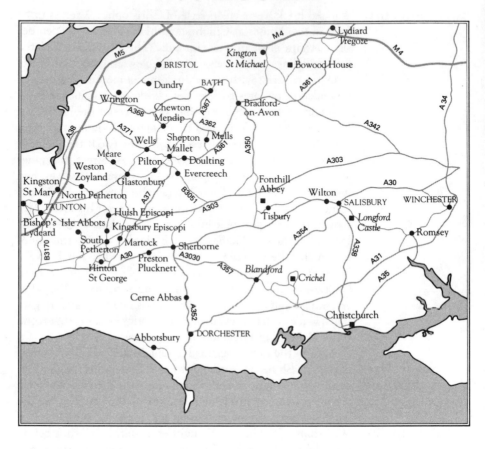

Winchester Cathedral Priory, a most venerable and ancient Benedictine foundation, is only not of the order of Durham or Ely, perhaps because of a more salubrious soil or setting away from, alike, the gales of the sea-coast and the mists and dampness of the East Anglian fens. But Winchester is marvellous for length of nave, largely, in the state in which we see it now, the work of the famous Bishop William of Wykeham; for its Perpendicular altar screen; but above all, for its chantry chapels, which are here in unrivalled number, several of them sited on the feretory or raised platform behind the reredos which was intended for the display of relics. Exceptional, too, and wonderful are the carved and painted ceiling-bosses in the nave at Winchester. As minute and intricate as Japanese *netsuke* carvings, and more to be admired than those, they show the arms of Bishop Waynflete and the Beaufort portcullis with much else beside, but are indeed only revealed in their full detail through a pair of opera-glasses.

Of the monastic buildings, there is only the site of the cloister and nothing left of the chapter house. But there are the choir-stalls which are of very early date, around 1300, darkened by the centuries and architectural of form as though their traceries were from the drawing board, and of an angular disposition and correctness. They are not, that is to say, particularly adapted for woodcarving, though their two-light arcading, and floreated and very pointed arches are of rich effect. The chantry chapels are to be seen ranged along both inner sides of the choir and along the south aisle, no less than nine of them in all. Three of them are outstanding. The chapel of that pre-eminent cleric, William of Wykeham, who founded New College, Oxford, as well as Winchester College, is the pattern of its kind, marvellous in elegance and lightness of design, and the embellishment not the obstruction of the space in which it stands. Filling a whole bay of the nave, with a two-tier grille of stone lights, then rising above that to a great height of emptiness, masked by slender pillars so that it forms a high three-light window with pinnacled hoods above that, that touch upon the clerestory. Within the chapel is the bishop's tomb, with three canons as 'weepers' sitting at his feet.

The chapel of Bishop Waynflete, founder of Magdalen College, Oxford, stands in the choir. It has an enclosure of three-arched openings, and an openness and emptiness above that, crowned on its exterior with great array of cusped canopies and niches. It is not as fine in conception as Bishop Fox's, which is on the south side of the choir. His is the perfect stone cage, to the degree that it could have been assembled or built outside, carried bodily into the cathedral and set up there. In its elegance it looks more portable than permanent. It is in two storeys; the lower built solid without openings, the upper of traceried window finished as to its top with pinnacles and crenellations like an ornamented chest, and with countless niches now statueless, save for the pelican feeding its young, which was Bishop Fox's emblem, both on the exterior and within. In a space to itself in the retrochoir is Cardinal Beaufort's chantry chapel. This most notable of English clerics with Thomas à Becket and Cardinal Wolsey, and ablest of the three – indeed the most able of the Plantagenets after the death of Edward III, since Henry of Agincourt, his great-nephew, was a fighting soldier, more than a great general – was the illegitimate son of John of Gaunt and Katherine Swynford. He was Bishop of Winchester for four decades, was made Cardinal and Papal Legate, and died in 1447. He was a Shakespearean character, dear to scholars of Shakespeare, so that he appears in paintings and drawings by the romantic Fuseli and might well, though in fact he does not, have a part in some Verdi opera. His chapel, as to its upper part is a maze of pinnacles and niches, with a great emptiness below that with low, indeed knee-high balustrading; and the high empty vault where his effigy but not the original can be seen, under fan tracery, but not of the first order of elegance or skill in execution. One carries away from Winchester Cathedral a very strong image of the English tomb-chambers which in their elegance give a lightness and ornament which yet do not detract from the solemnity of death.

A royal palace at Winchester was begun by Charles II, for which plans by Wren still survive. A street, two hundred feet in breadth, with nobles' and gentlemen's houses on both sides, was to lead from Winchester Cathedral to the palace. The frontispiece was of four Corinthian pillars and two pilasters. The centre was two hundred feet, and three hundred and thirty with the wings, which were joined by a colonnade. The staircase led to the great guard hall, with a filade of sixteen rooms, nine of them to the ending of the wing. There were to be three cupolas, two on the wings and one on the middle, high enough to see the men-of-war riding at Spithead. Two chapels, one for the King and one for the Queen; two piazzas; a terrace; a park of eight miles in circumference; and, beyond that, a forest without hedge or ditch. It is all gone. The Duke of Bolton begged the marble pillars given by the Duke of Tuscany, and all that was left was made into barracks after a fire in 1894.

CHRISTCHURCH   At Christchurch, not very far from Winchester, the whole church was, for once, retained for worship at the Suppression, with three storeys of male Norman arches for its nave. Here lies buried almost the very last of the Plantagenets, the unhappy Margaret Pole, Countess of Salisbury, who was daughter of the Duke of Clarence, and so niece of Edward IV. Her brother the Earl of Warwick, the last legitimate male of the family, had been beheaded by Henry VII, simply because of his origin, as early as 1499. She survived until 1541 when Henry VIII had her brutally beheaded, a harmless old lady who was more than seventy years old. Her son, Cardinal Pole, as a Catholic had taken the dangerous step of denouncing the King's marriages, as a result of which all his family including his mother were attainted. He was thus in some sense responsible for his mother's death, but escaped that fate himself by living abroad, though he returned in Queen Mary's reign to become last Catholic Archbishop of Canterbury, and dying in 1558 achieved safe burial in the cathedral. His headless mother lies still buried in the chapel at the Tower where she spent two years imprisoned. Her chantry chapel at Christchurch, though Gothic in its exterior arcading, is touched by the Renaissance and positively Tudor in its lower portion. Over that, above blind arcading, are two tiers of four-light windows. Within, despite the depredations of Thomas Cromwell and his Commissioners, there is an extraordinary and coffer-like richness of ornament. Three canopied niches rise up the wall; and the whole ceiling of this small, bath-room size cell or chapel is cobwebbed with fan-like spreads of stone though, as has been pointed out, it is not really a fan vault but of fan implication or suggestion,[1] and with a splendid, if mutilated carved boss in the middle of the ceiling, representing the Coronation of the Virgin. This little chapel with its heraldic devices and broken or chipped badges is the latest or last relic of the Plantagenets, and of a richness more to be associated with for instance the Cathedral or the Cartuja of Burgos, than with this former house of White Canons in the Hampshire meadows. But, at least, the

[1] 'Fan Vaults', by F. E. Howard, in *Archaeological Journal*, LXVIII, 1911, pp. 1-42.

King and Queen and the Infanta who lie buried in the Cartuja were this unfortunate lady's near relations, and there were many things they had in common.

ROMSEY

Romsey Abbey, where the Norman church with splendidly masculine choir of triple storeys of rounded arches is still in use, was a house of Black Nuns; with ninety nuns living in it early in the fourteenth century but only about a third of that number at the Surrender. Romsey is the largest of the nuns' churches that survive.

WILTSHIRE

KINGTON
ST MICHAEL

It could have been of any of these nunneries, but it was in fact of that of Kington St Michael, his native village in Wiltshire, that John Aubrey writes:

> Here ... the young maids ... learned needlecraft, the art of confectionery, surgery (for anciently there were no apothecaries or surgeons – the gentlewomen did cure their poor neighbours: their hands are now too fine), physic, writing, drawing, etc:

And in the words, almost, of one who could remember them, he continues:

> Old Jacques could see from his house the nuns of the priory come forth into the nymph-hay with their rocks and wheels to spin. He would say that he had told three score and ten, but of nuns there were not so many, but in all, with lay sisters and widows, old maids and young girls, there might be such a number. . . . This was a fine way of breeding up young women, who are led more by example than precept; and a good requirement for widows and grave single women to a civil, virtuous, and holy life.

SALISBURY

The spire of Salisbury, built towards the middle of the fourteenth century, is of ever to be recalled effect and prominence as one comes towards it from any direction over the downs. The setting, alone, puts it apart; and, conversely, the spire must have been conceived and designed especially for its particular background. Which we accept as normal; but in the dearth of descriptions of England by foreign travellers, it would be good to know the effect of this strange category of landscape scenery upon a sensitive and trained intelligence of alien blood. It is undeniable that the presence of Stonehenge upon the plain adds a primitive solemnity and strangeness both to first impression and to lasting memory. There it is, the great spire of England, seen from several miles away over the shoulder of a hill rising to more than four hundred feet above the roofs of the town. Or it can be the spire, just the spire, coming up out of the distance; the basic and for all time specimen of its kind; at once the unconscious pattern and cynosure of spires from every corner of the kingdom, and of a hundred villages and market towns. The proportions of it from far away are arguable, but not obvious. Like many works of art it is both gigantic and of ordinary size. Only on getting nearer is its huge stature to be apprehended; and in intimacy on emerging from the chapter house into the cloister. There it is, before our eyes, soaring up higher than the lark sings up above the downs; if, on nearer sight, a little dulled by copying itself over again as if not completely sure of itself in both storeys of its bell-chambers. It has turrets at the corners, and above that the octagonal spire starts up banded at three places, as though to keep itself to-gether for its leap into the air. I have been told that a family of falcons have nested up there from time immemorial, perhaps ever since the spire was built, though one cannot see any opening into that needle-thin stone structure. Perhaps it is below, in the bell-chamber that they have nested, but one would like to think of them up there where once there was human foothold, before the last scaffolding was taken down and the spire left alone in the wind and rain. Salisbury spire, with the stone circle of Stonehenge and the still stranger Avebury not far away, has some aura of sheepfold simplicity about it as though it is the dunce-cap spire coming out of the plain in Blake's woodcut illustrations to Virgil's *Pastorals*.

Salisbury, thanks to Wyatt, an architect and decorator of immense talent in his own field, but of fatal tendency when allowed to interpolate or sweep away, is no place in which to look for choirstalls, and the cloister and chapter house are lucky to have escaped alive. But the beauty of the cloister derives not so much from the cloister itself as from the cedar trees in its midst and the view of the incomparable spire from different angles along its walks. Even so, the chapter house has been to some degree 'hospitalised', i.e. by excessive zeal and scruple cleaned and cleared out until it appears empty of itself and more apt for the beds of a dormitory than for a synod. It is octagonal in plan, with many-shafted central column spreading out its

spandrels across the ceiling, pointed and uncomfortable-look-
ing sedilia along its walls under tall trefoil windows, but with a
beautiful two-arched and cusped entrance of noble effect. And
there is little left now of the cathedral's many former chapels.
The Hungerford and Beauchamp chapels were removed on
order from the dean and chapter, but there remains Bishop
Audley's chapel dating from early in the fifteen hundreds, with
balcony and cornice and half-cornice reminiscent of some
temporary pavilion put up from which to watch a tournament or
coronation procession. In particular, the columns at either end
and in the middle, rising above the chantry as though they are
sockets intended to hold flags or banners, give strength to this
illusion. Originally the vault of this chapel was painted, with
'deep blue panels shaded to green, and the ribs left plain except
for the fillets, which were gold'.[1] The heraldic bosses were
subtly dealt with; and in one of them the leaves of the roses and
the pomegranates were painted and gilded.

Emerging from the cathedral, we see Mompesson House, in
the quiet cathedral close, a beautiful example of Bucolic style
and manners. Is its name connected, one wonders, with Mr
Mompesson and the 'Drummer of Tedworth' in that most
curious of poltergeist hauntings?

WILTON   A few miles further distant we come upon the magnificence
of Wilton House, built for Lord Pembroke by Inigo Jones,[2]
wherein we may think ourselves in the unrealised interior of
Whitehall Palace, particularly, surrounded as we are by Van
Dyck's paintings. A good deal of the work of Inigo Jones at
Wilton has been destroyed, but there remain the state rooms
on the first floor with all their decorations, including the
Banqueting Hall and the Double Cube Room, a double cube of
sixty feet by thirty feet, with the frames designed by the
architect for Van Dyck's portraits. One entire wall is occupied
by the immense group of the Herbert family, containing ten
figures, and forming the most considerable portrait group ever
painted by the master. Here are the Cavaliers, made immortal,
even when we remember the haste with which Lord Pembroke
joined the other side. The mantelpiece in the Double Cube
Room is entirely splendid and of a heroic boldness. There are
splendid doors with broken pediments, and the wall panelling is

[1] F. E. Howard, op. cit.

[2] The building of the south block of Wilton involved, also, Isaac de Caus,
who worked with Jones at the Banqueting House, and, after a fire in 1647 or
1648, John Webb.

divided by great gilded swags of fruits and flowers, tied up with ribbons. The coved ceiling is painted, neither well nor badly, while a word of praise must be spared for some gilt furniture by William Kent which is exactly appropriate to Inigo Jones, his adored idol. The whole effect of the room is white and gold. For a comparison with the Double Cube Room we have to go to Italy, where the nearest equivalent is in the state rooms at the Pitti Palace, in Florence, that were frescoed and designed by Pietro da Cortona. The two are in fact contemporary, and perhaps both suffer from the same defects, of too much magnificence and too little feeling. No room like this had been built before in England, but it has moments, almost, of bad taste. The carving is heavy and not equal to the best Italian and there was no Pietro da Cortona to paint a fresco on the ceiling. We feel this to be the precursor of other heartless parade-rooms in the golden manner. But the time lag is abolished. English architecture has caught up with its foreign model and is no longer provincial and barbarian. As in so many other instances, in all the arts, nothing that came later ever surpassed the original. We may criticise the Double Cube Room for lapses of sensibility, but it may be that these are inseparable from rooms of state. They are softened, at least, by the proportion of Inigo Jones and the pencil of Van Dyck.

In the park at Wilton is the Palladian bridge, one of the most beautiful ideal structures imaginable, for which credit must be given to the ninth Earl of Pembroke, an amateur, even though he had the assistance of Roger Morris, a professional. This must be compared, for beauty, with Vanbrugh's Temple and Hawksmoor's Mausoleum in the 'pyramidal woods' of Castle Howard; and for a state of mind, with Vanbrugh's bridges at Castle Howard and Blenheim. Needless to say, Lord Pembroke had formed his taste in Italy. There is an oft-quoted, probably apocryphal, remark made by Canova to the effect that he would return to England, at any time, if only to look upon St Paul's, Somerset House, and the interior of St Stephen's Walbrook. The Palladian bridge at Wilton would have made his journey worth while from London into the country. It is the realisation of a project by Palladio that Palladio never executed; an architectural problem in double profile, as it were, the mystery consisting in how to accommmodate a colonnade, between a pair of porticoes, upon the three arches of a bridge. There were the frontal views to be considered, too, together with the architectural sensibilities of the person standing on the balconies at either end, or among the pillars of the colonnades. The solution is a structure so ideal that it has become mysterious, and far from being inhabited by Arcadian nymphs and shepherds its proper analogy is to Picasso's visions for the *Metamorphoses* of Ovid, wherein the bearded Ancient is a god reclining by a horizon that circumscribes the whole Mediterranean in a line of water, and the contour of the nymph could be blue-eyed Arethusa or the cumulus of white cloud upon a Classic day. But this Palladian bridge possesses, in itself, the gift of metamorphosis, for at Prior Park, near Bath, where it has been copied exactly, the poetry is quite other, and Virgilian.

LONGFORD CASTLE Longford Castle is not far from Wilton, and here, the wonderful paintings, one by Rubens, in particular, confer a distinction upon the house when it is in reality more curious than beautiful with its triangular plan and three towers at the corners. And there can have been few houses more worth FONTHILL ABBEY visiting than Fonthill Abbey, built by Wyatt for William Beckford[1] – if only for its perfumed coal in gilded baskets! – but how cold and haunted it must have been! – haunted, when brand new, and while the gangs of workmen were employed night and day upon the walls! haunted, when Nelson came to visit it; haunted the day the great tower fell down!

BOWOOD Wyatt's great rival worked at Bowood in the northern part of the county, though the house was altered, but not improved, by Barry. The Marquess of Lansdowne, who owned Bowood, was anxious that Adam should reproduce some portion of Diocletian's palace at Spalato, an awkward request of a sort that must be familiar to authors as well as architects, and Adam, selecting that portion of the palace which faced the harbour, complied with an Orangery which originally was a great portico upon the Adriatic. This is still called the Diocletian wing and has been preserved, although the main block at Bowood has been demolished.

LYDIARD TREGOZE At Lydiard Tregoze, a few miles beyond Bowood, the church has an array of masterpieces of superb craftsmanship. The north

---

[1] We learn something of Wyatt's reputation when we read in Farington's *Diary* that: 'Beckford is much dissatisfied with Wyatt, who perpetually disappoints him. He said if Wyatt can get near a big fire and have a bottle by him, he cares for nothing else.' And we add this postscript from William Windham: 'PS. Am I to expect the metal frames which you ordered in Sheffield will come at last when they are no longer wanted: or am I to understand only that what you told me is untrue, and that no such order was ever given?' Such dilatoriness on the part of the architect was so different, we may feel, from the diligent, untiring Adam, whose plans, perhaps even whose finished ceilings, would be ready almost before you realised you had ordered them.

side of the chancel is almost entirely occupied with a vast painted panel of all the arms of the family, arranged in the form of a family tree, with a female portrait in a roundel above. This opens to show a large painted family group. There is as well a kneeling pair of painted figures of Elizabethan date under a Corinthian canopy, slightly reminiscent in attitude and execution of the Hoby monument at Bisham in Berkshire. There is a 'conversation piece' of a Mompesson husband and wife sitting opposite to each other, and on the north side of the chancel is the superb 'Golden Cavalier' of Edward St John, in his bright gilding unlike anything in England, with painted figures on the curtains. But it is the great monument to Sir John St John which is most remarkable for its size and nobility, even though it is difficult to envisage it in its closely set gilt railings. Under a vast canopy lies the figure of the Lord in Cavalier armour, and slightly lower on each side are the figures of his two wives, one of whom holds a marble baby. Reminiscent, in their fine execution, of the Savage monument at Elmley Castle, in Worcestershire, and, it may be conjectured, by the same hand. There are eleven smaller figures of sons and daughters, some kneeling, at each end of the monument, sons at the head, daughters at the foot, one, like the elder Savage boy, with her hand upon her heart. Others are in roundels beneath on the sides of the tomb, including two small figures holding skulls. The four small Baroque statues, probably allegorical, at the corners of the canopy, are instinct with life and vigour.

DORSET

A beautiful feature of all this west of England are the monastic barns which are found nowhere else in Europe, being especially peculiar to this region, it has been suggested, because of the good building stone, the better climate, and the agriculturally richer monasteries. They are not to be met with in East Anglia or in Lincolnshire or Yorkshire, but only south-west of a line drawn between Birmingham and Brighton; farm buildings as they could be seen through the eyes of a painter of pastorals like Samuel Palmer, or in the woodcuts of pastoral scenes by Edward Calvert, subjects of strict limitation to a particular locality, dialect-pictures, even, of a countryside as of a poet writing in patois. Once seen, one knows them so well with their stone buttresses and stone-tiled roof, their high porches and the glorious 'ships' timbers of their ceilings. They are temples of Ceres of a peculiar and most English poetry inseparable from the landscape, even from the chalk figures on the downs. The monastic barns are scattered so widely over the west of England that it would hardly be possible to know them all; but how ABBOTSBURY beautiful is the great barn of Abbotsbury, where the Black Monks owned the swannery and made profitable commerce from quill pens and swan's down.[1]

SHERBORNE Sherborne, an ancient Benedictine abbey is still in use, and marvellously preserved with the lierne and fan vaulting of its ceiling. Here, the nave vault has ceased all vegetative resemblance and is undeniably made up and composed of fans. They are half fans, half wind vanes, and at the same time are shaped just like one half of the 'funnel' which you use for pouring liquid from one vessel into another. Their edges touch on one another, not altogether comfortably, and then there has to be a composed design of stone lozenges and quatrefoils to fill in between the fans spreading out towards each other from both edges of the ceiling. This vault was, again, coloured, the choir having panels of chalk and ribs of yellow Ham Hill stone, while the bosses in the nave and transepts were picked out in gold and colours.

CRICHEL To end, however, upon a note of fantasy and enchantment, we describe a work of art which is attributed, on no certain evidence but that of style, to James Wyatt. This is the dining-room at Crichel. It is, indeed, one of the loveliest of eighteenth-century rooms, not only in England, but of the whole of Europe. It is the doorways in the dining-room that yield the name of Wyatt, for with the painted lunettes over them they so much resemble the doors at Heveningham, in Suffolk. But this is a higher and bigger room. The walls have large painted ovals by Rebecca, framed in stucco garlands, light and graceful, that reach from dado to ceiling. And it is the painted and stucco ceiling that is superlative, in the soft Atlantic, quasi-Celtic light of Dorset. The corners of the coved ceiling have umbrella-like ornaments, like the section of a tent or parasol; and thence the cove continues with painted medallions between moulded candelabrum ornaments, in relief, that are

---

[1] Besides the great monastic barn at Glastonbury there are others at Bredon and Middle Littleton in Worcestershire; Frocester and Stanway in Gloucestershire; Doulting, Pilton, and Preston Plucknett in Somerset; Tisbury and Bradford in Wiltshire; Cerne in Dorset; Buckland and Torre in Devon; Enstone and Great Coxwell in Oxon; to which list we put again Abbotsbury. The barn at Tisbury, the largest of them all, belonged to the nuns of Shaftesbury.

joined by garlands. The flat of the ceiling has a large central garland, with intersecting circles and diamonds, and little painted medallions, as subjects to themselves, with little pairs of moulded sphinxes, back to back, above them. The walls of the room are a pale straw colour. The wall paintings are in blue-grey; and the colours of that exquisitely beautiful ceiling are green and white, with purple for the background of the painted medallions, and white for the stucco ornaments and the moulded candelabrum. The ceiling at Crichel, together with Adam's stucco ceilings at Syon, Mellerstain, Saltram, Osterley, and at 20 Portman Square, reached a height of finesse and delicacy which it is obvious will never be surpassed. They are among the beautiful things of the world of human beings, even though they are no more than coloured plaster.

SOMERSET

BATH It is earlier in the eighteenth century, and Bath is rising, street by street, in circles, in hemicycles, and in squares. The Woods, father and son, are the architects. The elder Wood, of local origin, was working in Bath in 1725, or soon after, an early date for the construction of such buildings. Their uses had been foreshadowed by Wren in his scheme for the rebuilding of London after the Fire, and Lincoln's Inn Fields, King's Bench Walk, the Middle Temple, were really essays in this manner, but in general their style was Dutch. Their pattern was the red brick houses along the canals of Amsterdam. At Bath, Wood made use of the local stone, and his treatment was the strict Palladian, or Classical. Queen's Square and the North and South Parades are among the earliest of these buildings, but space is lacking to follow up this architecture, bit by bit. Wood's own house, No. 15 Queen's Square, has the stucco-work by the brothers Franchini, who worked, also, in Ireland;[1] on the very Rococo stair is a framed panel of St Cecilia under an archway, and, in odd contrast on the other wall, the flaying of the satyr Marsyas by Apollo. The elder Wood was master, also, of the grand manner, for which it is only necessary to see Prior Park, built for Ralph Allen, with its Corinthian portico, and the vale pouring down like a cornucopia to the Palladian bridge below.

[1] They worked at Carton for the Duke of Leinster and at the Rotunda Chapel in Dublin. The staircase of 15 Queen's Square has been sold and is now in an American collection.

Far to the north he also designed the admirable Exchange at Liverpool.

The younger Wood built most, but not all, of the other monuments of Bath, for there were lesser architects like Thomas Baldwin. But he was responsible for the Royal Crescent and the Assembly Rooms, and he finished the Circus designed by the elder Wood. Lansdowne Crescent, however, was designed by John Palmer. The Crescent, high above the town, is well known from the Rowlandson print of fat men and women blown about in a high wind and chasing their wigs down the steep slope of the hill, also for its memories of Beckford, for his house still stands there, with its niche in the hall for the dwarf Pedro. And there is Adam's Pulteney Bridge, with shops on either side, which could be likened to a Classical interpretation of the Ponte Vecchio at Florence. Bath is the pattern of an age of order, and of a spiritual state in which it was quite impossible for the horrors of our time to happen. No person of an open mind could deny it, as he looks upon this architecture and the contagion of good building spread from Bath to Bristol, and to the smaller towns and villages nearby.

But the pastoral Arcadia of Somerset is to be explored in the late fifteenth century and early sixteenth century, and for prelude there is the fan vaulting in Bath Abbey where, indeed, considering its location in the West Country it would have been curious did it not appear. Both the choir and choir aisles have the fan treatment, the effect of which is like a recurrent dream of Palm Sunday. For they are palms, palms, and hardly fans at all. Less so, perhaps, in the choir aisles where the bosses, hanging down from stone roundels at the intersection of the fans, detract from this fantasy-marriage of Palm Sunday with the palms standing in corners of a Late Victorian conservatory and drawing-room.

Those years around 1500 were the time when the local wool trade was as valuable as in Suffolk or on the Yorkshire Wolds. There arose a direct competition, for it was little less than that, between villages and small market towns in the matter of church towers, to which perhaps the only living equivalent in our day has been the rivalry in Balinese villages over their gamelan orchestras and their troupes of dancers. There have been times in human history when equivalent fevers of creation have seized upon certain areas of population, and I am not thinking of Saturday football results. Something of exactly the same nature was happening in East Anglia in just the same years, but in Somerset it was the towers chiefly and particularly; while in Norfolk and Suffolk it was flint flushwork, immensely long naves lit with many windows, angel ceilings, and much else besides. In Somerset it has been estimated that there are fifty, or thereabouts, fine towers; and that they can be divided into three or four groups which, luckily, cohere together because each group tended to work out its own problems as though in competition, not against each other group, but in friendly rivalry among themselves.

The 'play', so to speak, or cup of contention was in matter of arrangement and display of windows and in the cresting and parapeting of towers, though never in the sense of aerial grandstands, or for choir-singing on May Morning. Not even, I think, particularly for convenience in hearing the church-bells, but only and simply to be looked up at and admired, with the details of other nearby church towers held in mind, and ready there to be compared. One group is near Wells; another group lies south of that, below the Mendips; while the other towers are in the Vale of Taunton. Within the limits of play it is certainly extraordinary the variety that could be worked into their towers; it being, also, an important feature that there were different building stones, sometimes even within the same small area, and that therefore the towers are to be judged by colour, too, and not only for their outline, disposition of windows, diversity in arrangement and display of pinnacles, and so forth.

MELLS
CHEWTON MENDIP
WRINGTON

Starting south-west from Bath, spread out fanwise over an area of some fifteen to twenty miles, are the towers, from east to west, of Mells, Chewton Mendip and Wrington. All three towers being in the neighbourhood of Wells, are of the type of the parish church of St Cuthbert, Wells, which church in that cathedral city seems to have been the pattern; long rectangular panels, that is to say, of blind arcading and bell-chamber above that, all expressed in restraint and calm. The beauty of the villages of Mells and Wrington is marvellously set forth and enhanced by their Perpendicular church towers. A few miles

EVERCREECH

south-east of Wells, and east of Glastonbury, is Evercreech which has another of these sedative and quiet towers, designed for confidence and calm in villages of thatch and beautifully coloured stone.

A second group of only slightly different character and detail lies a few miles from Yeovil, its fame deriving from the towers of Isle Abbots, South Petherton, and the matching, yet con-

ISLE ABBOTS

HUISH EPISCOPI
KINGSBURY
EPISCOPI

testing twins of Kingsbury Episcopi and Huish Episcopi. Isle Abbots looks to be a model of its kind winning on all points possible in this pastoral or Arcadian contest of towers, and South Petherton I have not seen. Huish and Kingsbury Episcopi, to write of them as brothers – and they are but a mile or so, or, as it were, a year or two apart – have indeed but the vaguest of facial differences by which to distinguish them and tell them apart, and one would have to run from one to the other repeatedly in order to feel at all certain as to wherein these differences lie. A few words of description of Huish Episcopi must suffice. Built of blue lias, a phrase which a little belies or exaggerates the visual truth, like its companion it is within a few inches of a hundred foot high; it has a large west window of four lights over its west door; ringing-chamber above that with three-light windows, and two-lighted bell-chamber; the whole, buttressed to this height with three tiers of attached pinnacles, diminishing and clasping the tower closer at each tier. Roof platform, nothing spectacular, but nicely pinnacled with quatrefoil battlement for rail. Huish and Kingsbury Episcopi are probably the most beautiful and typical of the Somerset towers, and are so beautifully matched as to be an architectural and aesthetic satisfaction, more than a sensation, in themselves.

NORTH
PETHERTON

BISHOP'S LYDEARD
KINGSTON
ST MARY

TAUNTON

A third group of towers is round Taunton, and includes North Petherton – the best part of twenty miles away from South Petherton – Bishop's Lydeard, Kingston St Mary, and St Mary Magdalene in Taunton itself. North Petherton, in fact, much resembles the Episcopis, if it is a little taller, and its tower is more richly parapeted and made into more of an aerial feature.[1] Both Bishop's Lydeard and Kingston are of red sandstone, of which latter village – and it is not inconsequent to the beauty of its church tower – the Arcadian fame was its Kingston 'black apple' from which a dark or even blood-red cider was produced; 'and it was the custom till within the last few years for rustics on Christmas Eve to go to every orchard and sing to the apple-trees to make them abundantly fruitful'. The tallest of all the towers is St Mary Magdalene at Taunton, which is one hundred and sixty feet high and rebuilt, moreover, but in exact copy, in Victorian times, except that the material is pink sandstone in place of the original grey stone. Above the five-light window over the west door there come two storeys of

[1] The tower at Probus, in Cornwall, strictly of Somerset type, closely resembles North Petherton, and were they set down side by side away from their villages it would be difficult to tell one from the other.

identical three-light windows, with bell-chamber over them which has still taller windows; the whole flanked by buttresses as high as the bell-chamber where they divide into tall pairs of pinnacles set at an angle to the wall. Where they stop, just below the parapet, there is an awkward thinning which makes top-heavy the exaggeratedly tall roof-pinnacles that in any case project themselves awkwardly as though thinned and then broadened out to no purpose. The top of the tower at Taunton, is, at once, too heavy and light; too large and looming, and yet pierced with openwork so that it is like a transparent crown. [1] The high detached pinnacles that balance themselves on the backs of projecting gargoyles add to the confusion of points and cusps, and are as though acrobats had been brought in to balance billiard-cues or other things of the sort upon their heads.

MELLS But it is at Mells that we find the extreme melodic beauty in local architecture, where, that is to say, it has the perfection of line and form of folksong. For the pale golden stone of Mells is unsurpassable. The church tower is indeed a thing of wonderful beauty which would be famous were it in any other country but in England. There is certainly no minaret, and I have seen most of the famous minarets of the Muslim, to compare to this. Its only sisters in beauty being the other Perpendicular towers to be seen in different parts of England. The architect of Mells, whoever he may have been, was the master of elegiac repose and calm, the attributes most needed in a living monument to the dead, if a church is to be something more than a mere charnel house of bones.

WELLS There can be no question that in every respect Wells is unique in this country, and the only rival in the West of England to the trio of Ely, Lincoln, Durham, that are the architectural wonders of the eastern region. Indeed, its chapter house is a work of art that can hold its own with any other in Europe of whatever date. It is a sensation in itself that it is approached, as you turn leftward before reaching the choir, by and under the inverted or strainer arches inserted to hold the weight of the tower in 1338-40, a feat of original genius that made a virtue out of necessity. The conception is of a boldness that puts the triumphs of twentieth-century engineering to shame. The arches, four sets of them to form the quadrilateral shoring up

---

[1] A tower that has manifestly that of St Mary Magdalene at Taunton well in mind is at Dundry, at the other end of the county, built as a landmark on a hill above the Bristol Channel.

the tower, rise from the floor with their brave mouldings, each pair of them intersecting in the manner that the larger branches of a beech tree of rare instance can grow through or into and out of one another, and continue upward on their course. In fact, in giant form they are as a pair, four pairs indeed, of bent trunks that have been trained and inculcated in this manner. And in the spaces left empty by their arching are huge pairs of round *ocelli*, like great portholes, with the same simple mouldings. But it is better still to put off entry into the chapter house until one has seen the Lady Chapel which is in the apse of the church behind the choir. It forms five sides of an octagon, but the play and interplay of its supporting columns – they are clustered columns – develops a theatrical richness and diversity of effect as one moves between them, and prepares one for the shock of entering the chapter house.

The chapter house has another prelude or fanfare which is the staircase leading to it. This is incomparable of effect and as a prelude, with its plantation or grove of wall columns all around, and age-worn steps. And so to the right into the chapter house, the mere entry into which is a sensation of the first order. It is a marvellous but frozen palm-house of organic growth, arrested, but still dormant and nourishing itself on air and water. The central column and its spreading palm-ribs hold the eye, but the chapter house is octagonal and as many more of the fan-trees of the oasis sprout and spread themselves upon the walls. But there is a static orderliness about this arboreal growth. All is trimmed and kept to order and proportion. This central shaft or bundle of columns, tied in with base and capitals, has thirty-six ribs rising in parabola from it towards the ceiling and the pollarding or lopping of its foliage. Round the octagon, beneath this arboreal springing of palm-ribs from all around, are tall two-light and trefoil windows and the stone seating. There is no surer or firmer conception and sensation in any stone archi-tecture than in the chapter house of Wells, which like its Lady Chapel can only be from the hand of a master.

It is an added satisfaction at Wells that there should be at least two chantry chapels worthy of their setting. Bishop Bubwith's chapel is set down in the nave like a beautiful little portable stone birdcage. A little blind arcading at waist height, and then just filling the bay in which it stands, up to the capitals of the clustered columns, graceful and light arcading, a two-light window in depth, and a pair of those longitudinally on each side of the fretted door-arch. Over that a graceful cornice for frieze and elegance of finish, and Bishop Bubwith's chantry could be raised on castors and wheeled away.

Dr Sugar, who was treasurer of the cathedral, built his chantry across the nave, and in little it is incomparable in richness, and a lesson to those modernists from Mies van der Rohe downward who are frightened and run for their lives from ornament. Here, their motto 'less is more' is flatly contradicted. The canopies of the five-fold or quintuple canopies on the interior wall, and the incipient fan or spray or inverted sun-burst rising from the middle one of the canopies in the midst of a vertigo of mini-ornamentation, with carved cornice after cornice above that, and here and there on the exterior and among the fans and other devices of the ceiling, the doctor's rebus of three sugar-loaves under a doctor's cap, are a lesson in delicacy of touch and a light and fearless hand.

GLASTONBURY   From hereabouts it is no great distance to Glastonbury:

> We assure your lordship [this from the Commissioners to Thomas Cromwell] that it is the goodliest house of that sort that ever we have seen ... a house mete for the kinges majesty and for no man else; which is to our great comfort. ... The house is greate, goodly and so pryncely as we have not seen the lyke; with 4 parkes adjoynyng ... a great mere well replenished with greate pylce, breme, perche, and roche; 4 faire manour places belonging to the late abbott, the furthest but 3 myles distant, beyng goodly mansions.

The end was swift and merciless. Abbot Whiting, accused of hiding treasure and being in possession of treasonable literature against one or other of the King's divorces, was tried and condemned. And dragged on a hurdle with five of his monks from the gate of his abbey through the streets of Glastonbury, and hung on a gibbet on Tor Hill. His severed head was then put above the abbey gate.

Only a few days before this Cromwell writes in his memoranda: 'The plate from Glastonbury, 11,000 oz. and odd, besides gold. The furniture of the house of Glastonbury. In ready money from Glastonbury, £1,100 and odd. The rich copes from Glastonbury. The whole year's revenue from Glastonbury'. Who, then, was the robber? And why should it have been Abbot Whiting who was hung on the gallows on Tor Hill? Glastonbury was the most sacred ground in England with a sanctity going back to pre-Christian times, the Apple-Tree Isle or Isle of Avalon of Arthurian legend. The skulls of King

Arthur and Queen Guinevere who were buried here, were on occasion put outside the shrine for the devotion of pilgrims. The incalculable treasures it contained disappeared almost overnight; and of monastic buildings, the George Inn apart – the old pilgrims' hostel built by Abbot Selwood with the arms of Edward IV over its gate, supporters the black bull of Clare and the white lion of Mortimer – what is there left which is not a ruin except the Abbot's kitchen, buttressed and lanterned, impressive in scale and ingenious in internal arrangement, for the manner by which the four fireplaces in its angles make the interior into an octagon? How beautiful was the sacred isolation of the Isle of Avalon! The Abbots of Glastonbury had a summer

MEARE house a little way away at Meare, where is the prehistoric lake village, on an island in a lake variously described as covering five hundred acres, or five miles round. There is, also, the Fish House where lived the abbey fisherman, and a field called Pool-reed where the abbots came by water and their boats were moored. The village could only be reached by a horsepath till Victorian times. The Apple-Tree Isle was in the middle of the reeds.

HINTON
ST GEORGE
There are other marvels in the churches of Somerset. For an instance, the Poulett monuments at Hinton St George, one of which pertains so entirely to the Baroque that it could have been transferred bodily from a church in Valencia or Palermo. Upon a floriated chest or sarcophagus, supported on lions and held at the corners by a hairy satyr, or 'wild man', and his mate, stands a figure with outstretched wings in the act of ascending into the heavens, under a swag of flowers and a draped curtain. Above, a pair of cupids, seated on the cornice, hold a crown above a coat-of-arms, and to either side there are the tapering columns and fluttering cornices of Sicily or Spain. Mrs Esdaile ascribes this strange monument to the seventeenth-century Bristol school of carvers, and it is significant that Bristol was the great seaport of England and that not a few of its population may have been to Portugal or Spain.

Then there are the timber roofs, less complicated of structure than those of East Anglia, if no less detailed in execution. Another kind of carpentry altogether is involved. These are 'waggon-roofs'; and if only Gypsy caravans were not now things of the past it would be easy to see why they are so called because

SHEPTON MALLET such a ceiling as that of Shepton Mallet does closely suggest one type, if one type only, of Gypsy caravan construction, though curiously enough it is not the interior ceiling of the caravan that it suggests so much as the exterior roof under which the Gypsies moved and lived between the hedges. In any case, it is a flat form of roof construction the placing of which must have entailed more hammering and less noise of sawing, much nearer to the *artesonados* of Spain than to the double hammer-beams of Suffolk and Norfolk.[1] There are winged angels, priests or presbyters along the cornice but they hardly obtrude, and although they have spread wings, seem flightless. But there is, also, the other type; of which the best specimen may be that of

WESTON ZOYLAND

Weston Zoyland of the delightful name, as to the latter part of it, which seems to contain in itself the local accent, and may recall to some readers that occasion when Pepys goes down to Somerset and teases the villagers in order to hear them speak. At Weston Zoyland the angel hierarchy are busy in the ceiling. There are tie-beams resting on the heads of angels, but they are the lesser of the tie-beams, and the larger, resting on full-length angels, carry the kingposts. In fact, angels are pressed into service to hold up the ceiling. In addition, fluttering in the middle of the tie-beams are angel figures, wings aflap, and reminiscent of the angel-rookery of March in Cambridgeshire, where you could almost listen in the silence and hear them moving on their nests, and if not their laughter, then, at least, their cawing.

[1] Numbers come into it again. On the 'waggon-roof' of Shepton Mallet are 350 panels and over 300 bosses, all of them different; while at Martock, on a tie-beam roof with kingposts, there are 768 panels in all, with only six different patterns repeated. If numbers do not make works of art, they on occasion do not impede them. Cf. *North Somerset and Bristol*, Harmondsworth, 1958, by Nikolaus Pevsner; and *Churches of Somerset*, London, 1952, by A. K. Wickham.

WESTERN ENGLAND

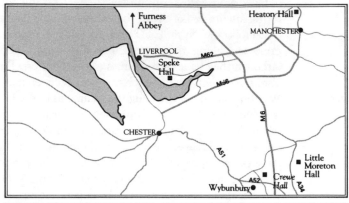

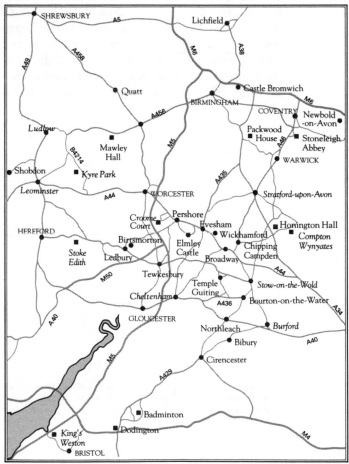

GLOUCESTERSHIRE

KING'S WESTON

The journey northwards up the western side of England begins at a group of houses in the neighbourhood of Bristol, starting with King's Weston, the most compact of Vanbrugh's houses, for it is a single block, merely, without wings, but betrays the architect by the huge dimensions of its Corinthian frontispiece built, apparently, for a patron who could not afford a portico, and by the characteristic device, used nowhere else, of linking together the chimney stacks and raising them into the air to form a square arcade, the effect of which is curious and singular more than beautiful.

BADMINTON

Badminton, for all its air of splendour in its twelve-mile belt of trees, has the tradition of being but a temporary residence, for the Somersets intended to build better. We can read, in Sir Roger North, of the extraordinary state kept by the first Duke of Beaufort. We can see Kip's print of its formal gardens, and read of its long avenues laid out, even over the neighbouring estates. The house was built in the reign of Charles II, but probably altered or recased by Kent, who made some alterations in the interior. There are some mantelpieces from his designs; the entrance hall, resembling that of Houghton, may be due in part to him; while it is tempting to identify his hand in the bold rustication of the entrance door. Three miles in a straight line from the house lies the Worcester Lodge of Badminton, set back in the great verge of trees. This is the open deer park down which we see the coaches driving in one of the pair of paintings by Canaletto, that were the first he ever did in England. The stone Lodge is the work of Kent, and a triumph of Palladian architecture in England. it consists of a room above an archway, beautifully decorated with stucco mantelpiece and ceiling within, and intended for supper on summer evenings. The arch has a short curtain wall on either hand, ending with a pair of little cottages or pavilions that have roofs shaped into a pyramid, in rough, Cyclopean style, forming an exact and appropriate ornament among the trees.[1] The English genius for park buildings, in which they rivalled the Italians with their fountains and their statues, is proved in the Worcester Lodge; and should we continue but a mile or two further down the road on which it stands, will be exhibited again in the circular,

[1] The pyramidal roofs may be a reminiscence of Vanbrugh's kitchen court at Castle Howard.

pillared lodges to Dodington, designed by James Wyatt after the pattern of the Roman temple of Vesta at Tivoli. We look through the archway of the Worcester Lodge, across the misty park, to where the Palladian house lies in the distance, and perhaps may imagine a typical scene in the last century, when its cold, aloof architecture would be enlivened by a joint meet of the Beaufort and Old Berkeley on the lawn before the house, when the blue and buff of the Beaufort followers would mingle with an occasional red coat from a neighbouring pack, and with the canary of the Old Berkeley.

DODINGTON   Dodington was the latest of Wyatt's great Classic houses, being finished, largely, after the turn of the century. We have already mentioned the circular lodges quite typical of his Classic manner, but Dodington, with its enormous Corinthian portico, is neo-Greek, and no longer eighteenth-century. It has a great hall and staircase with ingeniously inlaid marble floor; most of the rooms, which have fine doors and friezes, are carried out in gold and white; and Christopher Codrington, the wealthy West Indian landowner who was his patron, built a chapel attached to the house in an early Italian Renaissance manner, where Wyatt shows reminiscences, too, of St Mary-at-Hill, or other of Wren's City churches which have a Greek cross for plan, with a dome at the intersection. Another feature of Dodington is the dairy and stables by Wyatt; indeed the whole scheme, which involved its owner in enormous expense, shows Wyatt attending to the smallest detail.

GLOUCESTER   It was at Gloucester, the veritable cradle of the Perpendicular, our national style, that the fan vault was invented, in the cloister of the Benedictine abbey which is now the cathedral. In the cloister, 'with its stone winnows or fans forever opening along the cloister walks', though truth compels one to add that this is far from being the best of the fan vault ceilings. It is, even, rough and rudimentary both in design and execution, and far from rivalling as do its successors the 'apiarist work' of the Alhambra or of Isfahan. But the cloister ceiling at Gloucester contains the germ or beginning of the idea, and development was bound to follow in this fertile age. So it is with the multiple branching from the stems or columns in the Lady Chapel up into the ceiling, the design of which is much complicated by the roof-bosses which proved an irresistible temptation to the mediaeval craftsmen, even if the detail was all but invisible to those below. It is perhaps fair to say, then, that the fascination of the cloister at Gloucester lies more in its appurtenances or fittings than in its fabric, for does it not contain the fan-vaulted *lavatorium* for the monks with the stone troughs for the water, and even the towel-cupboards at the corners? Not only that, but the most complete set of carrels or reading cubicles set along the cloister walks, no fewer than twenty of them, but such incidental detail does not equate with beauty, and Gloucester is not a beautiful cloister. The fan-vaulting makes the abiding interest of it; but it is for indoors, not for the sun and shade.

Of another order are the cathedral's marvellous east window whether or not, but let us have it 'yes', in memory of Crécy, its 'fern-Gothic' canopy for murdered Edward II, and the awe-inspiring figure of Robert Courthose, Duke of Normandy, eldest son of the Conqueror, whose warrior form, of Irish bog-oak, and therefore of a material or substance prehistoric in itself, lies, hand on swordhilt, his mailed and coroneted head resting on a pillow, ready to rise up from his tomb, by clock-work, half-draw his sword, and lie back again.

TEWKESBURY   The grandest and most important of the western monasteries was Tewkesbury, an old town where the Severn and the Avon join one another, which is not without poetic and symbolic significance and portends at least that it is right in the middle of historic England. The abbey is still overwhelmingly impressive, and an extraordinary instance of the innate military manner of the Norman conquerors transmuted to other purposes, and this in the meadows and orchards of Gloucestershire, a county which in the Middle Ages was even famous for its monk-made, sweet red wine. Among its other beauties are three chantry chapels; the Fitzhamon Chapel built by the monks in his honour two hundred years after his death for he had been a personage of utmost importance, a cousin of William Rufus, of odd repute, and Lord of Tewkesbury, Bristol, Gloucester and Cardiff; a chapel correct in every particular, and leading on to greater things. To the Warwick Chapel built by the widowed Isabella le Despenser for her husband Richard Beauchamp, Earl of Worcester and Abergavenny, who was killed in the wars with France. It is in two storeys; the lower, once again, being delightfully irregular and varied in its height of stone screening; its base of blind panelling with figures of angels in the guise of mourners holding shields of heraldry. Above are open canopies ending in crown-like cornices, while the upper floor has an elaborately pendentive and almost stalactite ceiling.

But the great and abiding fascination of Tewkesbury is the chapel of Sir Edward le Despenser, who died in 1375, built by his widow; and not even so much the chapel, with its two-arched windows of five lights, as the canopied niche or tabernacle on the roof of the chapel, within which kneels the helmeted and mailed figure of Sir Edward le Despenser, kneeling with his face towards the altar. It is as effective and shattering in that silence as a trumpet blown from a tower in the dark of night. And, at that, some old cavalry call of the armoured horsemen. The kneeling figure facing the altar is there night and day, year in, year out, down the centuries, and indeed has knelt there for some six hundred years. It is not a life-size figure, being in fact no more than half-life-size. But if we walk round the choir so as to get the best view of him, which is from over the roof of the chantry chapel opposite, the effect, almost the sound of it, is as strange and haunting as that first time one hears the muezzin calling from a minaret, and we come out of Tewkesbury Abbey and back into the present enriched by an experience in its little way as marvellous and memorable as any shock of the suddenly revealed past in whatever other land.

CHIPPING
CAMPDEN

The Perpendicular style is to be seen in perfection at Chipping Campden. How often has the present writer come towards it through the Cotswold country that in his reckoning, coming from his direction, begins just the far side of the dark golden stone of Bloxham. And, at last, and perhaps the apple-orchards will be in blossom this time, we see the town of Chipping Campden with the Tudor gazebo of the old walled garden of the Noels beyond, and rounding the corner and taking the beauty of it for granted, we are beside the most reticent and beautiful of almshouses, a row of buildings that in their dignity could be said truly to make little difference between prince and beggar! To judge from its buildings Chipping Campden must have been something of an Arcadia of rich farmers and peasants in its day, but of course, as with the Perpendicular churches of Suffolk, the real wealth came from the wool trade, and at least in Suffolk it was another kind of Perpendicular. I think there was more of fancy and imagination at work there than in the Cotswolds perhaps only because it is near the coast and many persons will have heard tales of, or even have been to Bruges and Ghent. But the Cotswolds were untroubled by news of foreign parts. The row of almshouses at Chipping Campden, and the buildings and the number of little, they could almost be called Palladian, bridges over the stream at

BOURTON-ON-
THE-WATER

another village, Bourton-on-the-Water, argue a high level of sensibility and civilisation, though the effect, if not the truth of it, depends more than a little upon the warm-hued stone. There are no nerves or apprehensions in the architecture of Chipping Campden; or for that matter of Broadway, or Burford, and their attendant villages. This must be the most quiet and contented architecture in the world. And so it continues, through Bibury and Northleach and Cirencester and a hundred more villages and hamlets, down to what we can only look back on out of our time as yet another pastoral Arcadia.

TEMPLE GUITING

In the midst of which there is a wood, I think a wood of beech trees, between Stow-on-the-Wold and Winchcombe, at Temple Guiting. This is one of the rare woods where lilies of the valley grow wild in England. A country legend tells that the lilies were planted by the monks wherever they stayed for the night upon some journey. Whither, or where from, we are not told. Nor the purpose of the journey. Nor where else the lilies are found growing. The wood must be a lovely sight in May or June, so beautiful indeed that it calls for explanation, and this could be what gave rise to the legend. It speaks well of the monks. Or is it no more than a countryman's tale; like that which says the Milky Way across the heavens led to the shrine at Walsingham? Either reason or other, it is but a legend about a wood of lilies of the valley.

WARWICKSHIRE

HONINGTON HALL

Just across the county border from Chipping Campden is Honington Hall, a red brick Charles II house, with busts of Roman Emperors above the windows, which has a hall with Rococo stucco-work that may be by Charles Stanley. The great octagonal saloon is as magnificent as the work at Houghton or at Holkham. The eight-sided cove, or dome, frames Venus rising from the sea by Luca Giordano, while the shutters of the windows and the sash bars are most richly carved. It is possible that Stanley worked, too, on the saloon at Stoneleigh Abbey, near Coventry, in the same county, for the classical motifs are much the same.[1]

[1] The stucco-work at Stoneleigh Abbey is tentatively ascribed by Mr Geoffrey Beard (*Decorative Plasterwork in Great Britain*, London, 1975) to Artari and Vassalli, who worked with Smith of Warwick, the architect of Stoneleigh, at Sutton Scarsdale.

COMPTON
WYNYATES

Still in the Cotswolds is Compton Wynyates, a house that has a physical beauty that is not architectural. Nevertheless, to look down upon this house from the trees above it is to enjoy one of the most lovely visual experiences to be had in England. The church here has the finest collection known to me, personally, of heraldic hatchments. This very minor art seems to have flourished, particularly, between about 1780 and 1820.[1] The artists, it seems, were at this time coach painters; but, then, coach-building and the painting of coaches was an English art. We may call these hatchments the last display of heraldry, the final struggle of something that had come down from the Middle Ages. They are not far removed in style and execution from the Royal coats-of-arms that used to stand above the London shops, erected between 1820 and 1840, but, now, too often, unfortunately, destroyed or done away with.

WARWICK

The view of Warwick Castle from the bridge below it across the Avon has a sempiternal Englishness, as typical of England as the view of the Bay of Naples is of Italy. Warwick Castle is of the same antiquity as Windsor or the Tower of London. And the knowledge that Shakespeare, who was born by the same river Avon, must often have set eyes on Warwick cannot fail to give sanctity to its battlemented walls. In St Mary's church all that is left from the Middle Ages is the Beauchamp Chapel, with the tombs of the Earls of Warwick, but this is the most splendid and sensational of all chantry chapels in parish churches. Here is the tomb of Richard Beauchamp, Earl of Warwick, with a bronze effigy like those of the Plantagenet kings and queens in Westminster Abbey, except that this is not a portrait, but simply the 'image of a man armed', as contracted for by Will Austin, 'citizen and founder' of London, and it is a work of art not inferior to any known in Europe. But of added interest in the Beauchamp Chapel is the minute, indeed the mini-chapel leading from it which has one of the most exquisite and satisfying of all fan vault ceilings, small enough to have but three pendant fan-stalactites to a side, a little masterpiece of concise and perfect masonry, mathematically conceived, drawn, and carried out, more as if it were a carpenter's work and was a wooden ceiling. It is not much larger, and certainly no wider than the dining-car on an express train.

COVENTRY

Coventry was famous for its 'three fine spires', but the writer

[1] Armorial hatchments are to be admired, hung high up, in many old country churches; and they may be seen, also, in old Dutch churches in Holland, in Colombo, at the Cape, and in the East and West Indies.

of these pages stupidly and purposefully avoided going there although it is so near his home – near enough to hear the 'blitz' on Coventry and see the far off explosions – because it is an industrial town, and thus missed seeing the three hundred foot spire of St Michael's 'set upon its hill above its two attendant spires', a steeple that in the words of a great authority and writer upon mediaeval architecture, 'deserves mention as one of the wonders of the world.'[1] In palliation it could be said that St Michael's was of red sandstone, a building material that not even where it carves like sandalwood as at the red chapels of Banteai Srei, near to Angkor, where one could say that the stone almost is scented like sandalwood, does it justify itself so that it can be thought of as stone.

But there are survivals of both bombs and industry in this area around Coventry and Birmingham, to mention only the topiary PACKWOOD HOUSE garden at Packwood House, near the Forest of Arden, which represents, in yew, the Sermon on the Mount, or the rustic NEWBOLD-ON- Boughton monument at Newbold-on-Avon, with two delight-AVON ful figures who stand stiffly between a pair of fluted columns, under a canopy wooden or awkward in its folds; this was carved by John Hunt, a local mason of Northampton, who also carved the statue of Charles II over the colonnade at All Saints, in his native town.

WORCESTERSHIRE

WORCESTER At Worcester we find another local master, rescued from obscurity in that he may have studied under Wren, the genius of the age. This was Thomas White, who built the Guildhall of Worcester, a fascinating, indeed entrancing, red brick build-ing, with figures of Peace, Plenty, Justice, Labour, and – why? – Chastisement upon the roof, while, in niches, Charles I, Charles II and Queen Anne stand upon the wall below. The Guildhall of Worcester pertains to that civic fantasy which has given us Gog and Magog, the Lord Mayor of London's coach-man, the curious dresses of his attendants, the vestry of St Lawrence Jewry, and the swordrests of the city churches of London and Bristol.[2] I believe that of the Georgian churches of Worcester White is responsible for All Saints and St Nicholas

[1] *Gothic England*, by John H. Harvey, London, 1947, pp. 30, 31.

[2] Sure enough, the best of the iron swordrests out of London, the Bristol churches excepted, is to be seen in All Saints, Worcester.

but not old St Martin's or lovely St Swithin's no longer threatened but under repair.[1]

At Worcester Cathedral, of dark red sandstone, the Perpendicular cloisters are restored, and the decagonal chapter house is but the ghost or shadow of what it may have been. But Worcester has the tomb chapel of Prince Arthur, which is among the most beautiful of all chantry chapels and commemorates this elder brother of Henry VIII who at only fifteen years old was married to Catherine of Aragon, went after his wedding in his role as Prince of Wales to live at Ludlow Castle, and died within three months. Two years later the Spanish Infanta married Henry VIII. The stone screen of the chapel is elaborately beautiful in the Perpendicular manner, vying in interest with any *reja* or *retablo* in a church in Spain. It is in two storeys, the lower being of light stone trellis or arcading through which can be seen two other tombs left undisturbed at the building of the chantry. Above this is a wide band of stone panelling which is worked with heraldic badges: the portcullis of the house of Lancaster, the Tudor rose, and the falcon and fetterlock of the house of York. Over this is a high screen of three-light windows, but irregularly arranged and the better for that; and the chantry is topped with a cornice of open panels and tall pinnacles. The contrast between the open part of this stone screen and the ends of it, where the open traceries have become blind panelling, is most telling and effective. In the interior, the altar end of the chapel has four large canopied niches, still with their statues, and the ceiling has pendentives and is quasi-Tudor, in distinction to the exterior which is the ultimate in Perpendicular.

PERSHORE

Pershore Abbey is a wonderful relic of the long dead past, and before parts of it were torn down was a bigger, and some would say better work than Worcester Cathedral. But it must yield

EVESHAM

place to Evesham, which bears every sign of having been placed among the most fertile and pomiferous orchards in England. Indeed some of the cider apples of the district may date back to monastic days. Worcestershire was also famous for its wine until about 1300.[2] But how much of it was wine, and how much, verjuice (unfermented grape juice)? And, again, did they count

---

[1] Mr Marcus Whiffen (*Stuart and Georgian Churches*, London, 1947-8) has established that White designed the church of Castle Bromwich; particulars of the other churches which may be attributed to White or other local builders are also given in Mr Whiffen's book.

[2] Cf. Edward Hyams, *The Grape Vine in England*, London, 1949.

mulberry trees as vines? Or gooseberries, or red currants? Yet nothing of Evesham remains, only the feeling of its past, and the Perpendicular bell-tower but just finished before the Suppression, reminder of other towers in the buttercup fields down to the south – and, in the precinct, the two little chapels or churches of All Saints and St Lawrence, each with a chantry chapel built by the same abbot, and each with a fan vault ceiling.

BIRTSMORTON At Birtsmorton we again encounter Thomas White of Worcester, here as a sculptor of memorial tablets and of a reclining statue of an admiral, between pillars, with a sculp-

WICKHAMFORD tured man-of-war below.[1] While at Wickhamford is a pair of painted canopied tombs, from the first years of Charles I's reign, of Sir Samuel and Sir Edwin Sandys, with rows of their children, sons facing one way, daughters the other, sculptured below, coats-of-arms and small obelisks upon the roof line, but which resemble nothing else than a couple of grand old bed-steads dragged, without their curtains, into a corner.

ELMLEY CASTLE Of the same date, but of quite other import, is the Savage memorial at Elmley Castle. The babe in swaddling clothes in its mother's arms is closely paralleled in Nicholas Stone's monu-ment to Mrs Coke at Bramfield, in Suffolk, so nearly, indeed, that we may think the one sculptor must have seen it in the yard or studio of the other. At the feet of the mother and father kneel the four sons, in ruffs and doublets, three of them with clasped hands, but the eldest as making a declaration, with his hand upon his heart. These four sons we may regard as an attempted improvement upon the kneeling husband at Bramfield. The pose of the two mothers is nearly identical. The headdress at Bramfield is more beautiful, but the flounced collar at Elmley Castle, as the sleeve at Bramfield, are passages worthy of Bernini. Of the two babes in swaddling clothes, that at Elmley Castle is the more richly dressed and there is more of infant expression in its little face. And the Savage memorial (and if the one is a great work of art, so is the other) has the advantage that Sir Giles Savage, hatless, but in the complete dress of the Cavalier, in ruff and doublet, with slashed sleeves and wrinkled boots of softest leather, lies at her side. It is difficult, indeed, to choose between this pair of monuments. But at Elmley Castle

[1] White was the author of another monument to a mariner, Captain Samuel Skynner ('no mean proficient in maritime affairs') – and he looks that! – in the church at Ledbury, in Herefordshire. Close by is his monument to Anthony Biddulph, in loose cravat and periwig, and his wife. Beautiful works, both, in a country or secondary Baroque style.

there is also the superb tomb of Thomas, Lord Coventry, by the London sculptor William Stanton, a reclining figure, in the heaviest of periwigs, pointing with one hand, proudly, to the coronet beside him. The effigy is framed in four pillars with attendant, standing angels, ditto above, seated upon the broken cornice, and a fine coat-of-arms.

CROOME COURT

Stanton's monument was originally destined for Croome Court, the house of the Earls of Coventry nearby, but a family row led to its being placed in the church at Elmley Castle. According to a statement of Humphrey Repton,[1] on the authority of 'the late Mr Henry Holland, to whom at his decease he ["Capability" Brown] left his drawings', Croome Court, Worcestershire, house, offices, lodges, church, etc., 'were designed by "Capability" Brown for the Earl of Coventry.' This, as Mrs Esdaile observes, heads the long list of Brown's works, and may entitle him to rank high among the architects of his time. Nevertheless Croome is a very complex house; part is earlier; Adam and Chippendale worked, and, it is said, quarrelled, there, and Sanderson Miller may have been connected with it. The long gallery at Croome is by Adam, with a ceiling in his 'mosaick' manner of octagons and lozenges; the niches for statues resemble those in the dining-room at Syon, and there is an exceptional carved marble mantelpiece. But the most charming features of Croome are the Doric Orangery with the carved basket of fruit and flowers above the pediment, and the interior of the little 'Gothick' church which has been attributed, but on no certain grounds, to Adam. To return to Brown, Holland's own opinion is quoted and is very laudatory, and Brown may be unique in 'never having had one single difference in dispute with any of his employers'. Indeed, Lord Coventry raised a monument to him at Croome.[2]

KYRE PARK

Finally, at Kyre Park, we may admire an example of the West Country style of Rococo stucco-work, which is characterised, in the opinion of Miss Jourdain, by floral ornament, vines and hop poles. Another writer has remarked that 'as Rococo died in London, it sprang to life again in the West Country', quoting, for proof, the 'apple-green and scale-blue, the exotic birds and coruscating Japans' of the old Worcester china factory. Kyre Park, where the work may be by Thomas Stocking, the Bristol stuccoist, has hops for motif in the domed boudoir, where four

[1] *Observations upon Landscape Gardening*, 1803, p. 168. Our attention has been drawn to this by Mrs Esdaile.

[2] Cf. *'Capability' Brown*, by Dorothy Stroud, London, 1950.

groups of hop poles start the decoration, which is continued with flowers dropping out of cornucopias.[1]

HEREFORDSHIRE

SHOBDON   The Rococo-Gothic is to be found in the little church at Shobdon, and there is nothing else like this in England. It was built by Lord Bateman in 1753; and the architect may have been Sanderson Miller, or, more probably, Richard Bentley, the friend of Horace Walpole, who made the illustrations for Gray's *Poems*, which is one of the most delightful of English eighteenth-century books. In argument for this attribution, the uncle of Lord Bateman had been 'converted from a Chinese to a Goth' by Walpole, and Bentley designed a 'cloister' for him at Windsor. What is interesting in the church at Shobdon is the use of colour, and in particular, of a light or pigeon's egg blue with which the 'Gothick' cusps and trefoils are all painted.

STOKE EDITH   We would wish to be able to visit Stoke Edith, but the house was destroyed in a fire in 1927, for here the hall and stair were painted by Thornhill, and they must have shown him in his full capacity as decorator. Both rooms had painted walls and ceilings, and here we could see Thornhill in allegory and still life, in portrait, in arabesque, and in sham perspective. But a survival of the fire are the Stoke Edith tapestries.[2] These panels, four in number, were embroidered according to the story by the five wives successively, of one of the Foley family, a most peculiar instance, if nothing more, of aesthetic continuity. But the tapestries are obsessed by formal architecture. They depict a red brick house of the latest fashion in front of which ladies and gentlemen are promenading in a formal garden. The conventions of the needlework betray a particular delight in the joints of white mortar between the red bricks of the terraces, and in the orange trees and bay trees that are set out in big tubs of china. We may notice how the five wives of Mr Foley, or perhaps only one of them, in particular, had delighted in the shadows of the bay trees in their tubs, shadows attached

[1] The most typical example of West Country Rococo is the Royal Fort, Gloucester, with an all-over scheme of vines in stucco by Stocking upon the staircase walls, and dining-room with a door in the Chinese taste, Rococo overmantels, and wings of hunting subjects above the fireplace, all by the firm of Thomas Patey of Bristol.

[2] Needlework panels, strictly speaking, rather than tapestries, they are now preserved in Montacute House, Somerset.

by the stem to the tree root, but slanting at an angle, like the practice ball of the pugilist seen in simultaneous vision. Nowhere else, except on Tiepolo's painted ceilings at Würzburg and Madrid, do these vases or tubs of blue and white china appear in art,[1] but the Stoke Edith tapestries in their humble category are works of art of a high order. They communicate the health and sanity of a brand new, red brick Queen Anne building, and this is a convention or idiom as personal as a Douanier Rousseau painting. These needlework tapestries, aesthetically, are more valuable than the multitude of minor Dutch masters. But they are in fact only the masterpieces in a whole school of naïfs, for similar scenes can be met with upon damasked tablecloths, where ladies and gentlemen, conditioned by the stiff convention of the damasking, promenade by formal parterres with box borders, past the façades of red brick palaces, and by a splashing fountain.

SHROPSHIRE

MAWLEY HALL Mawley Hall is another place to find Rococo stucco-work, in an elaborate trophy of arms above the mantelpiece in the entrance hall. There is, also, a staircase with fine stucco panels, and a Chinese room with a delightful ceiling in delicate Rococo.[2] The architect was probably Smith of Warwick, who built Sutton Scarsdale. Attention must be drawn, too, to the handrail of the staircase, which is a serpent with a twisted tail, ending in a dragon's head. The diary of Mrs Philip Lybbe Powys gives a delightful account of Mawley Hall in 1771. She notes that

> The house has more chintz counterpanes than in one house I ever saw; not one bed without very fine ones . . . and . . . the three charming boys, the eldest not three years old, and a fourth coming. Never did three little creatures look so pretty; the two youngest in fine sprigg'd muslin jams, the eldest in a vest and tunic of tambour (Lady Blount's own work), large sprigs of gold on a thin muslin lin'd with pink.

QUATT Of earlier date, an example of the Baroque of the unknown

---

[1] We are indebted to Mrs Esdaile for the observation that, though this may be the only instance in English art of the blue and white china tubs, they have a permanent place in English literature, since 'the pensive Selima' of Gray's poem was drowned in what Walpole called 'the cat's vase'.

[2] Cf. *Decorative Plasterwork in Great Britain*, by Laurence Turner, London, 1927, pp. 222, 223.

master or the amateur, which, as might be expected of our English temperament, is often more extreme than that of the more famous name, is the remarkable white marble statue of Lady Wolryche at Quatt. She is lying, lute in hand, her hair dressed in somewhat of the ancient Roman manner, with a long inscription above, setting forth her claim to sing among the angels of the heavenly choir. Apart from this unprecedented appearance of a lute upon a monument, the statue is remarkable for its décolleté dress, as extreme a moment in fashion as the climax of the crinoline in 1864. But the date is 1668, and as yet no name has been suggested for the sculptor of this monument.

SHREWSBURY   At Shrewsbury is one of the most original buildings in England. According to the guide book, St Chad's has 'a tall and unattractive pagan façade'. This it may be; but the circular interior with its pillars and gallery is like a celestial concert hall. There is a round vestibule, an oval hall from which springs an elegant double staircase, after which you enter the unique interior. Hatchments and wall tablets are all arranged in proper order. All is gay and delightful. This strange church was built in 1790, but I would hesitate to name its style. It would be ideal for the performance of Haydn's and Mozart's Masses. Its purpose seems purely musical, and one leaves it wishing one could see the artists' room. [1]

With which in mind, let us cross the town to the Assembly Room of the Lion Hotel, for it was here that the great Paganini played on his way to, and from, Dublin in 1831. The Assembly Room, at the back of the hotel, though not actually designed by the brothers Adam, is a delicate and magnificent example of Adam decoration, as fine, in its way, as anything in the country. The colour scheme is in green and white, and there are splendid gilded mirrors upon the walls. At one end of the room, supported upon pillars, there is a fine gallery where the band would have played during dances. Shrewsbury, to this day, is a town of mediaeval half-timbered houses belonging, mostly, to the early seventeenth century, and this Assembly Room, in its midst, strikes a remarkable note of gaiety and delicacy. It must have been just as much in contrast with its surroundings a century and a half ago when Paganini drove through the streets.

---

[1] There is a galleried church a little resembling it at Whitby; but, in that, the atmosphere is nautical, and pews and staircases are like companionways.

STAFFORDSHIRE

LICHFIELD   The triple spires of Lichfield which at a certain distance – you cannot see them from far away – seem so near together, join the memory of seeing from the train-window the five square towers, in local patois, the bell-loud '*chongs clôtiers*' of Tournai against a darkening sky. But it is the multiple form of both cathedrals that makes the analogy, for there is no other point of consanguinity, and in fact Lichfield is built of dark red sandstone, not a favourite building material, and the blemish alike of Strasbourg and of many German mediaeval churches. Nevertheless, Lichfield is a grand performance in an unpleasing medium. It has an extreme homogeneity as though conceived and carried out in one flight of execution; west front with its three doorways, row of statues above that, rose-window continued within its lancet arch to the bases of the two west towers. Out of much-fringed arcading these spring up in duo as high as their bell-chambers, which have not the doubled lights of Salisbury, and further to the turrets above those bell-chambers, only, like any pair of twins, to be separated at some stage in their lives which is where each spire begins out of its tower. One of them in any case is very little smaller in girth than the other. Or is this so? Because from whatever angle one looks up at them, and plays or compares the one against the other, there is always some discrepancy and it is difficult to be certain. There is no cloister, and the chapter house – with a ribbed roof and central shaft – is not outstanding. But there is no effect quite like the clustered spires of Lichfield as they hover over the building on which they have settled, its red stone front carrying, not too happily, the burden of nearly a hundred statues and figures in niches, but the sculptures are restorations, there is niche upon niche and arcade upon arcade, and then the three spires rise, so worked with windows and blank openings and cusps and bands that one has in mind Madura and its lily-tanks, could there be a Dravidian temple in a cold climate, and not the bells of Lichfield, near the kilns and potteries of Staffordshire.

CHESHIRE AND LANCASHIRE

CHESTER   That there should be an ancient Benedictine abbey at Chester founded by the first generation of Norman conquerors, on a site which was an administrative centre even in Roman times, and always a border fort against the wild Welsh, is something only to be expected. The building is again of red sandstone, an unfortunate material even in the temples of Cambodia, a shortcoming for which the canopied choirstalls and the unusual state of preservation of some parts of the monastery, a perfect example of a slype among them, is little compensation. But the stalls are indeed remarkable, with two or even three spired niches superimposed on each other; and there is the dean's stall carved with the Tree of Jesse and a strange little figure in wide-brimmed hat sitting to the side of it, staff in hand, and reminiscent of the charlatan or necromancer in paintings by Hieronymus Bosch, though it may date from a hundred years before his time.

Cheshire is above all a county to admire the instances of 'magpie' building, timber houses built, as we would expect, in wooded districts, in the Weald of Kent and Sussex, and still more in Lancashire and Cheshire. Little Moreton Hall, in Cheshire, and Speke Hall, near Liverpool, are black and white

LITTLE MORETON HALL houses of great size. The outside of Little Moreton Hall, with its two storeys of oriel windows and its gables all facing inwards at different angles, is exceedingly picturesque; while the drawing-

SPEKE HALL room of Speke Hall has a magnificent stucco ceiling moulded into grape or acorn panels. Nothing could be more English than these 'magpie' houses. They show no foreign influence. At Little Moreton Hall the bay windows are signed and dated by Richard Dale, a carpenter, in 1559, which raises two arguments concerning such specimens of building. In the first place, they are so entirely indigenous and traditional in style that in the absence of definite evidence it is difficult to date them. It has been suggested that Speke Hall was not begun till 1598, and there are other cases in which the problem extends from late fifteenth to early seventeenth century, from the reign of Henry VII to that of James I. And, secondly, the beauties of such houses derive from carpenter and plasterer. An architect, as later ages understood that term, would hardly be employed upon these wood and plaster buildings.

At the same time, the crafts of the carver and plasterer were in their apogee. They were, in fact, in such houses, in advance of the walls on which they worked. In a sense, the appropriate architecture was not yet ready for them. We must remember, in looking at the beautiful lithographs of Elizabethan buildings and interiors by Joseph Nash, and at the books on Elizabethan

architecture and decoration by C. J. Richardson, both published more than a hundred years ago, that they were in
possession of better evidence than we can find ourselves. So
much has perished; so many buildings have been burnt down or
destroyed. Some houses, like Speke Hall, outside Liverpool, or
Aston Hall, nearly in the middle, now, of Birmingham, have
found themselves stranded like extinct monsters in the waste
lands, or in the public recreation parks. In any case, Nash and
Richardson could see colours that are lost to us. Of the plaster
CREWE HALL   mantelpiece in the carved parlour at Crewe Hall, Cheshire,
which was burnt down in 1866, Richardson writes that

> It represents the effects of Idleness and Industry. The
> former, dressed in rags, is asleep, his ground overrun with
> weeds and thistle, his house, unroofed, is falling to ruin from
> neglect; it is backed by dead and lifeless trees; a gallows, his
> final destination, is seen in the extreme distance. Industry
> . . . without his coat is represented at work to the left; in the
> centre is Time, presenting rewards and punishments.

And there is but small compensation in finding, in the
WYBUNBURY   neighbouring village of Wybunbury, the naïf memorial, with a
suggestion to it of the wild men or satyrs on the sculptured
palaces of Salamanca, to Sir William Smythe, with his shaggy
hair, one of the most strange and unaccountable of Jacobean
monuments.

HEATON HALL   Heaton Hall, less than four miles as the crow flies from the
centre of the town of Manchester, was one of James Wyatt's
earliest commissions and his first important house in the Classic
style. Built for Lord Grey de Wilton, it consists of a centre
block with a bay, connecting by colonnades with octagonal
pavilions. These octagons contain the kitchen and the library.
But the interest, at Heaton Hall, is the saloon in the bay, the
staircase, the billiard room; and, above all, the cupola room
upstairs in the upper storey of the bay. We would instance the
splendid mahogany doors of the billiard room, the overdoors
and ormolu door fittings, superb models of their kind; and the
plaster wall ornaments and overdoors upon the staircase landing. These last are beautiful designs, suggesting, somehow, the
crystal drops of a wall light or a chandelier.

The cupola room, upstairs, is in the Etruscan style, with walls
and ceiling painted entirely by Biagio Rebecca. The decoration
in fact is given over to Rebecca, and painted largely upon strips
of paper, though, of course, the form of the room and the doors

and pilasters are by Wyatt. Neither the Etruscan room, nor Heaton Hall generally, can be seen now at their best, because the Corporation of Manchester, who bought the house at the beginning of the century, allowed, incredibly, much of the specially designed furniture and many of the fittings to be sold 'quietly and quickly at the Coal Exchange'. Nevertheless, Heaton retains the marks of genius, and helps to explain how Wyatt sprang to fame.

FURNESS ABBEY   And our journey to the north-west ends at Furness Abbey on its promontory or *presqu'île*, founded here by monks from Savigny in Normandy on this spot, then called Beckansgill, or the Valley of Deadly Nightshade, and 'built of the red sand-stone of the district, the softness of which did not admit of that minute and elaborate ornamentation which distinguishes some of the other abbeys of England'. The monks owned coal, and this was a Cistercian abbey as one might guess from its isolation, and one large enough to have thirty-nine monks and one hundred other inmates, mostly servants, still in it in 1537. They worked iron, or had it worked for them, as well; iron ore found on Walney Island for which the monks put up two furnaces. The abbey owned malt-kilns, breweries, fishponds, a private army of twelve hundred including four hundred horse for use against the Scots, an estate as large as the Isle of Man, and presumably the shrimp-sands of Morecambe Bay; and here for four hundred years their abbots reigned in peace and plenty, doing, it must be conceded more good than harm. There were cloisters at Furness Abbey, though there are no remains of them, but they must have been in use as passages more than for recreation. For how many days in the year at Furness Abbey did one long for the peace and silence of the cloister, and perhaps a memory of the south, even Mercutio's 'dew-dropping south' having, maybe, had a taste of it in south-western France, or even Italy, and of the splashing waters of a fountain!

EPILOGUE

A bright stab of sunlight, that kind which comes out of the void of winter to live for a few moments only and remind you of its summer potency, came down through the windows and we were taken back again to the Northern streets, lit only by the beacon windows of public-houses, till we stood once more by a bed of yellow flowers that I have described, and at the edge of an asphalt path that wound away like a molten river through the grass. That cropped lawn seemed to run straight into the sky just a few feet in front of us, but no sooner did we walk out upon it than the horizon took a vast leap away from us beyond a huge surging bay, a kind of immense amphitheatre in which we occupied the highest seats, while below, the sea played to us with a listless and tired enthusiasm.

At this highest point of grass, upon a bench which was hot to touch and the brown woodwork of which was blistered and swollen by the sun, sat Colonel Fantock, listening to the brave music from the band below; but out upon the sands, and in front of the Spa and the gardens on the cliff, there stood a box-like, open booth, a small theatre upon trestles, with the cart and horses waiting to take it away again when the tide advanced against the sand. The dimly seen figures there were inaudible from above, and so we ran quickly down the long flights of steps to get the noisy music of the band behind us as we came near to watch this open-air theatre. Colonel Fantock we left at the top of the cliff, agreeing to meet him in a tea-shop in an hour's time.

In a few moments we were treading on the sands, though just near the shore they were so crumbled and soft as to make walking heavy and difficult. As soon as they had enough solidity to keep a definite footmark they became crisp and delightful to walk upon, and they stretched right away down to the bottom of the bay, for the sea was very far out at low tide. Every day I used to go to see that pierrot entertainment, and when the tide was too near in for them to play on the sands, or it was too windy, or began to rain, they gave their performance under the roof of the 'Arcadia', where they always appeared at night during the hours I was sealed hermetically within doors. By this frequency I got to know them by sight and learned to appraise their differing degrees of 'personality', a quality which can be present in the highest and fullest degree without in itself conferring any other excellence upon the performer.

It was a thrilling experience to arrive down there before the afternoon performance had begun, for the different actors strolled casually towards their occupation, and the only sign of their profession lay in an almost too marked affectation of the ordinary, so that they appeared out of this excess with something peculiar to them. Grey felt or straw hat was too considerately brushed, suit too pressed, walking-stick too unused, while there was a haunting and mordant vulgarity about their voices.

There were ten or a dozen of them, and they were to be seen walking in the same couples, or trios; they lived, obviously, according to this very grouping, in the same theatrical lodgings. I can never forget on these fine days seeing them coming along some quarter of a mile away down the sands that were as fresh and virginal as any island shore of which you could possibly dream. The lighting was admirable: there is never such a background for character, we know from Jacques Callot, as the actual boards of the theatre built with their cross-bars along the body, right up the limbs, and above the head. On summer mornings the sun had prepared just such a setting as this for their approach, and where his light was so perfect that every detail could be seen without the necessity of some other measure to give it scale, he had dispensed himself of the actual board-marks, rubbing out all those parallel lines in the sand and giving us just the lion-coloured sea-floor for foreground, wings, and background. It gave the effect of that casual entrance upon the stage which is one of the most perfectly finished products of theatrical technique.

A virtuoso who drew pictures on the sand with his toes was at work, as if upon the wings, of this scene. I do not think they are to be found anywhere else save in England, these developments of the pavement artist into something that approaches the feats of Hokusai; on this particular day it was Lord Roberts in a garland of victory over the savage Boers, and to see a comedian walking past the huge twists of that moustache, or by a blaze of medals, was in itself an experience of stage possibilities. Of course since the artist was at work a great square like the lines of a football field was scratched upon the sand, and he addressed indignant reproaches to anyone who endangered his picture by walking within its borders.

Just a few feet away, and nearer to where I stood, lay another of his sketches which had been more than half-destroyed by yesterday's high tide, though you could still distinguish Russians and Japanese, while every sporting instinct of our race was centred upon Admiral Togo. This scene, since it was old and done with, could be walked right through and its details knocked about or kicked with shoe or walking-stick.

The rest of their walk to the partitioned hut behind the stage led them past a photographer or two who held his tripod and black hood ready as though for a feat of necromancy; while the most considerable among them owned a primitive tin-built, pseudo-motor-car into which parties could climb to be photographed. More humble vendors stood by with baskets of beautifully coloured seashells, and trays of those strange marine creatures who seem to be half hedgehog and half doughnut. These last they would put for you as a final temptation into a pail of water, where they blossomed into a strange and glossy beauty.

A few moments later, when a whistle had been blown, the curtain was raised to show these actors in a strange mixture of character; for while the only two women were dressed in the conventional pierrot dress, half the men – like that variety of sea-shell? – were pierrots, and half, naval officers. It soon became apparent that only those members of the company who were not credited with being funny, and who relied upon a 'straight' song or recitation for their success, had adopted this latter excuse to favour. They stood at the salute, while their brothers and sisters remained rigid, hands to sides, when the curtain rose and till the piano had begun that inevitable doggerel song, a kind of musical legend of the company's activity. This, in itself, had a conventional horror which completely captured the attention. It seared and burned itself into memory, to remain there for ever.

The audience on their folding wooden chairs laughed as stupidly as ever; the pierrot at the piano played with lodging-house tone but with more than lodging-house pace. The rest of the company sit still, while through those draped curtains at the back of the stage a premonitory and powdered hand emerges, followed in a second by the whole figure of their 'lead', a young man with the calibre of cracked voice that would have enrolled him among the Sultan's private bodyguard, though those emasculate notes were really the result of a too premature appearance upon the stage with the strain of late hours and the effort of singing out above the cheap and noisy music. Both his parents were stage people, I expect, so that this tone of voice may even have been inherited, if one can inherit from a parent some quality which has been accidental in its origin, a tendency to melancholy, for instance, or a disposition to cry when you hear music. Despite all this, I remember such a performance as his for its gaiety – this young man had some inborn tricks and devices of the stage which made his acting professional and not amateur – and he contrived in a few seconds to evoke the whole 'seaside', as it exists to the Anglo-Saxon mind.

The turn of tide one did not notice, but over a great stretch of what had not long ago been sand, the blue sea now shook and played in its tidal strength. It would besiege one rock after another, running back again so as to have the pleasure of once more surrounding and taking it. The actual shelves of sand it ran down as quick as wind bends the corn, but even this easy conquest it repeated again for its pleasure. It was shaking a thousand cymbals, rattling a thousand silver coins in each wave that broke; and this slighter music came out above those tumbling, sleepy moves of its great mass.

There was now but room for people to walk abreast between the first plumes of foam left by the waves and the back of the stage where horses and carts stood in readiness. Even before the traditional seventh wave had time to raise its head, this narrow space was gone and a thin film of water lay in its place; it broke in little gurgling rings against the wheels of the carts, the horses' legs, and even, though this was the limit to its advance, ran below the trestles on which the stage was supported. Further than this, and among the audience, the sea was forbidden access by the traditions of high tide, according to which there must always be a few feet of rough, shuffled sand between water and shore.

These ghosts faded out of my mind to a rattling piano played above the sea's great mass, and the tunes fought bravely for life, that premonitory and powdered hand hung once more on to the curtain, though this was but a straw to hold to and the actor never came forth from his thin cloud. In place of that, I leave them there as I best remember them, in a waning afternoon when the tide upon the sands put an end to their performance.

SOURCES

Passages are included from the following books:
All Summer in a Day, Duckworth, London 1926 (*ASID*)
Liszt, Faber and Faber, London 1934 (*L*)
Dance of the Quick and the Dead, Faber and Faber, London 1936
   (*DQD*)
Conversation Pieces, Batsford, London 1936 (*CP*)
Old Fashioned Flowers, Country Life, London 1939 (*OFF*)
Sacred and Profane Love, Faber and Faber, London 1940 (*SPL*)
Splendours and Miseries, Faber and Faber, London 1943 (*SM*)
British Architects and Craftsmen, Batsford, London 1945; 5th ed.
   Pan Books, London 1960 (*BAC*)
Introduction to *English Church Monuments 1510 to 1840* by
   Katharine A. Esdaile, Batsford, London 1946 (*ECM*)
The Hunters and the Hunted, Macmillan, London 1947 (*HH*)
Cupid and the Jacaranda, Macmillan, London 1952 (*CJ*)
Truffle Hunt with Sacheverell Sitwell, Robert Hale, London 1953
   (*TH*)
Journey to the Ends of Time, Vol. 1, Cassell, London 1959 (*JET*)
Monks, Nuns and Monasteries, Weidenfeld and Nicolson,
   London 1965 (*MNM*)
Gothic Europe, Weidenfeld and Nicolson, London 1969 (*GE*)
For Want of the Golden City, Thames and Hudson, London 1975
   (*FWGC*).

Material used in the different chapters comes from the pages
indicated of the books listed above (references are to the fifth
edition of *BAC*, otherwise to first editions):
Prologue: ASID 42-49, 67-68, 70-72.
   1. Yorkshire and the North-East: *BAC* 43, 122, 125-129,
      148-150, 172, 177, 194, 200, 219, 224-225, 229, 241;
      ECM 5, 19, 22-24, 31; *JET* 382; *MNM* 26, 31, 35, 51-58;
      GE 17, 20-21, 31-32, 48.
   2. East Midlands: *ASID* 15, 22, 26-29, 75-77; *SM* 259;
      BAC 37, 47-53, 107-108, 117, 167-169, 201, 214-215,
      228; *ECM* 10, 16-17, 21, 25, 39, 40; *HH* 282; *CJ* 23-24,
      219; *TH* 146; *MNM* 38-40, 64; *GE* 15-16, 20-21, 31,
      48-49; *FWGC* 79.
   3. Lincolnshire: *BAC* 139; *ECM* 4-5, 13, 17, 24, 30; *JET* 380;
      MNM 41-44, 47-49; *GE* 15-17, 21-22, 32, 41, 73-78;
      FWGC 285.

4. Northamptonshire: *OFF* 12-13; *BAC* 39-40, 45-47, 98-99, 118, 148, 169-170, 246-247; *ECM* 4, 19-20, 26, 32, 39; *JET* 381; *MNM* 41-42, GE 15, 18, 21-22, 56.

5. Thames and Chilterns: *BAC* 38, 44, 65, 67-68, 77-78, 80, 82, 86, 91-92, 106, 125, 132-136, 145, 149, 164-165, 169, 173-174, 176, 183-185, 187, 192, 227-228, 244-247, 264; *ECM* 4, 6-8, 11-12, 17, 20, 24, 27, 30, 32, 35-37; *TH* 38, 181; *JET* 381; *MNM* 34-35; *GE* 18-20, 34, 43-44, 49, 57-58.

6. East Anglia: *CP* 67-68; *BAC* 30-32, 42, 63, 77, 79-81, 99-100, 131, 151-153, 162-163, 171-172, 186-187, 189-191, 194-195, 236-237; *ECM* 1, 4, 6, 8, 15-17, 20-22, 27, 31; *TH* 82-83, 117, 147-148; *MNM* 3-5, 31, 42, 44-47; *GE* 17-18, 22, 33-34, 37-39, 48, 50-54, 56-57, 67, 74; *FWGC* 285, 340-341.

Old London: DQD 4; *SPL* 250-257.

7. London: *BAC* 24, 60-61, 63-65, 82-90, 92, 95, 105-106, 117-118, 145-147, 151, 159-161, 169, 176, 185-188, 192-194, 196-197, 202, 217, 219-221, 223-224, 230, 240-244; *ECM* 2-3, 12, 18, 20, 25-27, 30-35; *TH* 122-123; *MNM* 34; *GE* 42-43, 59-61; *FWGC* 331.

8. The South-East: *BAC* 43, 72, 92-95, 137, 155, 164-166, 178, 191, 202-203, 215-217, 228-229, 259-260; *ECM* 6-8, 15, 17-20, 25-30, 33, 35, 39-40; *MNM* 32-33, 37-38; *GE* 66.

9. Wessex: *BAC* 37-38, 65-66, 91, 153, 169, 195, 198-199, 218, 225, 231, 239-241; *ECM* 5, 22-23, 26; *MNM* 60-65; *GE* 13-14, 23-25, 28, 30, 35, 39-40, 44-46, 56-57, 62; *FWGC* 285.

10. Western England: *L* 138-139; *BAC* 34-36, 38, 99, 101, 118-119, 121, 136, 140-141, 153-155, 171-172, 188-189, 191, 218, 234-236, 238, 262; *ECM* 2-3, 21-23, 26-28, 38-39; *TH* 125-126, 146, 281; *JET* 382; *MNM* 5-7, 43, 47, 58-60; *GE* 14-16, 22-23, 27, 30-31, 33, 46-48, 55-56, 130.

Epilogue: ASID 216-222, 224, 228-229.

INDEX